"_Then_ **Madden**
Said to
Summerall..."

"Then **Madden** Said to **Summerall...**"

The Best NFL Stories Ever Told

Matthew Shepatin

TRIUMPH
B O O K S

Library of Congress Cataloging-in-Publication Data

Shepatin, Matthew. Then Madden said to Summerall: the best NFL stories ever told / Matthew Shepatin.
p. cm.
ISBN 978-1-60078-265-7
1. Football—United States—History. 2. Football players—United States—Anecdotes. 3. Football players—United States—Biography. 4. National Football League. I. Title.
GV954.S44 2009
796.332—dc22

                                                           2009011390

This book is available in quantity at special discounts for your group or organization. For further information, contact:

Triumph Books
542 South Dearborn Street
Suite 750
Chicago, Illinois 60605
(312) 939-3330
Fax (312) 663-3557
www.triumphbooks.com

Printed in U.S.A.
ISBN: 978-1-60078-265-7
Editorial and page production by Prologue Publishing Services, LLC
Design by Patricia Frey
Photos courtesy of AP Images except where otherwise indicated

For my mom and dad.
And to Nana Ruth, for your compassion, your strength.

table of
contents

acknowledgments

I would like, first of all, to thank Tom Bast, editorial director at Triumph Books, for having the faith to start me in the big game. A heartfelt thanks is due to my friend and colleague, Allen St. John, for his generous support. I wish to express my gratitude to my editor, Adam Motin, for his invaluable help and encouragement. Everyone at Triumph has displayed All-Pro talent; their dedication is greatly appreciated. I'm also deeply indebted to Fred Koster of Koster Films; it was a sincere pleasure working with you.

I have a lot of friends and family who in some odd, cosmic way helped get this book written, and I give special thanks to them all. To my amazing, funky mom for supplying large quantities of love, laughter, Motown music, and Klondike bars. To Larry Sr., it's been a joy being your son and watching Giants games with you on Sundays since I was a wee tyke. Thank you for making the world's best tuna fish sandwich and helpfully reenacting L.T.'s sacks, despite a decided weight advantage. The question is, now that I've written a football book, are you willing to finally relinquish control of the clicker to me?

I want to thank my sister, Courtney, a bright shooting star. You're my friend—winter, spring, summer, or fall. Bonnie, for the gift of you. You are as strong as you are loving and kind.

My gratitude extends to Bill Hofheimer, Dan Masonson, Robin Brendle, Leslie Anne Wade, Mark Mandel, Frank Gifford, Phil Simms, Jerry Rice, Mike Haynes, Tony Kornheiser, Sal Paolantonio, and Greg Cosell. Special thanks to Eric Levin at *New Jersey Monthly*, Eric Gillin and Matt Sullivan at *Esquire*, Chris "Mad Dog" Russo, Mark Reiter, Richard Sandomir, Alex Balk, and Elizabeth Spiers. Much gratitude to Kyle Smith; Manon Roux; Tom Cuddihy; Jane and Lee Zanger; John Brooks and Courtney O'Brien; Roger Ziegler; Gabby Yung and little Jaslyn; Paul Lucas; Lilit Marcus; Dashiell Bennett; Dan Maccarone; Chris Rasmussen; Jeff Kurzon; Katie Baker; Larissa Phillips; Carl Bialik and Hunter Walker; Chris, Merel, Max, and Molly Monaco; Perry, Lisa, and Monika Julien; Bert and Adrienne Kestler; Pam Kestler and Emily and Jason Sagalow; and the rest of my extended family: Steve, Marilyn,

Dana, and Jen Monsein; Jamey and Randi Hamm; and the gang at Roots Café, Professor Thom's, and Destination. And, finally, thanks to you for reading this book. So say we all!

introduction

Are you ready for some football? I can't remember a single September when the answer wasn't, *Heck yeah, I'm ready!*

But with the NFL season kicking off, I'm feeling less ready than usual.

The last voice of my childhood is gone. He has stepped down from the booth. He's hung up his microphone. Rode his big cruiser off into the sunset.

John Madden has said good-bye to football.

For the first time in 30 years, the premier color commentator won't be working any of the games. Not Thursday night. Not Sunday night. Not Monday night. Not the Giants. Not the Steelers. Not the Patriots. Not the Packers.

No Boom! Bam! Whap! Doink!

Am I ready for football without that gruff voice, rumbling warmly like some beer pub sage, then suddenly bursting forth with the energy of a rambunctious bulldog? That's like asking a quarterback if he's ready to get sacked by Lawrence Taylor. It's like asking a wide receiver if he's ready to get hit by Jack Lambert.

Of course, I was blindsided seven years ago when the legendary broadcasting team of Madden and Pat Summerall split after 22 years together in the booth, thus ending the longest, most beloved partnership in the history of televised pro football.

On his own, Madden was still a pleasure to listen to. But Sundays would never be the same without the duo's effortless banter. Every great drama needs a great soundtrack—they were our soundtrack to our team's glory and agony, to their epic victories and crushing defeats. They were just one of the guys, a couple of funny, engaging pals hanging out in the den with me and my family.

Simply put, Summerall was Laurel to Madden's Hardy. Or to use an analogy closer to the field, Madden leaving Summerall in 2002 was like Deacon Jones departing from the Los Angeles Rams to join the San Diego Chargers in 1972. He was still great. But back when he was part of the Rams' defensive front four, along with Lamar Lundy, Rosey Grier, and Merlin Olsen—the Fearsome Foursome—forget about it. Together, they were the all-time best.

Madden and Summerall. The Dynamic Describing Duo. The Terrific Talking Tandem. The all-time best.

But what does that mean: to be the all-time best?

It means you probably had instant chemistry.

Well, in the case of Madden and Summerall, that's almost true. Working his first game with Madden, a Giants-Buccaneers tilt in Tampa in 1980, Summerall noticed how nervous his new partner appeared, sweating profusely through his clothes. Summerall wondered to himself if perhaps the former coach was really cut out for the job. Little did he know that Madden's uneasiness had nothing to do with on-air jitters; the high-in-the-sky booth had triggered his intense fear of heights. (Hence, why the big guy hasn't seen the inside of a plane since 1979.)

It wasn't long before the two men clicked. Fans loved their odd-couple chemistry, the way Summerall's smooth, understated style complemented Madden's call-it-like-I-see-it rants. Madden knew his football, but it was Summerall who had a way of teasing out his vast knowledge of the game—it was like Summerall snuck you into the Raiders' complex, down into the off-limits coaching offices, and let you watch Madden, the brilliant head coach, unfiltered, uncensored, breaking down game film, scouting players, and discussing war strategies. "He allowed John to fly wherever he wanted to in his sometimes-outlandish way," said the team's former producer, Bob Stenner. "Pat could always bring him in for a safe landing with a word or two. That gave John a sense of comfort to go further out with the chalkboard and other things."

It means you probably bring insights on the game that come from personal experience, fighting in the NFL trenches.

As a matter of fact, the two brought a combined 22 years of combat in the league when they were paired to cover games at CBS in 1981.

Prior to picking up a microphone, Summerall was a place-kicker and periodic tight end, first with the Detroit Lions in 1952, next with the Chicago Cardinals from 1953 to 1957, and then with the New York Giants from 1958 to 1961. He finished his standout career with 563 points and appearances in three NFL Championship Games, including the mythic 1958 title match, aka the Greatest Game Ever Played, which the Giants lost to Johnny Unitas and the Colts. However, his last-second miracle kick in a blizzard to defeat archrival Cleveland Browns on the last day of the '58 season and get them into the playoffs rates as one of the greatest plays in Giants franchise history.

Unlike his broadcasting partner, John Madden only played one year in the NFL, as a tackle for the Philadelphia Eagles in 1958, before a knee injury cut his career short. Where Madden made his mark was as head coach of the wild, colorful Oakland Raiders, who dominated opponents throughout the 1970s. In 1969, when owner Al Davis tapped the 33-year-old to be the youngest head coach in NFL history, he directed the Silver and Black to a record of 12–1–1 and an appearance in the AFL Championship Game. Over his decade-long Hall of Fame coaching career, he led the Raiders to a record of 103–32–7 for a regular-season winning percentage of .763, the best of any head coach in NFL history with more than 100 career victories. After enduring more than his fair share of playoff heartbreak, none more crushing as the defeat to the Steelers in the 1972 AFC playoff game on Franco Harris' last-second "Immaculate Reception," Madden finally got his ring in 1976, guiding one of the greatest Super Bowl teams of all time to a dominating victory over the Minnesota Vikings.

It means you probably announced some of the NFL's greatest games.

If you're going to cover your first Super Bowl together, you want Joe Montana playing quarterback. Your odds of a classic skyrocket. Luckily for Madden and Summerall, CBS paired them in the booth for the 1982 Super Bowl matchup between the San Francisco 49ers and Cincinnati Bengals. On cue, Montana put on an unforgettable MVP performance, including a pair of fourth-quarter drives that set up the game-clinching field goals and the 49ers' first championship. But the real winners were the millions of viewers who got to see this new sportscast tandem do their thing. Even with a slight glitch at the very start of the telecast—"I sat on Pat Summerall's headset," recalled Madden—it was at one time the most-watched Super Bowl telecast ever.

Over their broadcasting career together, they called eight Super Bowls (five for CBS and three for Fox). Summerall, who began his broadcast career in 1962, covered a record 16 NFL title games, beginning with Joe Namath's thrilling "guarantee" victory in Super Bowl III.

Football fans who hoped the broadcasting team's last waltz together would be memorable were not let down. In a doozy of a Super Bowl, the Patriots stunned the Rams 20–17 on a last-second Adam Vinatieri boot. Summerall, who had made his own fair share of dramatic kicks as a player, summed up the history-making event the way you would imagine he would—with succinct charm and class: "It's right down the pipe. Adam Vinatieri. No time on the clock. And the Patriots have won Super Bowl XXXVI. Unbelievable." Before parting ways for good, the men traded heartfelt words. "You're the spirit of the NFL," Madden said of his partner. "You're what a man and a gentleman is all about." In turn, Summerall said to Madden, "They can take me from standing next to you, which is going to happen, but they can't take away the memories of being with you [for so many years]."

They can't take away our memories, either.

It means you probably had a huge influence on the way the game is enjoyed and appreciated as never before, by millions of fans around the globe, both young and old.

John Madden is as much a part of American culture as he is football culture. For years he has lent his fun-loving, larger-than-life persona to the promotion of America's favorite game. With his "Madden NFL Football," the top-selling sports video game of all time, he has made grasping the beautiful intricacy of the game—the Xs and Os part, the tactical maneuvers, the defensive and offensive concepts—a passion for millions. He has hosted *Saturday Night Live*, turned up in an episode of *The Simpsons*, appeared in a U2 video, done some "tough-actin'" in films and commercials, and lent his voice for public service spots, including the Pacific Vascular Research Foundation of San Francisco.

Summerall. 40 years. Over 1,000 football games. Unbelievable.

It means you probably were the voice of football to a generation of fans.

Who could argue that John Madden and Pat Summerall weren't the voice of football to a generation of fans? (You might as well argue that there's no way to stuff a chicken in a duck stuffed in a turkey. Uh, turducken, anyone?)

But come this 2009 season, those voices will be silent.

For the first time in nearly half a century, that signature call from the booth will be missing. You can check every game on the NFL package and you won't hear that calm baritone capturing the drama of the moment with a few simple words: "Brady to Moss. 75 yards. Touchdown." You won't hear his gravel-voiced buddy exclaiming, "Boom! There's a football player who plays like a football player!"

For the first time in nearly half a century, you won't hear those two voices. Not in the living room. Not at the local bar. Not anywhere.

Madden and Summerall. The hole they leave behind is huge. Big enough for 30 "Refrigerator" Perrys to run through.

But if football teaches us anything, it's that heroes rise and fall. Careers explode and fade. Legends are born and die.

But the chains keep moving. The stories endure.

These are those stories.

The stories of those heroes, those careers, those legends.

These are the stories of the Punishers. The Playmakers. The Gunslingers. The Generals. The Big Gamers.

These are the stories of courage, pain, determination, and glory.

These are the stories of the NFL.

So, I gotta know.

Are you ready for some football?

chapter 1

The Gunslingers

What does it mean to be a gunslinger? Back in the early days of the NFL, throw over six passes a game, and you'd probably qualify. Consider trigger-happy Arnie Herber of the Green Bay Packers, whose league-high 37 completions and nine touchdowns in 1932 would have made him a fantasy league stud in those times. Imagine a quarterback today making first-team All-Pro with numbers like that, but Herber did, while also completing just 37 percent of his passes and throwing as many interceptions as touchdowns. Enter "Slingin' Sammy" Baugh, who, in the late 1930s and early 1940s, sent a jolt of electricity through the league, posting passing numbers that, back then, were ridiculous. In the first three games of the 1947 season, Baugh completed 47 passes, 10 more than Herber's 1932 league-high total for a *full* season.

The gunslinger legacy born with Baugh would bloom madly over the next 50 years, as NFL football evolved from a grind-it-out ground war to a game featuring enough wild and complex passing schemes to implode the mind of a first-time Madden '09 player. Over the game's many eras, gunslingers have come and gone, each with their own throwing style, their own flair for the dramatic. Sammy Baugh was Buffalo Bill—the flashy, tobacco-chewing sharpshooter. Bobby Layne was Sam Houston—the brash, swaggering Texan. Brett Favre was Billy the Kid—the irrepressible grin, the reckless streak. But all these quarterbacks share one thing in common: a knack for thrilling you with every shot they took.

Sammy Baugh

Over his 16 seasons with the Washington Redskins, Sammy Baugh lit up the scoreboard, throwing for a the-unheard-of 21,886 yards and 187 touchdowns while leading the league in passing six times—a record he still shares with Steve Young. Spectators watched with amazement as Baugh scattered the field with pinpoint passes, even from inside the 20-yard line, a virtual no-fly zone in those days. But Baugh wasn't just a cannon-armed quarterback, he also wowed fans as a ball-hogging defensive back and one of the all-time great punters. In 1943 Baugh pulled off a statistical Triple Crown, leading the league in passing, punting, and interceptions. (Steve Van Buren and Dudley Clark are the only other players to accomplish a Triple Crown.) From 1940 to 1943, he led the league in punting, averaging an NFL-record 51.40 yards a punt in 1940. His career punting average of 45.10 yards is fourth behind Raiders punter Shane Lechler (46.47). He's also the first player in league history to snag four picks in a game—a record that's been tied but never broken. By the time he retired in 1952, the forward pass had changed from an occasional weapon to the centerpiece of modern offenses. In addition, he gave the people in the nation's capital a new tradition decidedly more riveting than watching mealy-mouthed politicians deliver long-winded speeches about finance policy—of course, with it came an increased risk of pretzel-choking.

While he achieved iconic status for rifling footballs down the field at a time when young soldiers were rifling grenades into German bunkers, Baugh actually earned the nickname "Slingin' Sammy" for his powerful bull-whip throw to first as a star third baseman at Texas Christian. "He didn't have overly large hands," recalled former Redskins receiver and teammate Joe Tereshinski. "But his arm was so good he was going to play shortstop for the St. Louis Cardinals." Even after Baugh led Washington to the NFL title in his rookie season, he left to pursue his primary goal: a career in the big leagues. Signed by ex-superstar Rogers Hornsby, then a scout, he joined the Cardinals farm team, where he was converted to shortstop. "For some reason, he didn't think he would beat out Marty Marion, so he stuck with football," said Tereshinski. "And he and Unitas became the game's two greatest passers."

It was another lanky prospect, a 17-year-old by the name of Ted Williams, who caught Sammy Baugh's eye in the minors. "He'd go out to right field, turn his back on the pitcher, and do jumping jacks and crap like that," recalled Baugh. "He'd look over his shoulder for the pitch and do exercises in between. These old-school guys thought, *What a goddamned bush-leaguer.* But you know, that crazy sonofabitch would get up there and knock a goddamn board off the fence.... I always thought how a manager would handle him—not many would put up with that bullshit. But if you make the sonofabitch mad at you, he'd just leave. And how would you like to be the sonofabitch who let Ted Williams get away?"

Once he signed with the Redskins in 1937, it didn't take long for the Texas gunslinger to make an impact. In his first season, he led the Redskins to a 28–21 victory over the Chicago Bears in the NFL Championship Game. Once, during his rookie season, Redskins coach Ray Flaherty drew up a pass play on a blackboard. He told Baugh, "When the receiver gets to this point, you hit him in the eye with a pass." To which Sam replied, "Which eye?"

For 37 years Baugh held the record for completion percentage in a season, managing a gaudy 70.3 percent in 1945. Two years later Baugh

Snake Bites

Even Samuel L. Jackson couldn't have stopped this snake. Too wily was Oakland Raiders quarterback **Ken Stabler.** In the 1970s the reptile-nicknamed renegade was famous for raising hell on and off the field; a perfect leader for the anything-goes Raiders of that era. The strong-armed lefty used plenty of savvy to lead the Raiders to the Super Bowl in January 1977, but it was his quick-thinking action in a game against the San Diego Chargers during the 1978 season that resulted in one of the most discussed plays in NFL history.

Down 20–14, Stabler engineered a furious fourth-quarter drive down to the San Diego 14 with no timeouts remaining. On the key play, linebacker Woodrow Lowe hit Stabler. As the Snake fell to the ground, he "accidentally" fumbled the ball forward to the 8-yard line, where Pete Banaszak "accidentally" knocked it to the goal line, where tight end Dave Casper "accidentally" kicked it into the end zone and fell on it for the winning touchdown as time expired.

The controversy that ensued—Raiders fans called it the "Holy Roller" and Chargers called it the "Immaculate Deception"—caused the NFL to adopt a rule change that stated no offensive player could advance a fumble in the final two and a half minutes, except for the player who initially fumbled.

was involved in one of the greatest shoot-outs in league history, battling Philadelphia Eagles rookie receiver Pete Pihos on the opening day of the season. When the dust had settled in Philadelphia, a then-record 12 touchdowns had been scored and 87 points put on the scoreboard. It remains the most points ever for an opening-day NFL game. Unfortunately, Baugh came out on the short end of a 45–42 score. But perhaps Baugh's toughest loss ever was in the 1940 title game, when the Chicago Bears pasted the Skins 73–0 in the most one-sided score in NFL championship history. After the game, a reporter asked the QB if things might have been different had a Redskins tight end not dropped a touchdown pass in the end zone earlier in the game. "Yeah," Baugh drawled, "it would have made it 73–7."

Baugh would return the Redskins to the top of the football heap in 1942, knocking off Chicago 14–6 for their second title. Sadly, the team's next two trips to the championship game resulted in defeat: first to the Bears 41–21 in 1943, and then to the Cleveland Rams 15–14 in 1945. Win or lose, the colorful Baugh maintained a great sense of humor—even about getting clobbered by an opposing player. The story goes that when Baugh was asked to describe a devoutly religious linebacker, he responded, "He knocks the hell out of people, but in a Christian way." In 1940 he costarred in a 12-episode Western serial called *King of the Texas Rangers*, but he was far more comfortable on an actual Lone Star ranch than a Hollywood soundstage. "Ah, shit on celebrity," he told writer Dennis Tuttle in 1995. "It didn't make sense to be showboating all over Hollywood and spending a lot of money for a steak when I could take that money back to Texas and buy a whole cow."

His No. 33 is the only number the Redskins have officially retired.

Johnny Unitas

In the late 1950s the NFL emerged from the shadow of the college game—*all hail, Notre Dame!*—to become a major sport, turning regular Joes with names like Huff, Marchetti, Ameche, and Brown into national heroes. But of all the players thrust into the spotlight, none of them began so low and rose so high as Johnny Unitas, who went from shoveling coal in dirt-poor, rural Pennsylvania to a figure so universally beloved

Johnny Unitas won three MVPs and is still regarded by many as the greatest quarterback in NFL history.

that he no longer required a full last name. Like the *S* on Superman's chest or the *Z* that identified Zorro, one letter sufficed: *U*.

To be sure, Unitas was a superstar in the 1950s and '60s because he was a brilliant passer, a three-time champion, and one helluva clutch player; but what made him a "bronze statue in the making" were the broad-shouldered values he symbolized. Stoic confidence, grace under pressure, hard work, moral fiber, and, most of all, guts. Unitas was the last man to read a self-help book, do mind-expanding drugs, or listen to Dylan. Coal mills, cowboys, communion, commitment—that was Johnny U. Beer, bowling, bruising tackles, punishing blocks—that was Johnny U.

In a 1958 regular-season game against the Green Bay Packers, Unitas suffered three broken ribs after defensive back Johnny Symank kneed him in the chest. Unitas checked out of the nearby hospital so he could watch the rest of the game from the rain-soaked bench. A couple of broken ribs wasn't going to keep him from rooting for his teammates.

That night, back at his house, Unitas had trouble breathing. The next day doctors discovered he had more than broken ribs—he also had a punctured lung. Surgeons immediately operated on him. But that wasn't the end of his season, as Colts teammate Art Donovan recalled, "They put some kind of a steel cast halfway around John's body, and of course that weasel bastard Weeb [Ewbank] didn't inform the league. John was some kind of tough. That's how he led, really. Norm Van Brocklin had been an underwater demolitions guy in the Navy. Bobby Layne was a merchant marine gunner. But without having gone to war, John was a tougher quarterback than either of them, and a better leader. Most of the players had been in the service. You were used to being told what to do, and you did it. But to do it well, you had to respect the guy who was giving the orders. We respected Unitas most of all for his toughness."

> "I actually got to know Johnny Unitas when we went to Vietnam together. Pete Rozelle asked four of us players to go over, and we became the first NFL group to do a tour in a combat area. It was me, Sam Huff, Willie Davis, and Johnny."
> —Frank Gifford

"That crew-cut hair," a 25-year-old Joe Namath told a reporter days before the long-haired rebel—the anti-Unitas—would go on to deliver on his "guarantee" to upset the vaunted Baltimore Colts, for whom an aged Unitas still played, in Super Bowl III in 1969, "those high-top shoes. On Sixth Street in Beaver Falls, I wasn't Joe Namath. I was Joey U. My number was 19, too. For our away games in high school we didn't have a 19 jersey, so I wore 29. It wasn't even a quarterback's number, but it was the closest I could get to him." Namath wasn't the only future Hall of Fame quarterback who grew up in western Pennsylvania revering Unitas. There was also Jim Kelly, Dan Marino, and Joe Montana, who also wore No. 19 as a kid.

Today players like Peyton Manning still look to Unitas for instruction on how the game should be played. "I wore black high-tops at Tennessee because of him," Manning said. "If you call a play you believe in, what does it matter if it's first-and-10 on the opening drive of the second half, or if it's fourth-and-5 with 30 seconds to go? If this is the play you believe in, this is the play you call. You make it work. That's Unitas."

Bobby Layne

Here's a shocking revelation: Detroit didn't always suck. Hard to imagine after 2008's record-setting act of futility, a perfectly putrid 0–16 record. But here's the crazy thing. The Lions used to be cool. And nobody was cooler than Bobby Layne, a blond Texan who always managed to pull off some improbable victory no matter how tough the odds, mean the defense, or brutal the hangover. The hard-partying gunslinger led the Detroit Lions to a glorious dynasty in the 1950s, highlighted by back-to-back championships in '52 and '53 and one more in '57. But he was more than just one of the NFL's greatest money players, as *Detroit News* sports columnist Jerry Green explained, "He was the symbol of this city. The toughest and the best. He played without a face mask, and he was at his finest against the clock.... When the Lions were on the coast, dinner would be permitted to turn cold until Bobby coaxed the Lions to their victory in the final minute."

Indeed, Bobby Layne is sort of the Godfather of the Two-Minute Drill. Long before Elway, Montana, and Brady, it was Layne who mounted a drive for the ages in the 1953 championship game. The Cleveland Browns were leading 16–10, and Layne was starting at his own 20-yard line with just over four minutes left in the game. The Browns' legendary quarterback Otto Graham stood helpless on the side-line, huddled in his parka, as his devil-may-care adversary worked his magic, moving his team down the field with one great pass after another. Not all his throws were beauties, to be sure—some wobbled in the air like a wounded duck. But as usual, they found their target. One of those targets was Jim Doran, a defensive back who had come in as an emergency receiver. The story goes that he kept telling Layne that he could beat his guy deep. Layne ignored his pleas the whole game. The Lions had driven down to the Cleveland Browns' 33-yard line. Two minutes

Wilted Leaf

Worst draft choice in NFL history? People seem to be in agreement on this one: it's San Diego Chargers 1998 first-round pick **Ryan Leaf**. After voting him one of the "Top Draft Busts of the Last 20 Years," *Sports Illustrated* stated: "The one-time Washington State star redefined the term 'bust' in his brief NFL career. He wasn't No. 1 overall—the Colts chose Peyton Manning—but his spectacular decline caused lots of problems for the Chargers, who traded up with Arizona to select Leaf. In 18 starts for San Diego, Leaf finished 4–14 with a 48.8 passer rating. And off the field Leaf alienated teammates and the community with his brash behavior." Added the *Bleacher Report*: "Next to the creation of the XFL, he is the worst professional sports disappointment ever! That's as bad as it gets."

on the clock, everything on the line. After calling a timeout, Layne met the Lions head coach Buddy Parker on the sideline to discuss the crucial play. After Parker gave him the call, Layne told him in his cool southern drawl, "Know what I think? I think a cigarette sure would taste good about now." In the huddle, Layne turned to Doran. "Can you still beat that feller?" Doran smiled to himself. He was ready. Layne dropped back, spotted Doran rushing down the field, and released the ball. As Doran sprinted past the cornerback, the ball sailed through the air—not one of those perfect, tight NFL Films spirals but a shaky bomb defying the laws of aerodynamics. Doran hauled in the pass and ran into the end zone for the game-winning touchdown. Few NFL fans had ever seen such a heart-stopping late march down the field. Layne was so great under pressure because, well, that's the way he was built—Captain Sparrow in cleats. "If I'd had overthrown Doran or if he'd dropped the ball or if I'd gotten my ass buried by Lenny Ford and a couple others, there wouldn't be nobody feeling sorry for themselves," said Layne. "We'd have gone out and had something cool to drink anyway."

And we're not talking about one or two drinks, either. Even as Bobby Layne was racking up Hall of Fame numbers, he seemed to be on permanent shore leave. One story goes that before a game two linemen had to hoist Layne up by his ankles and drop him in a barrel of ice-cold water to get him coherent enough for battle. Former teammate Harley Sewell recalled, "When I was a rookie, I went with Layne to get a tube of toothpaste and didn't get back for three days." And good ol' boy Don Meredith once said, "In my next life, I want to come back as Bobby Layne's chauffeur. He stays out late, goes to interesting places, and tips well."

Amazingly, Layne, a man so intent on victory that he'd go to church to pray for a win, never let his partying effect his play. Actually, Layne believed just the opposite. "Maybe I'm a better player," he once said, "because I start having fun at midnight, get to bed when everybody else is waking, and sleep all morning. Makes me fresh as a daisy for the game." At the University of Texas, Layne was not just a great football player but also a dominant pitcher. One time he cut his foot on broken glass horsing around with his roommate. Already on thin ice with his head coach, he didn't let on that his foot was in agony when he took the mound the next day against archrival Texas A&M. To get through the game, he had the student manager bring him beer on the mound. Spotting Layne's limp, the Aggies beat their drum as loud as possible. After the game, Layne thanked the Aggies players with a one-finger salute. That was, of course, after he had thrown a no-hitter against them.

Whether it was quarterback of the Texas Longhorns or Detroit Lions or later the Pittsburgh Steelers, Layne was always the ringleader, on and off the field. "Once you were on the team, you were part of the gang," explained former Lions defensive back Jim David. "There would be a spirit party of sorts. There was rookie afternoon at some showbar in town. If you didn't show, we'd send a taxi for you. Bobby was the leader, and we all followed. He knew the game and he knew people and he knew how to have a good time. There were some nights he'd be throwing $100 bills into a saxophone 'til all hours, and there were other nights when some of us would kinda commandeer a trolley for a while. But when it came time to play, we were ready. They'd tell jokes that, when we'd form the huddle, you could smell liquor and stuff like that. But that never happened." He paused. "Not during regular season, anyway."

Mickey Mantle famously said once, "If I knew I was going to live so long, I'd have taken better care of myself." But the line actually came from his golfing buddy, Bobby Layne. Like the Mick, Layne's liver took more physical abuse than, say, a modern Detroit Lions quarterback. Both men paid the ultimate price for all the years of punishment on the "other" field of play—the barstool. Mantle died at 63. Layne was just 59. But nobody earns Hall of Fame status for their prowess drinking. During his playing days, Layne was a fearless leader who called his own plays, and when he retired, he held many of the league's passing records. It's just that he did it his way. "They don't make them like Bobby anymore," said Buddy Parker in 1960. "He's a case of 'Don't do as I do but do as I tell you.' He's a one-man team who goes against all the rules. But, by golly, it works."

So will Detroit keep sucking? Will they ever return to the glory days of Bobby Layne? One man thinks he has the answer. He started a website called the Curse of Bobby Layne. Legend has it that when Layne, the heart and soul of the organization, was traded to the Steelers in 1958, he said, "Detroit won't win for 50 years." Those possessing superior math skills will realize that this means the "curse" ended in 2008. Perhaps that year's winless season was just the grand finale of pre-ordained failure? Let the apologies to Matt Millen begin.

Joe Namath

Everybody knew that there was no chance in hell of it happening—the cocky kid was just writing checks his ass couldn't cash. So was the general consensus when Joe Namath made his "guarantee" in 1969 that his New York Jets—an 18-point underdog representing the second-rate AFL— would beat the NFL's dominant Baltimore Colts in Super Bowl III. Such a ridiculous boast was not worthy of public outrage or media hype. (Today ESPN would almost have to start a new channel to give the story the necessary airtime.) It was only after it *did* happen, only after the Jets beat the Colts 16–7, that people went into momentary shock. It was only after the upset had earned the AFL instant respectability that the Super Bowl became the big-time showdown we've come to know. It was only after Namath trotted off the field, finger raised up toward heaven, that the Guarantee became legend, along with the young, shaggy-haired quarterback who made it.

While delivering perhaps the greatest upset in NFL history— Giants fans might dispute that fact, presenting David Tyree's head as Exhibit A—Namath's impact went beyond the league, reaching far into society. "Namath was the first of his kind," explained Mark Kriegel in his excellent biography *Namath*. "An athlete whose place in culture owed as much to television and the sexual revolution as it did the point spread.... For an entire generation, he became a spectacular voluptuary of booze and broads, a guy who made bachelorhood seem an almost sacred calling."

In 1972 Namath's popularity landed him on the cover of *Time* magazine. In the feature, he's described as some "20th century counterpart" of Victorian swordsman Tom Jones. There were photos and stories about his bachelor pad on Manhattan's East Side, which featured a white llama rug, and, purportedly, some of the unholiest debaucheries since Petronius' last house party.

> "It wasn't that Joe Namath was so rebellious. He just didn't like to get all dressed up and go to fancy places. He was a fun-loving guy, a single guy, he loved gals, and they loved him. But pretty soon he became this mythological creature that the sportswriters created. But he's really just a quiet guy."
> —*Frank Gifford*

No American beauty could regard her career as complete without a date with "Broadway Joe" (a bad geographical misnomer, because Namath's favorite haunts—Dudes 'n' Dolls, Mister Laffs, P.J. Clarke's—were many blocks and light-years away from Broadway). He made guest appearances on television talk shows, where writers provided him with merry bedfuls of double-entendres. He starred in a Grade Y potboiler called *The Last Rebel* (in which he actually said out loud, "All right, men. Guns on the table!") and a Grade Z film, *C.C. and Company*, with Ann-Margret.

Called one of the three smartest quarterbacks of all time by Don Shula, the Hungarian Howitzer was always ready with a smart-aleck quip, many of which appeared in his 1969 literary masterpiece *I Can't Wait 'til Tomorrow... 'Cause I Get Better Looking Every Day*. It featured chapter titles such as "They Probably Would Have Told Our Lord to Cut His Hair" and the Bode Milleresque "I Never Drink at Halftime." In one of the book's more self-reflective passages, Namath confided, "I like my girls blonde and my Johnnie Walker Red." Almost 30 years later, he reflected on his views in an interview with a local Florida TV station: "I was stupid.... At that time, I was probably dating a blonde-haired lady, so let me apologize to redheads, brunettes, whatever."

A household name in the late '60s and early '70s, Namath endorsed everything from pantyhose (which he himself wore in the huddle to stay warm) to razors (Shick paid him a then eye-popping $10,000 in 1968 to shave off his celebrated Fu-Manchu moustache for a 1968 television ad). "I can scramble better now," said a clean-shaven Namath. "I'm a little lighter."

There was a story of a man named Brady...who met a man named Broadway Joe. Of course, I speak of the *Brady Bunch*, which featured the quarterback. Barry Williams (aka Greg Brady) recalled: "Unfortunately for me, the episode called "Mail Order Hero" focused around little Brady brother Bobby. I didn't let that get in the way of playing receiver of his passes in patterns of down and outs and going long in-between takes. Joe was, simply put, a gracious guy. He didn't avoid everyone by staying in his dressing room until he was called, he didn't sit in the corner waiting to get it over with, he was social, friendly, and oh, yeah...pretty good with a football. I ate it up. I probably could have run more plays with him if Florence Henderson didn't keep jumping up into his arms." Years later, Namath was offered his own starring role as a retired athlete on a sitcom. Broadway Joe passed, and the role went to Ted Danson. The show was called *Cheers.*

Sometimes lost in the legend of Broadway Joe, the world's most famous bachelor, the guy who bagged the most beautiful blondes and threw back whiskey shots with Frank Sinatra, was his big-game passing acumen. "Namath must have peripheral vision," recalled Jets receiver Eddie Bell in 1972. "Most quarterbacks wait until their receiver makes his break and then they throw. Namath throws before you break, and the ball comes right down into your arms. Somehow he anticipates what guy is going to be open." Added Hall of Fame coach Bill Walsh, Namath was "the most beautiful, accurate, stylish passer with the quickest release I've ever seen."

The only thing quicker than Namath's release—which he used to hit favorite target Don Maynard and rack up almost 28,000 career passing yards—was the time it took a woman to get splayed out naked on his white llama rug. "When we won the league championship," recalled Namath. "All the married guys on the club had to thank their wives for

The Escape Artist

Long before Randall or Steve or Mike or Donovan, there was Scramblin' Fran. The first great running quarterback, **Fran Tarkenton** was as adept at buying time to make a throw (his 47,003 passing yards is fifth all-time) as he was scampering for a first down (he rushed for 3,674 yards). He was Houdini in a football uniform, escaping the most impossible circumstances, slipping away from the grasp of the entire defensive line.

"He had eyes in the back of his head. I'm thoroughly convinced of that," Deacon Jones told NFL Films. "You could approach him from the rear, and he's looking downfield, but he feels you and sees you. And he would react."

His weekly magic act resulted in his Vikings making three trips to the Super Bowl (VIII, IX, and XI), but that's where the magic stopped. Minnesota lost all of them. Still, his backfield improvisations were worthy of Baryshnikov, and thus provided a new vision of how the position could be played. Even Tarkenton recognized he was ahead of his time. "I must have looked like a kind of lunatic loping [from sideline to sideline]," he said, especially compared to other signal-callers of his era, who were "about as mobile as 16-inch shore batteries."

putting up with all the stress and strain all season. I had to thank all the single broads in New York." He dated famous women, from Barbra Streisand to Raquel Welch. Even hippie-chick Janis Joplin once rerouted her tour in hopes of landing the Crown Royal–drinking, country club–golfing, white fur–wearing bachelor—the noble rogue was good enough to oblige. Another time, Namath was at a Manhattan bar when two gorgeous girls who had been making eyes at him all night followed him outside. Namath took the beauties back to his penthouse for a night of partying, leaving their two dates sitting alone. Don't feel too bad for the lads—they were Mick Jagger and Keith Richards.

Great parties don't end with a whimper but burn out in a blaze of glory—leaving you wanting more. So it was with La Festival de Namath. The first sign of trouble came in 1969, when NFL commissioner Pete Rozelle forced him to sell his interest in a Manhattan pub called Bachelors III because of its ties to mobsters like Tommy "Tea Balls" Mancuso. But it was a premature case of bad knees that really dimmed Namath's sparkling career. It's a credit to the five-time Pro Bowler's mega-watt charisma that while his injuries shortened his football career they couldn't diminish his legendary status. It seemed that everyone wanted to live vicariously through the glamorous, free-wheelin' athlete, even the man who signed the Alabama star to a then-unheard-of $400,000 contract, Jets owner Sonny Werblin: "Joe likes excitement. He's single and young and doesn't have to be at work until noon. You can't ask a man like that to sit at home and read a book."

In 2009 Academy Award–nominated actor Jake Gyllenhaal will star in a film recounting how Namath went from a steel-worker's kid in Beaver Falls, Pennsylvania, to a Super Bowl MVP awash in the bright lights of Madison Avenue and the adoration of a young generation seeking brash, fearless heroes.

Terry Bradshaw

Terry Bradshaw is one of the most easygoing and funny people to ever put on an NFL uniform, but if you think the road he traveled from a small town in Louisiana to the Hall of Fame in Canton, Ohio, was smoothly paved, you'd be wrong. When the Steelers made him their No. 1 draft choice in 1970, he was hung with the burden of high expectations. After all, the "Blond Bomber" (a name given to him, albeit, by a disliked college teammate) had all the raw material to be great: he was a big, tough, 6'3", 215-pound quarterback with an arm that earned him the nickname the "Louisiana Rifleman"—because of his cannon arm and uncanny resemblance to Chuck Connors, who played the Rifleman on television.

While he showed glimmers of brilliance, Bradshaw's first few years in Pittsburgh were marked by inconsistent play and far too many interceptions. The reaction he got depended on the person, but it was universally bad. His coach, Chuck Noll, who was the polar opposite of his affable, free-spirited quarterback, didn't trust him enough to let him steer the ship, precipitating a fierce quarterback controversy between three men: Joe Gilliam, Terry Hanratty, and Bradshaw. As for his teammates, they chaffed at the young, brash southern boy who delivered long-winded speeches in the huddle. "You want your quarterback to be a Bugs Bunny type," said one Steelers teammate in 1973. "Or Daffy Duck. A guy who's got the sneakiness, who's got that sneakiness. That's Hanratty. Bradshaw's too much like Elmer Fudd."

Terry Bradshaw and the Steelers won four Super Bowls in a six-year span in the 1970s.

If his coaches and teammates were disapproving, that was nothing compared to the Steelers fan, who practically forced Bradshaw into the witness protection program. "Booing Terry Bradshaw became a favorite sport in Pittsburgh," recalled the big-grinned quarterback. "'Hey, what do you guys want to do tonight? Let's go boo Terry Bradshaw.' The situation got so bad that my mom came up to stay with me for several weeks. 'It can't be that bad, Terry,' she said. I took her with me to a hockey game, and they booed us. They booed my mother! When my brothers and I booed her at home, that was one thing, but at a hockey game? They were booing her for giving birth to me. How awful is that?"

In 1974 Bradshaw managed to lead the Steelers to their first conference championship in their 42-year history and first Super Bowl ever.
However, you might be surprised to learn that he was benched as late as
November of that 1974 campaign, and it wasn't until after the last
regular-season game against Cincinnati that Chuck Noll told Bradshaw
that the job was his for good. And despite the Super Bowl title, the
doubters would not be silenced, especially those in the local media who
caricatured him as the "Bayou Bumpkin," an oafish hick who didn't have
the smarts to lead. Naturally, Terry Bradshaw was hurt by these accusations, which didn't hold much water considering that Bradshaw was one
of the few guys back then to call his own plays. "I played quarterback
unplugged," recalled Bradshaw. "I ran my team. I had the on-field
responsibility for our offense. Kenny Anderson had his plays sent in from
the sideline. Most often Tom Landry sent in plays for Roger [Staubach].
Vince Lombardi called plays for Bart Starr. I was the one whose elevator
didn't go to the top floor—but I called my plays."

In the run up to Super Bowl IX against the Minnesota Vikings, the
media teased him mercilessly about his brain power, comparing him
unfavorably to opposing quarterback Fran Tarkenton. Before Super Bowl
XIII against Dallas, Cowboys linebacker Thomas "Hollywood"
Henderson said Bradshaw "couldn't spell *cat* if you spotted him the c
and the a." All Bradshaw did was turn in an MVP performance, throwing for 318 yards and a record four touchdowns, eclipsing Bart Starr's
previous record of 250 yards. "Both Bradshaw and the Steelers had
arrived," recalled Dan Rooney, chairman of the Steelers. "That business
about him being dumb—people wish they could be that dumb. Next to
Johnny Unitas, I think Terry Bradshaw is the greatest quarterback in
history."

The "Blond Bomber" had silenced his critics, leading the 1970s-era
Steelers to four Super Bowls, one of the great dynasties in NFL history.
Bill Nunn concluded, "I go along with the Chief's [owner Art Rooney's]
analysis, which was: we won the first Super Bowl despite Bradshaw and
the last two of those four Super Bowls because of Bradshaw." He finished
his career with 27,989 yards passing and 212 TD passes, taking home
the MVP award in Super Bowl XIII and XIV, and winning the NFL's
MVP in 1978. He was elected to the Hall of Fame in 1989 in his first

> ## Armed Force
> The term "a Hail Mary throw" has become part of the American lexicon, used by everyone from Norman Schwarzkopf to describe a military operation during the first Gulf War (touchdown accomplished) to Elizabeth Dole's campaign manager, Marty Ryall, explaining the desperate, last-minute attack ad on her opponent, Kay Hagen, in 2008 (incomplete pass: she lost).
>
> While Doug Flutie's pass in a 1984 Boston College–Miami game is considered by many to be the ultimate Hail Mary, the original one occurred in the 1975 divisional playoff between the Cowboys and the Vikings. With seconds left in the game, Dallas' **Roger Staubach**, a former supply officer in the Navy who did a tour of duty in Vietnam, heaved a 50-yard bomb downfield. Cowboys receiver Drew Pearson beat Nate Wright to the ball (Vikings fans swear he pushed off), trapped the ball against his hip, and stepped across the goal line to complete the miracle play and advance Dallas to the next round with a 14–10 win.
>
> In a postgame interview, Staubach, who's flair for late-game dramatics earned him the nickname "Captain Comeback," told reporters, "I closed my eyes and said a Hail Mary prayer." Staubach had been knocked down on the play, so that's about all he could do. "Sister Sloan, my first grade teacher, contacted me," said Staubach. "You can't believe the number of nuns and priests who have told me how proud they were that I threw a Hail Mary. Or course, my Baptist friends say I should have called it the Hail Jesus pass."

year of eligibility. Since retiring, he's owned a cattle ranch, released several country-western albums—including the 1976 debut classic "I'm So Lonesome I Could Cry" (no word yet on a T.O. remix)—and achieved one of the most successful careers in sports broadcasting history. Guess the elevator did go to the top. Well, just about.

Dan Marino

The poor New York Jets. In 1983 they used their 24th pick in the first round of the NFL Draft to acquire quarterback Ken O'Brien, passing on perhaps the best pure passer in NFL history. Oops. Of course, I speak of the curly-haired quarterback out of the University of Pittsburgh, Dan Marino, selected by the Dolphins three picks later. In defense of Gang Green, Marino did have a less-than-stellar senior year, plus there were worrisome rumors floating around that he was a pothead. Still, Dan Marino. Oy.

In 1984 Marino had what might have been the greatest regular season in NFL history. Not only did he throw for more than 5,000 yards, but he also threw 48 touchdowns, shattering the old mark by 12. "How much did I like touchdowns?" asked Marino, who won the league MVP that year. "Well, I named my dog Touchdown, proving it was this man's best friend." In the fifth game of the season, he broke a club record with

Brothers in Arms

Manning versus Manning would be the ultimate Super Bowl matchup. But what if you had two Mannings on the same team? One MVP Manning passing to another MVP Manning. How could this be? Well, it almost happened. Once upon a time, the Greenies of Isidore Newman, a New Orleans private school, featured the dominant passing tandem of 10th-grader **Peyton Manning**, rifle-armed quarterback, and senior Cooper Manning, all-state wide receiver. The plan was for Peyton to follow his older brother to Ole Miss, where the tandem would resume their successful partnership.

But before the tight siblings ever got a chance to hook up on a single pass play, Cooper was diagnosed with spinal stenosis, a serious condition that forced him to quit football forever. "I believe Cooper handled it much better than Peyton did," said their father, Archie Manning. (The College Hall of Famer and Saints quarterback's legend is so immense at Ole Miss that his uniform number, 18, is the official speed limit on campus.) "Cooper just thought it was how life went. Peyton was angry; he thought it wasn't fair. They talked it through between them. Their relationship, their love for each other, makes me proud, even very emotional sometimes because the years have a tendency to go by." Peyton Manning chose to wear No. 18 in the pros, but not because it was the number his dad wore at Ole Miss, but because it was the number his favorite target wore at Isidore Newman.

When he arrived in Indianapolis, Peyton Manning was paired with wide receiver Marvin Harrison. That worked out okay. Over a decade playing together, the duo won a Super Bowl and set NFL records for completions (953), receiving yards (12,766), and touchdowns (112). Dan Pompei of the *Chicago Tribune* believes theses records could become "the football equivalent of Joe DiMaggio's 56-game hitting streak." He added, "In 11 years, between regular-season and postseason practices, training camp and preseason practices, and off-season workouts, Manning probably threw more than 44,000 passes to Harrison based on an estimation formula Manning and I worked up." In 2008 the Colts released Harrison, but the marriage produced one of the very finest quarterback/receiver combos in NFL history. No one is more proud of this fact than big brother Cooper.

429 yards. With seven games left in the season, he already held the Dolphins' single-season record for TD passes and yards. Marino guided the Dolphins to Super Bowl XIX, where they faced off against Joe Montana and the mighty San Francisco 49ers. They got beaten 38–16. Despite remaining the most prolific passer in the league, this would be Marino's last shot to play in a Super Bowl.

In 17 years Marino played on a team with a 1,000-yard rusher only once. His name: Karim Abdul-Jabbar. And no, he didn't have a devastating jump hook. After losing in the 1997 playoffs, offensive coordinator Gary Stevens vented his frustration, shared by legions of Dolphins fans, over the dismal state of their ground assault: "Name me a great player we have besides Danny," said Stevens. "You can't. We were No. 2 in the passing game. No. 2 in the passing game! How did we do it? With our players, you tell me, how did we do it? We have to throw. We couldn't run. And do we have a great running back? No."

Perhaps Marino's finest moment in the regular season came during a *Monday Night Football* game in 1985, when he led the Dolphins to an upset victory over the then-undefeated Chicago Bears. Against defensive coordinator Buddy Ryan's vaunted defense, Marino put up an unthinkable 31—by halftime. As usual, the Monsters of the Midway charged at the quarterback with reckless abandon, but Marino had such a lightning-quick release, they could never get to him in time. He was like a gunfighter who always got off the first shot—and didn't often miss. "We were so precise," recalled head coach Don Shula, "I later heard that Mike Ditka and Buddy Ryan nearly came to blows at halftime arguing how to defend us in the second half." Shula spoke for all Miami fans, past and present, when he expressed gratitude to Marino for insuring that the undefeated 1972 Dolphins he coached "wouldn't have any company."

According to sports writer Tom Fiedler, some medical doctors so marveled at Marino's arm strength and quick release that they studied the matter and discovered that he had an unusually high number of "fast twitch muscle fibers." As abundance of these fibers is great for a pigskin-throwing gunslinger, they are bad for a Tour de France cyclist traveling a great distance. In fact, a prevalence of "fast twitch" muscle fibers as opposed to "slow twitch" ones was something Lance Armstrong had to overcome on his way to becoming a cycling legend.

One time after he had retired, Marino was golfing in Ireland. Through the whole round, the caddies followed him around, star-struck. Marino didn't think too much about it—plenty of people recognize him. After all, he's one of the greatest NFL quarterbacks in history. Finally, Marino asked them how long they'd been Dolphins fans. Their response: "Who are the Dolphins?" Marino cocked his head slightly. "You were in that Jim Carrey movie!" they excitedly blurted out. Immediately, Marino realized that they knew him from his, um, performance ("Okay, I didn't get me an Oscar," quipped Marino) in *Ace Ventura: Pet Detective*. To this day, wherever he travels, people shout out to the Hall of Fame quarterback, "Hey, Dan, laces out!" Later, Marino passed on a cameo in the remake of *The Longest Yard*. Who knows? He could have been recognized as the guy in that Adam Sandler movie. Jets fans could give a crap either way.

Brett Favre

As he scrambles for his life in the backfield, dodging foaming-at-the-mouth defensive ends, one thought dominates your mind: he's going down. But before you can say Don Majkowski (the most famous trivia answer in Wisconsin), the football is whizzing down the field like it was on a rope. Seconds later, it hits a receiver in full stride. The quarterback who rifled the ball is lying flat on his back, having been crushed by a 250-pound beast. The next two images happen quickly: the receiver leaps into the screaming throngs behind the end zone; the quarterback rushes down the field, leaping up and down like a kid in a playground. The name of the receiver has changed over the years. The name of the quarterback hasn't. Neither has the number on his green-and-yellow jersey. It's No. 4. Brett Favre.

Some men are born and raised to be gunslingers. Favre was not one of them. The story goes that he spent his playing days at Hancock North Central High School perfecting the hand-off. Hampered by a head coach who employed a run-dominant wishbone offense, he was lucky to get off more than five passes per game. Nonetheless, Mark McHale, an assistant coach at Southern Mississippi, was convinced that Favre could shine as a college quarterback. The problem was convincing Eagles head coach Bill Carmody. This would be difficult, not only because of Favre's puny passing numbers, but because Carmody already had three quality quarterbacks on his Southern Miss squad and two more on their way. McHale persuaded Carmody to come watch Favre in person, but only by selling Favre as a prospective defensive back. The next step in McHale's scheme was to convince Favre's high school coach Big Irv to let his young quarterback air it out the last game of the season. "I said, Irvin, I have a head coach coming to see Brett.... I need you to let Brett throw the ball and show what he can do." Big Irv had another reason to open up the offense so his quarterback could show off his arm to the visiting Southern Miss coaches—Brett was his son. And so with Carmody and McHale watching in the stands, Big Irv Favre called his most aggressive game of the season, letting his quarterback attempt more passes than he had all year. A grand total of six.

Just the same, Favre got a scholarship to go play at Southern Mississippi. Despite being at the bottom of the depth chart, people soon began to take notice of his high-powered arm. "He split my hands open a couple of times during practice," recalled Eagles receiver Chris McGee. "We used to have a set route where the receiver runs a five- to seven-yard route and sits, the quarterback takes a four-step drop and hits you. The first time Brett got into the rotation to work with the receivers, he threw the

---

The Fab 40

When back-up Patriots quarterback **Doug Flutie** entered a 2005 *Monday Night Football* game against the Jets, opposing quarterback Vinny Testaverde must have been flooded with nightmarish flashbacks.

Twenty-one years earlier, the redshirted Miami Hurricanes quarterback had watched helplessly from the sideline as Flutie found roommate Gerard Phelan among the sea of players in the end zone, lifting the BC Eagles to an improbable 47–45 win. But by the time 43-year-old Flutie came into the nationally televised game, which coincidentally was the final telecast of *MNF* on ABC, New England was already coasting to victory. By then, there was a little that the 42-year-old Testaverde—who himself was a late-game substitute—could do, although he did manage to throw a touchdown.

As for Flutie, he only attempted one pass, resulting in a two-yard completion. Nonetheless, it proved to be another historic throw for Flutie, as well as for his college rival Testaverde, as it marked the first game in NFL history in which two quarterbacks over the age of 40 completed a pass. In the final game of the season against the Dolphins, Flutie would again make history, becoming the first player since the Bears' Ray "Scooter" McLean in 1941 to convert a drop kick for points.

ball, and Darryl Tillman moved out of the way. I said, 'Tillman. What are you doing?' He said, 'I thought he was throwing the ball down the field!'"

There are times when Brett Favre resembles a regular Joe rather than a future Hall of Fame superstar. He's always had this fun-loving, down-home exuberance. Once, in college, he earned the special distinction of being allowed into the tight fraternity of offensive linemen. "Brett was one of us," recalled 270-pound lineman Chris Ryals. The main perk of belonging to this club: you could eat pickled pig's feet with the guys in their dorm rooms. Eagles teammate John Brown recalled how, after two years in the club, he was barred simply because he was moved from offense to defense. "When I went back, they said no more pickled pig feet."

One can expect plenty of good-natured hijinks with Favre around, including stuffing his teammate's clothes with ice bags. "He's big on stink bombs every once in a while, too," recalled Packers teammate Mike Flanagan. "You would never know he is a $100 million guy. He just likes to have fun." While it's his humor that has kept his teammates loose, it's his toughness that's earned the respect of his teammates in college, as well as the pros. Prior to his senior year, Favre got into a car wreck that forced doctors to remove 30 inches of his intestines. Most assumed he was lost for the season. "He must have lost 50 pounds for the surgery," recalled Brown. But Favre only missed one game before reclaiming his spot on the field. "He had a drive that most people can't understand," said Brown.

Favre's first win as a Green Bay Packer reflected the heart-stopping, missile-launching, topsy-turvy career of the NFL's purest gunslinger. Favre came in during the first quarter against the Bengals to complete 22 out of 39 passes. Then he nearly gave the game away with four fumbles. But with 13 seconds left in the game, he threw a 35-yard touchdown pass for a wild 24–23 victory. Mike Holmgren got his first win of his NFL coaching career but lost a few years of his life in the process. Holmgren deadpanned, "Nothing he does surprises me, good or bad." His *good* performances are lore in Green Bay: the famous "throw across his body" to beat Detroit in 1994, the game-winning nine-yard scramble against Atlanta that same year. "There were several guys chasing me who were faster than me," recalled Favre of his all-or-nothing dash, resulting in the last touchdown ever scored in Milwaukee. "But at that point, I was running pretty fast." And perhaps his greatest gunslingin' moment was his improbable scramble and pass to

Made-for-TV Life

It's the kind of story that gets Hollywood producers bopping excitedly in their BMW convertible: grocery store stock boy becomes Super Bowl MVP (where he threw for a record 414 yards). Only then his career spirals downward as the ravages of age and injuries take their told. But at 37 years old, the washed-up veteran finds new life and proves the naysayers wrong, leading his 9–7 Cardinals to their first Super Bowl appearance and the team's first championship game since 1948.

This is the improbable but honest-to-god true story of **Kurt Warner**, who last year became the oldest quarterback to ever play in the Big Game. And to think, back in 8th grade the Iowa product was ruled too fat at 140 pounds to play any offensive position but lineman. A slimmer Warner came back the next year, intent on getting to touch the ball—as a tight end. But his coach at Regis High School in Cedar Rapids, Jim Padlock, showed up to training camp in desperate need of a QB. "He asked everyone to throw the ball, and I could throw the farthest, so he gave me the job," wrote Kurt Warner in his autobiography *All Things Possible*. "I was totally bummed out."

Andre Rison for the first touchdown of Super Bowl XXXI in 1997, which the Packers went on to win over the Patriots. Summing up the crazy play, Favre said evenly, "It made me look like I knew what I was doing."

What makes his NFL-record 269-consecutive-games streak so amazing is that for all the good fortune it required, it also depended on unfathomable will power. Looking at a partial list of injuries that Favre has played through since it began in 1992, it's hard to imagine anyone else, even iron-man Cal Ripken, making every single start:

- first-degree separation of his left shoulder (1992)
- severely bruised left hip (1994)
- severely sprained left ankle (1995)
- tendinitis in right elbow (2000)
- sprained lateral collateral ligament in left knee (2002)
- broken right thumb (2003)
- torn biceps tendon (2008)

After coming up short against the Giants in a thrilling 23–20 NFC title game in 2007 (his interception in overtime set up Lawrence Tynes' dramatic 47-yard game-winning boot), the ageless warrior concluded his impressive 17-season run with the Packers. But Favre's life of retired

---

The Reich Stuff

Frank Reich will forever be remembered as the man who put the wild in Wild Card weekend. On January 3, 1993, starting in place of an injured Jim Kelly, the Bills' quarterback rallied his team from a 32-point deficit in the third quarter to defeat Warren Moon and the Houston Oilers by a final score of 41–38. A field goal by 32-year-old Steve Christie completed the greatest comeback in NFL history.

The Oilers' defense had clearly not watched the 1984 game between Reich's Maryland Terrapins and the Miami Hurricanes. Reich was actually a back-up in college to Boomer Esiason, but naturally it was Reich that day who led the Terrapins, trailing 31–0, to the greatest comeback in college Division I-A football history.

---

leisure didn't last long, as he emerged for a final curtain call on Broadway, grabbing the helm of the New York Jets. Upon his arrival in 2008, Favre injected Gang Green with a shot of energy and excitement, leading the squad to a surprise 8–3 record, but a shoulder injury reduced his powerful rifle to a mere squirt gun as the Jets collapsed short of the finish line—and the playoffs. One again, No. 4 retired. A skeptical media and public watched as Favre spent the summer of 2009 flirting with the Minnesota Vikings, the Pack's longtime division rivals. Eventually, Favre decided to stay retired to the delight of Cheeseheads through out the Midwest, who now wouldn't have to burn their Wranglers in effigy.

Time will tell whether the gray-bearded sharp-shooter has hung up his holster for good, but he can take comfort in knowing that he's already in possession of many of the NFL's most famous passing records. Here are some that you might not be aware of: in 2004 he recorded his 26th straight game throwing a TD pass against the Chicago Bears, a team record. His 222 starts without a shutout was a record that ended September 2006. Brett Favre's first ever receiver? Brett Favre. He caught a deflected pass for a seven-yard loss. But for all his passing records and scintillating performances, he's most remembered as a fearless player whose tenacity is only eclipsed by the joy with which he performed his job. "He's a gunslinger," former Cleveland Browns quarterback Tim Couch said. "He may throw three picks in the first half, but he's still going to come out giving it all he's got in the next half, and he may throw three touchdowns and pull the game out in the end."

Then Phil Simms Said...

To this day, Phil Simms holds almost every New York Giants passing record. But it's what he did 22 years ago at the Rose Bowl in Pasadena that secured his place among the all-time great New York sports figures. On that late-January date he completed an unconscious 88 percent of his passes, including 10 straight in the second half, to lead the Giants to their first-ever Super Bowl victory—a 39–20 win over the Denver Broncos. After the game, he picked up some MVP hardware, with just enough time left over to be the first in a long tradition of players to grin at the camera and say, "I'm going to Disney World!" The legendary quarterback and veteran broadcaster told us about his Super Bowl glory days, getting chewed out by Bill Parcells, and keeping Lawrence Taylor from sacking people on the golf green.

You earned MVP honors in Super Bowl XXI as the New York Giants defeated the Denver Broncos 39–20. What's your greatest memory from that game?

The greatest feeling came just before we were introduced as a football team. We were standing in the tunnel at the Rose Bowl, looking out over the stadium. Just standing there going, *Wow, it's everything I dreamed it would be.* It was everything I dreamed it would feel like. It was my best moment in sports.

And then you went out there and completed 21 out of 25 passes.

Twenty-two out of 25.

I didn't mean to shortchange you by one. Still, that's a ridiculous number. Where would you rate that MVP performance in all-time Super Bowl history?

I don't think about it. I don't worry about it. And I'm surely not going to rate it. It was just a great moment, and I feel like I got a chance to get into TV and do what I'm doing now because of that Super Bowl. It gave me credibility.

Phil Simms quarterbacked the Giants to a Super Bowl championship in 1987 and is now a well-regarded analyst for CBS.

In that game, you threw a key 44-yard flea flicker to wide receiver Phil McConkey. But it's your fourth-quarter touchdown pass to him off Mark Bavaro's deflection that remains the most memorable image of that Super Bowl. What do you recall about that play?

The play was to get it to Mark Bavaro before the defense had time to react. Just like the coaches drew it up. It didn't work exactly like we hoped it would. They were both coming to the inside. Bavaro was open, and the ball hit him in the face. And McConkey, who was always on Bavaro's coattails, was there to catch the deflection for the touchdown. But I've heard Bavaro say many times, "The heck with Phil McConkey." That was his best friend, but he wanted to catch another touchdown pass. And he dropped it.

Wasn't McConkey also a Navy helicopter pilot?

Yeah. He was a daredevil. He played like a daredevil. All-out. Full-speed. I remember the year he came to training camp, he was catching every-thing. His forearms were raw—no skin left—from all the diving catches he made. So being a helicopter pilot in the Navy was perfect for him.

I always thought of him as the Giants' Vince Papale. Do you agree?

Yeah, that's a good analogy. He was small for a football player in the NFL. He returned punts. He took a lot of big hits in his career. At least twice a week at Giants Stadium I would hear the crowd go, *oooohhhhhh*, because Phil McConkey had just got run over. And when he was all done, he went back to the Navy.

You were nearly drafted by Bill Walsh to play in San Francisco. Do you ever think about how your career would have been different if you had played in his West Coast offense?

Sure. I've thought about it a lot. I remember he worked me out twice at Morehead State. He came down there himself. As I look back on all those things he said to me that day at Morehead State—about the rhythm and timing of being a quarterback and all that stuff—to have somebody teaching me like that through my career, it would have no doubt changed me. Would it have made my career better? I don't know. I can't say that. I do remember, after about seven years in the NFL, watching the 49ers play the Falcons on film and thinking, *God, the 49ers are making it look easy.* Joe Montana, man. It crossed my mind for a second, *Damn, that could have been me.*

Of course, you ended up having an outstanding 14-year career with the Giants. What was it like playing for Bill Parcells?

He had extremely high expectations of most guys. There was not much you could do that would satisfy him. He believed in practicing hard. Practicing perfect.

Can you describe what those practices were like?

He drove us hard mentally. Extremely sarcastic. Extremely verbal. You better not have touchy feelings. If it was your day to be picked on in practice, it was going to be a rough day. It could be the offensive linemen's turn. It could be Lawrence Taylor's turn. If it was my day, I just took it. But he was just trying to make you a better player.

There's a story of how quarterback Bart Starr once stood up to Vince Lombardi during one of his infamous locker-room tirades, and the coach actually backed down. Did you have any similar moments with Coach Parcells?

That wouldn't have worked with Bill. He said to me one day during training camp, while we were walking to the practice field, which was about 200s yard from our locker rooms, he said to me, "Hey, you're doing great. You're having a great training camp. I'm proud of you. You're practicing hard. You're playing well. You're being a good leader." And I'm thinking, *Wow.* I say to him, "Thanks, Coach." Then he says, "But listen to me, today I'm going to get on you like I have never got on you before." And I said, "Why?" He said, "I want the rest of these guys to see that if I can get on my quarterback, then I can do it to them."

So how bad did he get on you?

Oh, it was a show. Everything was going well, then mid-practice I throw an incomplete pass, and he goes into an unbelievable tirade. He starts cursing, "Simms, #%*$#!%." It just went on and on. The thing was, with Bill, if he was yelling at you, the other 49 guys were allowed to laugh. And I'm standing there, thinking, *Man, this is unbelievable. It's all preplanned. And I've gotta take this.*

On the other hand, Lombardi would let Paul Hornung get away with things he wouldn't let anyone else on the team get away with. He was like the prodigal son. Did Parcells have a similar relationship with Lawrence Taylor?

Sure. Absolutely. First, he was a great player. A greater player than Paul Hornung. Sometimes with guys, like Lawrence, there is a different set of rules. But it didn't bother me at all. I was all for Coach doing whatever he had to do to keep Lawrence performing the best he could for our football team.

I heard that on occasion L.T. would come to practice hungover.

Well, sometimes he'd stay out the whole night and he didn't have any sleep. He would come in and sit in meetings all day long. And then he'd go out to practice, and nobody could block him, nobody could stop him. And we'd laugh, and he'd say to me, "That was the only way I could get through it. I had to go crazy."

That's amazing he could still perform at such a high level.

There were a lot of us who've said, if he had taken care of himself and worked out all the time, what would he have been? But I don't know. Maybe he wouldn't have been as good. That was part of his mental makeup.

You and L.T. shared an intense competitive spirit?

Oh, yeah. He was the man who could do everything. We would get into foul-shooting contests. Lawrence could throw a football 50 yards into a trashcan. Of course, he's the only guy I know who thinks he can throw it into the trashcan on every throw.

I heard you guys even played golfed together. Any good stories from the links?

When Lawrence and [Giants nose tackle] Jim Burt played against each other, that was quite a pair. There was nobody else walking the course that looked like them, that was for sure. They wore their golf clothes and looked like football players playing golf.

They were so competitive, and they wanted to beat each other *so bad* that I had to make sure to stand in between them. You didn't know if they were going to start tackling each other and throwing each other down on the green.

Who was the biggest prankster in the Giants' locker room?

Our center Bart Oates was by far the worst. He would put a dead fish deep down around you car engine where you couldn't find it. You'd think, *What the hell is wrong with the car? It stinks.* One time I was driving home and I had this cop following behind me, and I'm thinking, *What's going on? This is ridiculous.* I got home, got out of my car, and saw on the back of the car there was a big sign that said, "I Hate Cops."

Who was the toughest defender you had to deal with as quarterback?
Reggie White, without a question. And I had to face him twice a year for most of my career. That was every bit as bad as facing L.T. twice a year. That's for sure. When I used to have to play Reggie White and the Philadelphia Eagles, I knew it was going to be rough and I was going to be hit a lot. Before the game I'd sit in the locker room, and I give myself a pep talk and say, "No matter how rough it gets today. Hang in there. Be tough." It wasn't like I was thinking, *Make the right read*, or, *Make the right throw*. It was all about staying tough.

chapter 2

The Gridiron Generals

George Halas

First consider this: the NFL would've likely folded—forget becoming a wildly popular, multibillion-dollar operation—if not for George Halas. Heck, it might not have even gotten off the ground. It was Halas who gathered with a small group of investors at the Hupmobile showroom in Canton, Ohio, in 1920 (a shortage of chairs meant a few had to plop down on vehicles) to form a professional football league, reorganized a short time later to become the National Football League. At the historic meeting, Halas represented the Decatur Staleys, which he would relocate to the Windy City and in 1922 rename the Bears. This, after he first considered calling them the Cubs; a thank you to the baseball team for sharing Wrigley Field. (Dick Butkus? Mike Ditka? Brian Urlacher? Not bears, but cubs? Hardly!)

You have to remember that in the 1920s pro football was barely a blip on the screen. In those days, people were hooked on the college game and a giant named "Babe" crushing little white balls out of Yankee Stadium. In a move that probably saved the league, Halas signed college's biggest star and one of the country's most famous athletes, Red "the Galloping Ghost" Grange, and then brought him around the country on an exhibition tour, shining a national spotlight on the league. As the tour concluded, Halas recalled making one last stop: 1600 Pennsylvania Avenue. "Senator McKinley of Illinois sent his limousine to take Red and me to the White House to meet President Coolidge," said Halas. "The senator introduced us, 'Mr. President, this is George Halas and Red Grange of the Chicago Bears.' President

George Halas was a founding father of the NFL and remains one of the most iconic figures in all of sports.

Coolidge replied, 'How are you, young gentlemen? I have always admired animal acts.'"

George Halas didn't get his nickname because, as writer Jeff Davis said in *Papa Bear*, he was "loveable and cuddly." For Davis, the nickname fit because he was "a grizzly, flesh-and-blood Ursus Horribulus: surly, snarly, sinister, and smart." Another journalist described him as "a shambling, disheveled fellow given to flamboyant outbursts of rage and delight." Many others have commented over the years on his famously stingy nature, including Mike Ditka, who once remarked that he "tossed around nickels like they were manhole covers."

In 1940 Halas was coaching the Bears to a 73–0 victory over the Washington Redskins, the largest blowout in NFL championship history. The Bears had kicked so many extra points, and sent so many footballs into the stands, that the refs were down to practice balls. Meanwhile, Halas was getting heartburn on the sideline, mentally tallying the cost of buying new footballs. The story goes that Halas ordered Clyde "Bulldog" Turner to muff the snap on the next extra point to save another ball from disappearing into the crowd. "I told Halas I wasn't going to make a bad snap, not in no championship game," Turner recalled. So Halas went to Plan B: he told the holder it would be in his best interest to mishandle the ball. "The next day in the paper," Turner grumbled, "they say the point was missed due to a bad pass from center. Hell, I never made a bad pass in my life."

While Papa Bear, whom a journalist once described as having "all the warmth of breaking bones," seemingly reveled in his well-deserved reputation as a frugal curmudgeon, he also had a very generous side, albeit far less publicized; for example, he took care of the medical expenses of Brian Piccolo, the back-up Bears running back who died of cancer at just 26. Piccolo's best friend, the legendary Gale Sayers, describes having an almost father-son relationship with Halas. "In 1967 or 1968," recalled Sayers, "I was growing a moustache. 'Gale,' he said, 'I know people are growing beards today. I don't think you look good in one.' I cut it off. I think that built our relationship. I was talking to his secretary one day. 'Gale, you know what?' she said. 'George Halas gave you this little bonus for many different things, because of your skills and everything, but he really appreciates your cutting off your moustache.'"

The Heidi *Game*

On November 17, 1968, the Raiders scored two touchdowns in the final 50 seconds to complete a stirring comeback win over the New York Jets. Too bad everybody in the country missed it. Instead, they saw a little girl traipsing through the Swiss Alps. Why? NBC had switched over to the scheduled movie *Heidi*.

After the game, Jets head coach **Weeb Ewbank** got a congratulatory call from his wife, who, like most people, didn't realize the Raiders had won. He furiously slammed down the phone. Angry fans reacted by flooding the NBC switchboard; meanwhile, the next day's headline in the *New York Daily News* announced: "Jets 32, Raiders 29, Heidi 14."

The next time you have to suffer through the conclusion of a blowout, you can thank this blunder, which caused the NFL to insert language into its TV contracts guaranteeing that games would be shown to their completion.

Papa Bear built his legacy as a resolute, hands-on owner—early on, he reportedly sold tickets before the game—but he was also a fantastic athlete. Not only was he an outstanding tight end for the Bears for 10 years, Halas was also briefly the switch-hitting right fielder for the New York Yankees before incurring an injury sliding during a spring-training game. (Many people don't know that 49 years later, in 1968, Halas had what was then a revolutionary hip replacement. Speaking of replacement, the man who took his spot on the Yankees roster: Babe Ruth.)

Halas, a deeply religious family man who neither smoked nor drank, was nonetheless known as a world-class curser. When archrival Green Bay Packers fans would heckle him from the stands, he would turn around and shoot back an ungodly stream of expletives in his thick Midwest accent: *You, Cacksuckers! Go fackin choke on a kielbasa!* Papa Bear had a Belichick sneakiness to him, employing an army of spies, while keeping a framed motto in his office that read: "Never go to bed a loser." Ditka recalled how Halas did things his way, no apologies or excuses: "There were times when he went out of his way to really aggravate the shit out of you. He knew he was doing it, but you know what, that was his way of doing things, and who am I to say it was wrong? It's like, you'd ask him, 'Coach, why do we practice on Sunday?' He'd look you right in the eye and say, 'You know why we practice on Sunday?' 'No.' 'Because we practice on Sunday.' That's exactly what the hell he'd say. That's the way it was.

I loved that man." Fed up with seeing the Bears struggling badly, the 86-year-old owner emerged from his semi-hibernation in 1981, and with a final roar announced without consulting his GM that Ditka would be the new coach, leading to a ninth title in 1985.

While few dispute his monumental role in building the NFL, especially up until the national televised event that was the 1958 Championship Game, his greatest achievement arguably came as coach of the Chicago Bears for 40 seasons. Over his career, Papa Bear won six championships and amassed 324 wins, a record that stood until Don Shula broke it in 1993. Halas won his first title at the age of 26 and his last one at the age of 68—the Bears' first title in more than a decade. He won coach of the year at the age of 68 and again at 70. To be sure, he never lost his passion for winning or his moxie, as demonstrated by an encounter that Halas, now in his advanced years, had with Ray Sons, a reporter for the *Chicago Daily News*. The Bears had held a secret practice, and Sons had reported it in the newspaper. The next day Halas took Ray Sons aside. "Ray," he said, "Wrigley Field is our home. What you did when you printed that story was walk in our house and shit on our living room carpet." "Yes," Sons would reflect after years had passed, "he was foul-mouthed, but he was a holy man." Today, and for as long as the Chicago Bears exist, his initials are emblazoned on every black and orange uniform.

Paul Brown

Paul Brown was sort of the Sun Tzu of the NFL: a master at the art of war, except his battlefield was between two end zones. It was his unbending philosophy in the importance of not just outplaying, but outsmarting your opponent that led to one of the greatest dynasties in pro sports: the Cleveland Browns of the 1940s and 1950s.

A former English teacher at Washington High in Massillon, Ohio, Brown shunned running endless football drills. His practices went 90 minutes. Maximum. (Lombardi's troops would just be finishing their "warm-up.") Playing for Brown was far from a cakewalk, however; few coaches in history demanded more of his team. He handed out notebooks to his players on the first day of training camp and expected them to make good use of them, a novel concept in an era before face masks.

Brown's obsession that his team learn the finer points of the game through "a total mental and physical effort" led to some key innovations—year-round coaching staffs; intelligence tests for players; detailed scouting reports, both for other NFL teams and college players entering the draft; and a revolutionary offensive system where the coach, and not the quarterback, called the plays via rotating "messenger guards." Critics accused Brown of being the world's oldest quarterback, while some of his own players chaffed at his tight-fisted control—today, it's rare the coach who doesn't call the shots on the field.

Then there were his many technical innovations—face guards, radio-equipped helmets (well, they kinda worked), and—perhaps most impacting—the use of game film. "His coaches used a hand-cranked moviola machine," said NFL historian Jack Clary. "The same kind that Hollywood and television film editors used to dissect scenes and splice them together to form the finished film—for their evaluations. It enabled Brown and his staff to study in slower motion and more precise detail exactly what had happened." He also drilled them over and over again on the playbook, giving them quizzes that tested their knowledge of his groundbreaking air attack.

Paul Brown's first game coached in the NFL would prove to be a microcosm of his brilliant 17-year run in Cleveland, in which he appeared in six straight title games, winning three, while suffering only *one* losing season. Forming the new team from scratch, he promptly led the Browns to four straight titles in the upstart All-America Football Conference. But as good as the Browns were, their annual challenge to the NFL champs to play a winner-take-all contest was denied. "For four years [when we were in the AAFC], Coach Brown never said a word. He just kept putting that stuff on the bulletin board," said quarterback Otto Graham, whom Coach Brown had brought with him from the Navy. "We were so fired up, we would have played them anywhere, anytime, for a keg of beer or a chocolate milkshake. It didn't matter."

In 1950 NFL commissioner Bert Bell, a Philly native, set up an opening day match-up between the Browns of the now-defunct AAFC and the two-time repeat NFL champion Philadelphia Eagles. *That would put those pretenders in their place,* was the prevalent attitude of many fans and most sportswriters. It was also one shared by Eagles coach "Greasy"

Gypsy King

The 1990s-era Buffalo Bills lost four straight Super Bowls, but they weren't always championship chokers. On the contrary, the Bills teams of the early 1960s were powerhouses, taking home back-to-back AFL titles in 1964 and 1965. The team benefited from a talented quarterback tandem of Jack Kemp and his reliever-of-sorts, Daryle "the Fireman" Lamonica. However, the lion's share of credit goes to **Lou Saban**, a former Indiana University football player, who arrived as head coach in Buffalo in 1962 after being unceremoniously fired by the Patriots in the middle of the previous season.

Considering his habit of bouncing from one job to the next—he was nicknamed the Gypsy Coach—it would seem unlikely he'd build a winning tradition in Buffalo. But in no time at all, Saban brought a level of professionalism and pride that the organization had never seen before. When the Bills sped out to a 9–0 record in 1964, everyone, from players to fans, started to believe.

But for all their success, Saban was not satisfied until he could vanquish the Patriots team that had fired him, and who since then, he could never beat. The teams would meet in the season's final game with the Eastern Division title on the line at Fenway Park, where more than a foot of snow had fallen the morning of the game. Saban still had to decide which of his two quarterbacks to start. "If you start me, I guarantee that I'll win this game for you," promised Kemp. After the future presidential candidate won the only vote that mattered, Lou Saban's, he went out and delivered the best performance of his career, throwing for 286 yards despite the wet, frozen conditions.

Following Buffalo's 24–14 triumph, an overjoyed Saban rushed into the celebratory visitors locker room and shouted, "My everlasting thanks to you for beating Boston. This is the greatest victory I've ever had, especially after all the nonsense from this city. There will never be another victory like this for me." These words would prove tragically prophetic for the Bills, one of 15 NFL franchises to never win a Super Bowl.

As for Saban, he would return to the college ranks as head coach of the Miami Hurricanes (his cousin, Nick Saban, is the controversial coach of the Alabama Crimson Tide). True to his "Gypsy Coach" name, he only stayed at Miami from 1977 to 1978, but long enough to recruit a promising quarterback from East Brady High School in Pennsylvania. Jim Kelly, of course, would go on to become the starting quarterback of those Bills teams that lost four straight Super Bowls in the '90s. Saban passed away in March 2009 at the age of 87.

Neale, who said of the Browns, "The high school kids are coming to play in the pros."

When it was over, the record crowd of 71,237 looked up at the scoreboard at Philadelphia's Municipal (JFK) Stadium: it read 35–10. The Browns hadn't just beaten the reigning NFL champions, they had demolished them. "They did things we had never seen before," Eagles defensive star Chuck Bednarik said. "They shifted into different formations. They sent backs in motion. It did confuse us very much."

Bednarik would soon have plenty of company. Over that season and the next five, the Browns compiled a .817 winning percentage, the highest for any six-year period in the last 60 years. And over the next two decades, Paul Brown would continue to devise Mozart-like game plans that would boggle the minds of his opponents while inspiring countless coaches for generations to come. Bill Walsh, who spent eight years as Brown's assistant coach in Cincinnati, credits Brown for inventing the modern passing game, which would help him to formulate the West Coast offense.

Many would assume Bill Belichick is a Lombardi guy. But days before his Super Bowl victory in 2005, a reporter asked him to name the coach he looked up to the most growing up: "Paul Brown," he answered. In fact, almost 50 years after the steely-eyed technician patrolled the sideline looking very un-Belichick—stately overcoat, suit and tie, trademark fedora—the Patriots coach still adheres to Brown's methods. "The same schedule, the same philosophy, the same approach to getting your team to perform to the highest level on the practice field, in meetings, in strategy, in game situations. The level that he was at, I think was way ahead of the competition at that point. And it's very, very much the blueprint for the way the game is played today."

Vince Lombardi

When you think of the term "winning tradition," you think Vince Lombardi and the Green Bay Packers. And rightfully so. His teams won.

With that said, it would be inaccurate to say that he lived by the famous credo: "Winning isn't everything. It's the only thing." For one thing, he didn't even originate the line. It came from a John Wayne movie called *Trouble Along the Way*. The plot involves an out-of-luck football coach, a role for which the Duke seemed ill-suited. He's hired to rebuild a college football program. Desperate to win, Wayne violates several league rules, including hiring ringers to come play for him. His new girlfriend looks on disapprovingly, but Wayne's 11-year-old daughter defends his immoral actions, telling her, "It's like Steve says, 'Winning isn't everything. It's the only thing.'"

Lombardi was enormously driven to succeed, but he knew the difference between "the price to win and winning at any price," explained David Maraniss, the author of the brilliant *When Pride Still Mattered*. He had a reputation for going ballistic after a win if he felt that his players didn't play to their full potential. Bob Skoronski recalls being in the locker room after an exhibition game in which

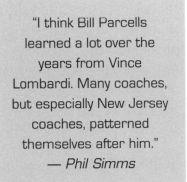

"I think Bill Parcells learned a lot over the years from Vince Lombardi. Many coaches, but especially New Jersey coaches, patterned themselves after him."
— *Phil Simms*

the Packers won 41–14 over the Cardinals as Lombardi stood on a chair, screaming at them at the top of his lungs: "I thought I was in the wrong locker room. I thought we had won."

Paradoxically, after a Green bay loss—which wasn't often—Lombardi was more likely to pat his players on the back than harangue them. Before he came to Green Bay, Lombardi was the offensive coordinator of the New York Giants, who suffered a heartbreaking loss to the Baltimore Colts in the 1958 NFL Championship Game, which is often referred to as the Greatest Game Ever Played. Frank Gifford, the Giants' star running back, fumbled twice, probably costing his team the title. Gifford recalls Lombardi coming up to him in the locker room after the game: "Frank, we wouldn't have got here without you." After every game, he would invite players and friends back to his house, serving drinks with a smile, win or lose. "Our greatest glory is not in never falling," Lombardi said, "but in rising every time we fall."

Lombardi believed that your level of pride, passion, and inner strength determined if you were a winner or a loser, not the numbers on the scoreboard; however, the only way to accurately gauge that level was by pushing his players to their utter limits. "Everybody has ability, but pride in performance is what makes the difference. Now how do you develop pride? Pride is developed from a winning tradition." Every morning at 8:00 AM, Lombardi went to church, occasionally filling in as an altar boy. By the middle of practice, he'd be pacing the field, putting his players through a series of back-breaking drills with names like "the Nut-Cracker" and letting loose a stream of expletives that would make a nun faint (by the way, the majority of his 50-seat allotment went to local nuns). Steve Sabol of NFL Films recalls filming the Packers as they prepared for the upcoming season: "As Willie Davis and Ray Nitschke led the team in drills, a little dog darted onto the field, rubbing up to his players, a sideshow that brought gales of laughter from fans. Then Lombardi appeared, bellowing, 'Get that dog off the field!' and the dog scampered away. It was the power of that voice. Any animal would respond."

Tom Landry

Tom Landry was more than just the man in the tweed fedora. More than just the stoic coach who, in a career that spanned 29 years, led the Cowboys to two Super Bowl victories, 20 consecutive winning seasons, a record 20 playoff wins, 13 division titles, and 270 victories, the third-most behind Don Shula and George Halas. Through the force of his convictions, he made the Cowboys more than just winners in the 1960s, '70s, and '80s—but a full-blown cultural phenomenon complete with adoring fans and clever (if slightly gimmicky) nickname: America's Team. While not everyone bought into their wholesomely heroic image—*darn, those cheerleaders and their strategically placed stars*—it's clear that Landry deserved credit for reshaping the expansion franchise he took over in 1960 into the gold standard of the league. More than any one person, Landry also helped restore the image of Dallas, which had been tagged in people's minds after 1963 as the place where JFK was assassinated. Reaching five Super Bowls in the 1970s made the Cowboys the class of the NFL, but it was Landry and the values he embodied—honor, class, and consistent excellence—that turned them into national sweethearts (well, except perhaps in Washington, Philadelphia, and New York).

Years before the auto mechanic's son from tiny Mission, Texas, got behind the wheel in Dallas, he was one of the 250,000 Americans to strap himself into the cockpit of a B-17 bomber during World War II. And he was very nearly one of the thousands of pilots, including his older brother, Robert, who were killed. Flying 30 missions from November 1944 to April 1945, Landry went from, in his words, "a scared college freshman, lost on his university campus, to a grizzled war veteran of 21." In 1981 Landry discussed with radio host Mark Oristano the harrowing time his plane ran out of fuel and was forced to crash-land in the French country-side. "Tom said the plane had both wings sheared off by trees," recalled Oristano. "He said one tree ended up a foot in front of his face. Everyone walked away. There were no fires or explosions because there was no gas. Nobody got hurt. I knew then why third-and-long didn't scare him."

Paul Brown was the man who created the template for modern offenses in the 1940s. It was Tom Landry who, as a New York Giants player/coach and then–defensive coordinator from 1954 to 1959, came up with the defense to beat it. Seeking to shut down Otto Graham and Cleveland's high-powered aerial assault, Landry created a defensive scheme where the linebacker was moved behind the linemen. Known as the 4-3-4, the alignment revolutionized the way the game would be played, making legends of the hard-nosed enforcers who patrolled the middle: Sam Huff, Mike Singletary, Ray Lewis, and so on. Landry also came up with a play called "Red Dog"—an all-out linebacker blitz fea-turing the hard-hitting Huff—that stirred excitement in the New York

Screen Play

Sid Gillman, the father of the modern passing game, came up with the innovation of studying game film while he was a young kid in Minneapolis working as a movie theater usher. He would cut out football clips from the newsreels shown to audiences prior to the main feature. The company that supplied the theater with the newsreels was far from pleased when they got back their chopped-up film.

To his young wife's dismay, an unfazed Gillman poured over hours of film, projected on a white sheet that hung inside their house. "During our honeymoon in 1935, Sid bought a projector for $15 at a pawn shop," recalled his wife, Esther. "He was only going to make $1,800 that year [in his first coaching job], and we couldn't afford it. I thought I would kill him."

Years later, Gillman, whose best years coaching came in San Diego, where he won the 1963 AFL Championship 51–10 over the Patriots, built a football-shaped pool with tiles for laces and stairs that looked like a tee.

Coaching Aches and Pains

The pressure of winning can take its toll on an NFL head coach. Vince Lombardi suffered from digestive problems and heartburn. In fact, his wife feared his terrible nerves would lead to a heart attack, which is exactly what happened to the short-fused Mike Ditka during the 1988 season. A bleeding ulcer was said to have contributed to Hall of Fame coach **John Madden**'s abrupt decision to walk away from coaching after the 1978 season. "He took a lot of Maalox," recalled former Raiders linebacker Phil Villapiano. "I think he was addicted to it."

crowds, who had always showered all their affection on the offense but now began chanting, "De-fense, De-fense!"

One practice, Giants star Rosey Grier was swaggering off the field after stuffing a run play. The 6′, 200-pound Landry, arms crossed, said to him stoically as he walked past him on the sideline, "If you hadn't made that play, the linebacker would have. The defense was designed for him to make it." *Oh, really*, thought Grier. To prove the coach wrong on the next run play, Grier just stood up and watched the runner pass him by. Then he heard, *Bam!* He swiveled his head back to see the middle linebacker, Harland Savare, had flattened the runner. "That's all I needed to become a believer," recalled Grier.

In Dallas, Landry evolved the 4-3 into what he called the Flex defense, but once again he had to first convince his skeptical players, who called him Ol' Stone Face behind his back. While it's true that talent on the expansion team was harder to find than sunlight underneath the white top of a Dallas Cowboys cheerleader, the team couldn't even manage a single victory in Landry's inaugural season. Once he had the skilled personnel to run his innovative plays, however—guys like Roger Staubach, Chuck Howley, and Bob Lilly—Landry transformed the Cowboys into a perennial powerhouse. Furthermore, his players grew to respect him as a rock-solid leader, on and off the field. "Coach Landry turned back around, faced the blackboard, and began writing a list of priorities," Bob Lilly said, recalling one locker room meeting. "God, family, and football. Every guy—and I mean every guy—in that room turned around and looked at each other in amazement. We all thought the same thing. *Coach has his priorities backward....* It took us awhile for us to get it, but in the long run we found that Coach knew what he was talking about and, as usual, he was right."

Prior to a game in 1979, the hated Redskins sent Dallas defensive end Harvey Martin a funeral wreath. After the Cowboys won, Martin ran into the visiting locker room and, to the amusement of his teammates, threw the wreath inside the door, hitting a Redskins player in the noggin. A few days later, Landry, who taught Sunday school in the off-season, called Martin into his office to tell him that he'd let down him and the organization. "But, Coach, they sent it to me," Martin recalled the exchange. "'Now Harvey, you know we don't do things that way,' he said. 'Harvey, I want you to apologize to them.' 'To the Redskins?' 'To the Redskins?' I went home and sent telegrams to the Redskins organization and to the newspapers apologizing just like Tom wanted. It hurt to do it. That was the kind of guy Tom was. He was first-class. Although they were the enemy, we weren't allowed to act like that."

As for his famously placid demeanor, it could have been a result of his youthful wartime experience, or perhaps it was born from having developed a speech impediment as a child. According to sportswriter Hubert Mizell, Landry modeled his trademark cool, methodical conduct after Texas golfing legend Ben Hogan. "People ask me, did I ever see Coach Landry smile?" former Cowboys running back Walt Garrison said. "And I tell them, 'No, but I only played there nine years.'" However, Don Shula, whom Landry beat in the Super Bowl in 1972, recalled how he had a great sense of humor, even about his own straight-faced notoriety. On one occasion, the two coaches, and eventual golf buddies, came together to shoot a promotional spot for NFL Films. Shula recalled, "Well, we were supposed to be playing a chess match against each other, one-on-one, like we had done in Super Bowl VI. Part of the deal was that every time a chess piece moved, we were supposed to change expressions. Tom couldn't do it. They wanted all these different expressions, and Tom had just that one. Later on, we had a big laugh about it."

Bob Lilly remembers the granite façade cracking on at least one occasion—after the Cowboys defeated Shula's Dolphins to win their first Super Bowl. "As we carried Landry off the field on our shoulders," Lilly said, "his stone-faced demeanor had transformed into an exhilarating expression of joy and delight.... It was the first time I saw Coach really smile. In fact, he smiled for many days to follow."

Don Shula

"Success is not forever, and failure is not fatal." This is just one of the many aphorisms from the winningest coach in league history: Don Shula. It also speaks to how the face of the Miami Dolphins franchise has remained an "island of consistency and dependency" through the dizzying highs (1972's perfect season) and cavernous lows (losing three of five Super Bowls) of a 33-year stint in the NFL.

As a teenager, Shula caddied at a municipal golf course in Grand River, Ohio, near Cleveland. According to golf journalist Elisa Gaudet, "His responsibilities included providing course knowledge to his players, the location of their ball, yardages, reading the greens, and telling the player what club to use or how to play a hole." On one occasion, the coach had his swing videotaped and then analyzed. "I could not believe what I was seeing; all the faults," he said. Later, he was asked how he thought it compared to Charles Barkley's swing. "I have problems," he said. "But not to that proportion!"

In high school, Shula once forged his mother Mary's name so he could play football. Cleveland Browns coach Paul Brown drafted him in the ninth round of the 1951 NFL Draft. He would later call Brown, along with George Halas, the man he eclipsed in the all-time wins department, the "two most important people in the NFL."

Shula got his first shot at being a head coach in 1963 when, at just 33 years old, he took over the Baltimore Colts. From the start, Shula made it clear who was in charge, replacing 30 percent of the roster in his first year. Just one season later, Shula led the Colts to a league-best 12–2 record and a title game against the very team who drafted him, the Cleveland Browns. While the Browns won 27–0, it would be the city's last major sports championship. Meanwhile, the losing coach would go on to coach the Miami Dolphins to two Super Bowl titles and 24 of 26 non-losing seasons.

One of those Super Bowls came in 1972, when the Dolphins capped off a perfect regular season with a 14–7 victory over Redskins in Super Bowl VII. What some people forget is that in just Week 5, Shula was forced to replace star quarterback Bob Griese, who had broke his right

Everybody Hates Herm

Herm Edwards pulled off the rare feat of pissing off an entire city as a player, then duplicating the accomplishment as a coach in a different city. After leading the Kansas City Chiefs to an abysmal 4–12 record in 2007, he told the fuming faithful to "get over it." The advice didn't sit too well in the Heart of America, and Edwards quickly issued an apology. The next year, the Chiefs responded with a 2–14 record, surpassing the franchise-worst 2–12 mark set in 1977. The team got over Edwards by firing him.

Of course, Giants fans still haven't gotten over Edwards' fumble recovery for a touchdown at the end of a game against the Philadelphia Eagles in Giants Stadium on November 19, 1978. All the woeful Giants had to do to secure a 17–12 upset over the hated Eagles was take a knee, but inexplicably quarterback Joe Pisarcik tried to hand it off to running back Larry Csonka, resulting in Edwards scooping the fumbled ball off the turf and taking it back 26 yards for the winning touchdown.

The man who had the most reason to be bitter was Giants rookie DB Odis McKinney. With about two minutes left, he intercepted a pass thrown by Ron Jaworski, the potential goat with three interceptions. Not only was it the first pick of his career, it would have made him the hero of the afternoon.

leg, with Earl Morrall, a 38-year-old veteran quarterback whom Shula had claimed off waivers before the start of the season. Not only did he quickly mold together a young team of mostly anonymous players and AFL leftovers, Shula adapted his offensive strategy after the Griese loss, creating one of the most devastating running attacks in history, one that featured the steamrolling Larry Csonka. When asked why the '72 team was so tough to knock off, Dolphins kicker Garo Yepremian explained, "Quite a few teams had more talent than us, but they didn't have the coaching, the preparation, and the kind of enthusiasm that we had." Houston Oilers coach Bum Phillips, who battled Shula in the mid- to late '70s, put it in a more colorful way: "He can take 'hisins' and beat 'yourins,' or he can take 'yourins' and beat 'hisins.'"

Part indomitable motivator and part cunning psychologist, Shula was able to wring out every last drop of talent from his players, even those who may not be naturally gifted. Shula could recognize a "football player" when he saw one, guys like Nick Buoniconti, a key member of the No-Name Defense, a fearsome no-holds-barred defensive unit that took pride in their overachieving status. "Technically, he wasn't big

Don Shula remains the only coach in NFL history to guide his team to a perfect season.

enough, fast enough, or strong enough to play linebacker," said Shula. "But with his great determination, enthusiasm, and love for football, he was one of the best to ever play the game."

Shula was a strict disciplinarian who did not change with the times. Meanwhile, many players in the late '60s reflected the free-spirited nature of the age. This made for a combustible mix on the practice field. In 1967 first-round draft pick Bubba Smith, who later joined Steve Guttenberg at the *Police Academy*, showed up to training camp with a huge Afro and love beads. When asked by a reporter if he was worried that Shula would make him trim his locks, Smith responded, "Is he my barber or my coach?"

Few others dared to be so cavalier toward Shula, who would challenge his players, even get in their face if he had to. "He scared the crap out of me," recalled wild child tight end Jim "Mad Dog" Mandich. "He had me off balance right from the beginning. I came to camp driving a '62 Valiant with flowers painted all over it. I was wearing love beads and had long hair. I walked into his [Shula's] office, and he took one look at me and said, "You're Mandich? You were the captain of the Michigan football team?" After a rough start, Mandich learned to respect Shula for maximizing his talents and eventually became a key member of two Super Bowl teams. "Lots of leaders want to be popular, but I never cared about that," Shula said. "I wanted to be respected. Respect is different than popularity. You can't make it happen or demand it from people. The only way to get it is to earn it. Not by talking, but by doing things that make sense to your team." Even Bubba Smith, who at first resented the way Shula challenged him by moving him out of his natural position and calling him out at practice, realized he was going to lose the battle of wills. So he worked his ass off until he proved to the coach that he deserved to start. Smith later said, "If a nuclear bomb dropped, the only things I'm certain would survive are AstroTurf and Don Shula."

Even late in his career, Shula was getting the most out of his players. Consider that in 1994, a year before he retired, the Dolphins won a division title with back Bernie Parmalee, who let's just say was no Larry Csonka. "In regards to Miami's running game," said sportswriter Brad Adler, "Shula turned chicken shit into chicken salad." On the other hand, Shula was the first to admit the importance of having a threat like Dan Marino on his team. When Shula was asked about the role luck played, he responded, "Sure, luck means a lot in football. Not having a good quarterback is bad luck."

Looney Tune

Nothing sent chills up the spine of NFL coaches like the name **Joe Don Looney**. The screwy, authority-hating fullback played for five different teams in five years despite his exceptional talent. In the fourth quarter of a tight contest against the 49ers, Detroit Lions coach Harry Gilmer asked Looney to send in a play to the quarterback. Looney replied, "Coach, if you want a messenger, send for Western Union." He then ambled over to the bench and took a seat. The next day he was traded to the Washington Redskins.

Shula would reach the Super Bowl for the last time in January 1985 with the prolific Marino, losing to the Bill Walsh/Joe Montana–led 49ers 38–16. "A while back," Shula recalled, "I tried to give Dan Marino a what-if scenario. I said, 'We've scored on the last play of the game. This puts us one point behind. We can kick the extra point to tie the game and force overtime, or we can go for the two-point conversion, and win or lose. If you lose, everyone says, "Why didn't you go for the tie?" If you go for the tie but lose the coin-toss in the overtime (we lost 10 out of the first 12 tosses in 1994) and don't get a good kick, the game could be over quickly with your opponent's field goal. When this happens, everybody says, "But we could have won it with a two-yard play!" What's your call, Dan?' he just smiled and said, 'Coach, this is why you get paid so much.'" Even in defeat, Shula maintained his positive perspective. After all, success is not forever, and failure is not fatal.

Bill Walsh

Many people in history have come to the Bay Area looking for gold. Bill Walsh, on the other hand, brought gold to the Bay Area. When he took over the 49ers, they were in a sorry state of affairs. Using his revolution-ary West Coast offense—just how many teams did Joe Montana beat into submission with short, precise throws?—he built San Francisco into the team of the '80s, leading them to three Super Bowls and six division titles. His legacy goes beyond the dynasty he erected in San Francisco, sprouting roots across the league. In 2007, 21 of 32 NFL teams were coached by someone linked to Walsh—not coincidentally, many black coaches came out of his forward-thinking universe, including Dennis Green, Tony Dungy, and Mike Tomlin.

As serious as Walsh was about winning, he also had a wonderfully comical side. "When we first went down to play the Rams," recalled 49ers receiver Mike Shumann, "he was concerned that we were going to get influenced by Hollywood and break curfew and go out, so he got [assistant coaches] Bobb McKittrick, Sam Wyche, and Denny Green to dress up as a hooker, a pimp, and a drug dealer, just to show us what we had to stay away from. Can you imagine telling Bobb McKittrick, 'I need you to find a wig and a dress?' Those guys had to be thinking to themselves, *What is he doing?*"

On another occasion in 1982, days before they would play the first Super Bowl in 49ers' history, the coach showed up at the hotel an hour before the team and paid a bellhop $20 to borrow his uniform. As the players departed the bus in Detroit, the distinguished Walsh stood outside the hotel, dressed in cap and coat, saying to his players, "Let me help you with your bags, sir." Many of the players declined help from the pushy, grabbing bellhop and his insistent requests for a tip. "I went up to Joe Montana, and he wouldn't give me his bag," recalled Walsh. All of a sudden, defensive tackle Lawrence Pillers recognized him, and the entire team broke out in hysterics. Except, perhaps, receiver Mike Shumann, who had forearmed the white-haired bellhop when he tried to grab his bag. Later, while riding the elevator, a teammate asked, "Did you see Bill Walsh dressed as a bellhop?"

"That was Bill?" Shumann gulped. "I'll never get in the game now."

With Walsh having broken the tension with his bellhop routine, the team was loose and confident moments before going out to face

"I remember he [Bill Walsh] told me at Morehead State, 'We're going to draft you, and you're going to be the leading passer in the NFL as a rookie.' I made a facial expression. He said, 'You don't believe me?' I said, 'Yeah, sure, Coach. I believe you.' And then he started citing all the quarterbacks that he'd had over the years that had been the leading passer in college or the pros—Kenny Anderson, Virgil Carter, Guy Benjamin, Steve Dils, and so on. That was interesting." —*Phil Simms*

Cincinnati. All they needed now was some rock 'n' roll music to get them fired up. A jovial Walsh broke his rule about blaring loud music in the locker room, allowing Joe Montana to play any song he wanted on his boombox. Walsh told Dwight Hicks to crank up the volume as the team rocked out to the song, playing over and over again, until they were ready to burst through the doors and kill the Bengals. The song: "This Is It" by Kenny Loggins and Michael McDonald. The team went on to beat Cincinnati 26–21. Now, everybody footloose!

It may appear that Bill Walsh has led a sunny, breezy life, but he did suffer the occasional setback, perhaps none so shocking or painful as when his mentor, Paul Brown, passed him over as his replacement as the Bengals' head coach. As a longtime assistant coach in Cincinnati, Walsh worshipped his boss, who in return, made comments to his

Revenge of Chucky

During a game in Oakland against the Seahawks in 1998, Raiders running back Harvey Williams was supposed to run "96 Seattle." Instead, he ran "97 Seattle." Busted play. When he got back to the sideline, head coach **Jon Gruden** tore into him. Williams told reporters, after the game, it was like looking at Chucky, the evil, possessed doll from the horror flick *Child's Play*. The next day the local newspaper ran side-by-side photos of coach and psycho doll.

"Until then, I had never heard of the movie," remarked Gruden in his autobiography *Do You Love Football?!: Winning with Heart, Passion, and Not Much Sleep*, which includes a chapter about how he met his wife, appropriately titled "Bride of Chucky." "I don't think the comparison is a negative thing," Gruden said, "although when I finally saw the movie, it was clear right away that he wasn't a really good guy."

As for accusations that he plays up to the camera during games by making crazy Chucky faces, Gruden said, "Give me a break.... If I'm closing my eyes or twisting my face, it's because I'm thinking, I'm concentrating—or I'm just pissed. I guess I've always been kind of a natural squinter anyhow."

Of course, Al Davis had another nickname for Gruden: Butch. "I never knew why," said Gruden. Chucky would exact his revenge on Davis for firing him, as well as critics who accused him of being a slick phony, when in 2003, in his first year as coach of the Tampa Bay Buccaneers, he delivered the historically dismal franchise their first ever Super Bowl victory over the Raiders. In 2009 Gruden is taking a breather from sideline fire-breathing to join Ron Jaworski and Mike Tirico in the booth for ESPN's *Monday Night Football*.

44-year-old offensive guru to indicate he was his heir apparent upon his retirement. But on New Year's Eve, of all days, a local sports columnist called Walsh and asked him to respond to the news that offensive line coach Bill Johnson had been named head coach. As David Harris explained in *The Genius*, Walsh was speechless. "Sometimes, I didn't think I could live through it," Walsh said. "At that moment, I was truly broken. It was crushing. I was very, very lost." A friend recalled, "He didn't know if he could even continue in football."

San Francisco running back Roger Craig, who played alongside Montana and Jerry Rice in all three of Walsh's Super Bowl victories, could see how some people might incorrectly confuse his cerebral, laid-back demeanor for a lack of forcefulness. "One of the funny things about Paul Brown's decision to pass over Coach Walsh for the head-coaching vacancy is that he doubted Walsh was tough enough to wield that kind of power," explained Craig. "This was a guy who fought more than 100 amateur boxing matches, and Paul Brown said Walsh was not tough enough!" In fact, the ripped running back and silver-haired coach would shadowbox before practices. Craig recalled: "He'd throw a left hook and say, 'That one would have gotten you.'"

Walsh earned a reputation with his players for running plays for as long as it took to execute them with effortless perfection. If practice had to run into the night, then so be it. On one occasion, it got so dark that tight end Russ Francis taped a flashlight to his helmet. As the other players noticed the shining light in the dark huddle, they slowly looked over at Francis. "Russ was the one guy on the team who could get away with that because he wasn't intimidated by Bill. We were all laughing." Walsh called practice—but not before running a few more plays.

Walsh's complex offensive schemes were the stuff off legend as running back Bill Ring recalled: "Bill's playbook was five times the size of the playbooks I had when I was with the Steelers or in college." However, there is such a thing as being over-prepared. "In college, we were called the Dateless Wonders," recalled longtime friend Marty Connelly. "We'd go out to a beer joint, and even then Bill would map out a plan to go to a table full of girls. By the time we executed, they were gone."

Bill Belichick

Beyond his recognition as a great coach, Bill Belichick has attained something rare in these days of nonstop media coverage: the image of a shadowy, almost mythic figure who achieves domination through the agency of a genius mind and possibly even a little black magic. Now, reconcile this mysterious, cloaked overlord obsessed with football glory with the reality of a man who once went on tour with his pal Jon Bon Jovi. "Bon Jovi wants to be a head coach," Belichick's friend Rob Ingraham said. "And Bill wants to be a rock 'n' roller." He also enjoys palling around with Sir Charles Barkley, tossing the lacrosse ball around with his kids, and cruising down the highway with the radio on. Somehow it's hard to imagine the miserable-looking, grey hoodie–wearing tyrant cruising down I-95 humming along to "Sad-Eyed Lady of the Lowlands," but it makes strange sense that he would be a fan of Bob Dylan. They are both self-possessed captains, full of contradictions, boldly charting a visionary course, damn the naysayers.

Bill Belichick got his start as a $25-an-hour assistant on head coach Ted Marchibroda's Baltimore Colts staff. In those days, he lived for free in a Howard Johnson. The story goes that Marchibroda traded the hotel owner game tickets for four rooms. After that, he became tight ends coach for the Detroit Lions. Belichick, or as the staff called him, Little Billy, was such a bad dresser—clashing colors and ugly khakis—that head coach Rick Forzano took him to a clothing store and got him a $50 pair of stylish pants. For the next several months, Belichick grumbled about their discomfort. "We were supposed to wear a shirt and tie every day to work," fellow assistant Floyd Reese said, "and you can imagine what some of the combinations look like when you really don't want to do it and probably don't have a lot of resources. I'm here to tell you that you can make a shirt and tie look a whole lot uglier than that hooded sweatshirt."

For anyone who enjoys a classic battle between mentor and protégé, it doesn't get much better than the aforementioned Bill Parcells and Bill Belichick. Like some renaissance architect, Belichick designed defenses that helped Parcells to win two Super Bowls (1986, 1990) with the Giants, and reach a third one with the Patriots in 1996. Yet Belichick resented that his boss, who while appreciating his considerable talent, never failed to put him in his place, even occasionally berating him in front of players and

The Gridiron Generals   53

staff. As one Jets player recalled, "He'd always walk away with his head down, cursing under his breath." But they didn't become mortal enemies until the soap opera that erupted in the winter of 2000: Belichick spurned the Jets for the rival Patriots—this, after Papa Parcells had anointed him his successor in New York, no less. In 2003 Parcells took his 7–2 Cowboys into Gillette Stadium to face Belichick's 7–2 Patriots in a game billed as the Battle of the Bills. In a pregame locker room speech, Belichick gave his team guidance on how to view the rivalry game that was both blunt, yet almost philosophical. "Don't get distracted by irrelevant aspects of this game," Belichick told his players. "Belichick versus Parcells? We're both assholes. We started coaching together when some of you were in diapers.

Bill Belichick has presided over a modern dynasty since taking over the Patriots in 2000.

The last time we coached together was five years ago. What were you doing five years ago and what people were you doing it with?"

That same year Belichick guided the Patriots to an exhilarating, last-second Super Bowl victory over the Carolina Panthers. During the team's warm-ups, Belichick was standing on the field with Richard Seymour when they noticed that some of the Panthers players were staring them down. By the time it came to give the pregame speech, Belichick was uncharacteristically worked up. "It's a bunch of bullshit," Belichick told his team in the locker room. "They're not what we are. They can't be what we are. *We* are what we are." New England guard Damien Woody recalled the reaction of the team: "This is going to sound weird since it was a lot of expletive. But it was touching. We saw a different side of him. We had never seen him that emotional before. He got me ready. I felt like going out there, strapping it up, and playing with one leg."

As Patriots head coach, he would go on to win one more Lombardi trophy, making it three titles in just four years, a feat that no other coach in history has accomplished. Not Lombardi, not Walsh, not Parcells. When you consider that he stewarded this dynastic run in the modern era of free agency, it's even more unbelievable. Only Lombardi has a better playoff record then Belichick, and his 14 playoff wins in the 2000s matches the record held by the mighty dynasties of the 1970s: the Dallas Cowboys and Pittsburgh Steelers. In 2007 he became the first coach in history to lead a team to a perfect 16–0 record. Perhaps most amazing: of 22 starters on this Super Bowl–bound team, 21 were acquired since Belichick became head coach in 2000.

> "I think Bill Belichick is the best coach in the game today and has been for a long time. He gets beat up a lot because he's not the most personable guy. He doesn't do a lot of politicking. He never has. But as far as I'm concerned, he's the finest coach. He's a coach's coach, is what he is. Most of them are psychologists, or think they are. And then they let a staff of 24 do the rest of it. Not Belichick. He coaches the team."
>
> —*Frank Gifford*

Allen Town

Spygate may be the most recent act of team espionage, but cloak-and-dagger tactics are nothing new in the ruthless and competitive world of the NFL. Which is why, back in 1971, **George Allen** became the first coach to hire a full-time security man. His real name: Ed Boynton, retired Long Beach, California, police officer. Codename: Double-0. His main job was to patrol the Washington Redskins' training facilities, rooting out any and all spies.

"Redskin Park had the secrecy of the CIA with the aura of a mental institution," wrote offspring Jennifer Allen in her 2000 memoir, *Fifth Quarter: The Scrimmage of a Football Coach's Daughter*. On one of Boynton's walking inspections of the facility, which the media nicknamed Fort Allen and Park Paranoia, he spotted an unidentified person and gave chase. It turns out he was a student coming from the chemical lab of the nearby high school.

Despite all his celebrated success, in the end Belichick remains a contradiction. He's a product of some of the best learning institutions—including Phillips Academy, where he was a classmate of Jeb Bush. His love of studying the game of football, its strategies as well as its history, is unparalleled. He's a funny, thoughtful man, seeking input from his staff and giving credit where credit is due. He once performed a rocking rendition of "Love Potion No. 9" at a private gathering with friends and family. At the same time, he curses like a sailor. He's crustier than stale sourdough. His style sense is Modell's. He doesn't believe in fate. He doesn't allow for mistakes. He's a hard despot who rides his players and coaches by whip. He's a former center. He's dickish to the media. He's a cheater. *Esquire* editor Eric Gillin even went so far as to compare him to Chairman Mao. "This is a man who looks like he sleeps in (and chews on) the clothing he wears on game day," said Gillin. "This is a divorced guy with nothing to lose and nothing left, a man so completely consumed by football, he is somewhere out there right now in a very dark room, watching film. Like an obsessive-compulsive in a Slinky factory, chronically restless, tinkering with his life's work, getting closer and closer to perfecting football's version of socialism, an efficient, victorious machine that sublimates the individual for the greater good."

So who's the real Bill Belichick? We may never know. What's beyond refuting is that he belongs on the short list of greatest coaches in NFL history.

Then Tony Kornheiser Said...

Over his 35-year career, first as a sportswriter for the *Washington Post*, where his "Bandwagon" columns immortalized the Washington Redskins' 1991 Super Bowl season, and later as cohost of ESPN's *Pardon the Interruption*, Kornheiser has a style all his own. Acerbic but not abrasive—he is the gentle grouch. His knack for funny, idiosyncratic observations has garnered him legions of supporters. In 2006 Kornheiser became only the third non-jock color commentator to join the famed *Monday Night Football* broadcasting team since its premiere back in 1970. After three seasons in the *MNF* booth, Kornheiser stepped down last May, citing his fear of flying as the reason for leaving. (Well, I guess that beats the "Spend Time With My Family" excuse.) While not everyone mourned his departure—okay, a few haters were downright cheerful—Kornheiser remains one of the most enjoyed sports personalities in television. He took some time out to talk about that dominant Redskins championship team, filling the big shoes of Howard Cosell, and why Frank Gifford is the most handsome man ever. (He's less crazy about bloggers, or "little toads," as he once referred to them.)

In 1991 the Washington Redskins had one of the greatest seasons of any team in the history of the NFL. After the team pasted the Lions in Week 1, 45–0, you began chronicling every step of the team's epic run in a string of columns called "The Bandwagon." It became such a phenomenon in Washington that there were even bumper stickers, hats, T-shirts, and for a grand finale, a 33-foot "Bandwagon" RV that you drove all the way from the Capitol to the Super Bowl in Minneapolis, Minnesota.

Phenomenon is really an overblown word. It started the first game when they beat the Lions 45–0. People said, well, they don't have Barry Sanders, and I thought, *He was going to score seven touchdowns?* So after Week 1, I said, whimsically, they're going to the Super Bowl. By Week 3, I had this sense I could pull this off for a while and began talking about a "bandwagon." The coverage of football didn't matter. The only thing that mattered was this cocoon-like village we pushed along each week.

Former Washington Post *columnist Tony Kornheiser joined the* Monday Night Football *broadcast booth in 2006. He was replaced by Jon Gruden in 2009.*

But that Redskins team did have a pretty great season.

Yeah, but I never expected that they would go 11–0. Not in my wildest dreams.

In the "Bandwagon" columns, you referred to Joe Gibbs in a loving, somewhat derisive way as "Coach Joe."

He never called himself Joe Gibbs. He always called himself Coach Gibbs, which is idiotic. These coaches take themselves far too seriously.

What do you recall about the road trip to the Super Bowl in the mobile-home-turned-bandwagon?

The No. 1 memory was that there was a bed in the back, and as soon as I went to lay down on it, the RV was swaying all over the road. So we never went in the back again. None of us. The No. 2 memory I have is going to a hotel in Indiana. Freezing cold. I mean, like, sub-zero. And this was not the Ritz-Carlton. This was just a regular roadside motel. And they had put on the welcome sign out front, "Welcome Tony Kornheiser and The Bandwagon." *(laughs)* I thought that was a hoot. And then they had an apple on my bed that had frozen solid.

What happened when you got to the Super Bowl in Minneapolis?

The television news crews from D.C. were all there when we stepped off this crazy RV. And it was, like, are they kidding me? Are you people serious? Is this what being a rock star is like? *(laughs)* This is insane.

What about the "Bandwagon" bumper stickers and T-shirts?

In those days, nobody used the phrase "feel-good story." And neither had I. And this was a real feel-good story. It allowed me to be subversive and sarcastic, which are the two ways I like to write most of all. And at the same time, have a great amount of fun and do something that people responded to in an incredibly—and with unanimity—positive way. It was great.

Were you worried that the Redskins might lose to the Buffalo Bills and ruin your happy ending?

No, no, no. If they lose, I blame them. If I win, I get all the credit.

Tough Start

Roughest head coaching debut? In 1971 **Dan Devine** began his tenure in Green Bay by losing a heartbreaker to the Giants 42–40. But that wasn't the most painful part. While rooting on his troops in the fourth quarter, he suffered a broken left leg in a sideline collision.

Have you heard from any of the guys who played on that Super Bowl champion team?

Mark Adickes was a substitute offensive lineman. These were in the days of the Hogs, when the Redskins offensive linemen were the stars of the team. He would say all the things that [All-Pro] Russ Grimm wished he could say, but he wasn't as glib or as smart as Mark Adickes. He called me about 10 years ago to tell me that he had just graduated from Harvard Medical School. He's now an orthopedic surgeon. A football player: 6'5", 320. Harvard Medical School! I mean, I couldn't have done that. That's great.

How do the Hogs rate among the great units in NFL history?

The Hogs were great. And none of them are in the Hall of Fame. Come on, how can Russ Grimm and Joe Jacoby not be in the Hall of Fame? Look at the Redskins over that 10- or 12-year period. Four Super Bowl appearances. Three wins. They're comparable to the 49ers. They're comparable to Dallas. They have a thousand guys in the Hall of Fame. How can the Redskins not have any Hogs? It's an injustice.

Why did you call Russ Grimm "the Flea" in your columns?

Because it's such an insane nickname. He's 6'2", 340. He's not the flea. That's crazy! But you know, he was a quarterback in high school. He was actually the Redskins emergency quarterback. Russ Grimm, baby.

How about a current player who belongs one day in the Hall of Fame?

Kurt Warner is going to the Hall of Fame. By getting to a Super Bowl with a second team. By becoming only the second player [quarterback] to do that. By having what F. Scott Fitzgerald said you couldn't have in America, "a second act." By having a second act, especially after the way Kurt Warner was drummed out of St. Louis and drummed out of New York, and basically told you're going to fill in for Matt Leinart until he is ready. By then getting to the Super Bowl, he walked into the Hall of Fame.

His story is uniquely compelling.

He was bagging groceries in Iowa. He was an Arena League quarterback. He was a minor league quarterback. He was a Europe quarterback.

And then he lit up the sky in St. Louis. And he wasn't even going to be the starter. Trent Green was. You were tempted to say the system worked for him. He was just a meteor. And then he faded and cooled off and he left. But you can't say that now.

What do you think of 2008's Super Bowl champion Steelers?
Pittsburgh went through the most brutal schedule of anybody last year and came out of it by winning games close and winning games late. So I really respect that Pittsburgh team.

When you sit around with your pals, do you talk about football?
No. We talk movies, politics, great novels. I don't sit around and talk about sports. I do that for a living. So I don't sit around with my friends and do that. I don't.

Top five best NFL players-turned-actors?
I don't know. Were any of them in any good movies? I'm not a guy who makes lists of great sports movies or great athletes in sports movies. I can tell you there have been movies that I loved with sports themes like *Bull Durham*, *Raging Bull*, and *Chariots of Fire*.

Any football-related ones?
North Dallas Forty.

Growing up in Long Island, who was the NFL player you most idolized?
When I was really young, it was Frank Gifford. Because the Giants were the only team. And when the AFL came around, it was Namath.

I don't think people now realize what a huge and glamorous star Frank Gifford was in the late '50s and early '60s.
Handsomest man in the history of the world. He's it. Matinee idol. Handsomest man ever. Frank Gifford.

You and Frank Gifford have both had stints in the legendary *Monday Night Football* booth. What do you think is the legacy of that show?

> ## Jilted Gilbride
> Just before halftime of the Houston Oilers' nationally televised 1993 season finale against the Jets, Houston quarterback Cody Carlson fumbled the ball on a pass play. How did Oilers defensive coordinator **Buddy Ryan** express his displeasure with the play call? On the sideline, he socked offensive coordinator Kelvin Gilbride in the face.
>
> This wasn't the first time Ryan flashed his red-hot temper, almost coming to blows with Mike Ditka during a 1985 Dolphins-Bears game in which Chicago lost their bid for a perfect season. Later, as head coach of the Philadelphia Eagles, he once said of his running back Earnest Jackson, "Trade him for a six pack. It doesn't even have to be cold."

You have to go back to Roone Arledge and Howard Cosell and the decision to take sports out of the weekend to put it in a primetime setting—that's had a profound effect on the way television is scheduled and on the integration of sports into the culture at large. It was something that could no longer be consigned to afternoons on the weekends. Or in the male province of the den. It changed everything. It's very hard now for a man or a woman who has no knowledge whatsoever of sports to get into a whole bunch of conversations in America. You better know sports because sports is the currency of the country.

You mentioned Cosell. Now, you got to meet him many years ago. What did you find most surprising about him?

The most surprising thing about Howard Cosell from people who met him was how tall he was. He was about 6'3", and nobody expected that. Big, strong, broad-shouldered guy. Cosell.

Did you feel any pressure to live up to Howard Cosell?

I'm not Howard Cosell. I mean, I'm not a jock, but I'm not Howard Cosell. I've been a sportswriter for 40 years, so I have some sense that you get six points for a touchdown and three for a field goal. I don't need to be taught that. But I'm not him, and if people think I'm him, they're wrong. He's, as they say in Latin, *sui generis*. One of a kind.

When Cosell died, you wrote, "He carried a glow that always suited television. In his passing, the picture is already a little dimmer." What do you think was Howard Cosell's most memorable on-air moment?

Cosell's greatest moment or the thing you remember most is when he announced that John Lennon had been shot. It was December 8, 1980. I'm sure if Howard were alive today, he would say of all the moments on *Monday Night Football*, that was the one that meant the most.

Where were you when you heard Cosell make the announcement?

I remember exactly where I was. I was sitting in my living room watching the game in Washington, D.C. Within five minutes, I got a phone call from the editor of the *Washington Post*'s Style section. He said, "Can you write?" And I said, "What's the deadline?" He said, "Twelve-thirty." I said, "Yes, I can."

How hard was that column to write?

That's what you do. You push aside all the personal feelings of loss you have, you push those aside until you're done. And when you're done, you think about those things. As they say in *The Godfather*, "This is the business we've chosen."

chapter 3

The Big Gamers

By what standards do we determine which NFL players merit Big Gamer status? The first question to ask is: do they "bring it" against the backdrop of high stakes or do they collapse under the weight of the big moment? Of course, the ultimate test of nerves is a title game. The person who can rise to the occasion in the pressure-cooker of a championship game or Super Bowl warrants total stud stature. But does that mean we discount those whose stellar exploits late in the season or in the playoffs merely got their team to the final showdown but fail to result in a trophy? The 1958 championship game is called the Greatest Game Ever Played—but how many people remember that the Giants don't even make *the playoffs* if not for Pat Summerall's last-second 49-yard "miracle kick" in a blizzard to beat the Browns in the final game of the season? So, yes, it takes big gamers to get to the big game. The last point is that luck has something to do with it. Proving your mind-blowing clutchability can be a formidable challenge for players stuck on a mediocre team. Surely, we would be celebrating the performances of Dick Butkus, Archie Manning, and Barry Sanders in the big game had they actually been in any. So big gamers can't find the onramp to the main stage by themselves. Of course, once they are front and center, with the spotlight trained on them, they know exactly what to do.

Otto Graham

Ten consecutive championship game appearances. I repeat, *10 consecutive championship game appearances*. If that doesn't qualify Cleveland Browns quarterback Otto Graham as a big-game performer, then I don't know what does. Need more proof? How about three NFL titles in six years? Four straight AAFC titles? In some people's minds, these triumphs qualify him for another accolade: greatest quarterback of all time. The late Giants GM George Young said this to sportswriter Peter King, "How can any quarterback be better than Otto Graham? All he did was quarterback his team to the championship game of his league every year he played." Paul Brown, who coached Graham for the entirety of his career, from 1946 to 1955, had this to say: "The test of a quarterback is where his team finishes. By that standard, Otto Graham was the best of all time."

There was this kid growing up in Cleveland who would sit shivering in the frigid stands to watch his idol Otto Graham play. The kid grew up to become good friends with Graham—he also grew up to become owner of the New York Yankees. "I remember a game against the San Francisco 49ers where he got hit, and the whole side of his face was split open," recalled George Steinbrenner in 2003, on the day Graham passed away at the age of 82. "He had a scar the rest of his life." One of Graham's finest feats of aerial wonder came in his very first NFL game— the 1950 season-opener against the Philadelphia Eagles. Given that the Browns were playing their first game in the NFL, facing the defending champion Eagles on the road, most people predicted pain for the Brownies. Sure enough, on his first drive Graham connected with his receiver Dub Jones for a 59-yard strike. Graham owned the Eagles all day, throwing for 346 yards and three touchdowns in a 35–10 rout. "No one gave us a chance," recalled Steinbrenner. "We went in there and whipped them." In 1998 Graham told *Sports Illustrated*, "After the game against the Eagles, their coach, Greasy Neale, said we were nothing but a basketball team. Pretty good basketball team, huh?" When Graham could no longer play, it was Steinbrenner, who 13 years earlier was just a 17-year-old fan rooting him on, who helped land him a job as athletics director and football coach at the U.S. Coast Guard Academy.

It's almost too incredible to believe, but Otto Graham might never have ended up in the Hall of Fame if he didn't play intramural touch football as a college freshman. Graham had come to Northwestern University on a basketball scholarship. For fun, he joined his Alpha Delta Phi brothers on an intramural squad. Ade Schumacher, the

Otto Graham led the Browns to the championship game in each of his six NFL seasons. Photo courtesy of Getty Images.

Wildcats assistant athletics director, recalled how Graham was plucked from obscurity: "After hearing rumors of a freshman throwing long, accurate passes and throwing all over fraternity competition, Lynn 'Pappy' Waldorf, Northwestern's head football coach, asked me about Otto and accompanied me to the IM championship game to see what the fuss was about." Waldorf convinced Graham to come out for spring football, although Graham was skeptical because, according to him, the "football squad already had the best running back in the state on its roster in Bill DeCorrevont." The accomplished music major—he studied the oboe, the English horn, French horn, piano, cornet, and violin—stuck with football and ended up breaking every Big Ten passing record on his way to becoming an All-American in two sports, football and basketball.

In 1946, the year he turned pro, he played on title-winning teams in basketball for the Rochester Royals and in football for the Cleveland Browns. Graham was the first player to ever win world championships in two major sports in the same year, but, then again, he was the first to do many things. For example, he recorded an Illinois state record as the biggest baby ever born—14 pounds, 12 ounces. He was the first player to wear a face mask, thanks to a late hit in the jaw from 49ers linebacker Art Michalik. "That's my real claim to fame right there," Graham told *Bernie's Insiders* magazine. "I was the first guy who ever wore a face mask on any level of football. We got this piece of plastic and wrapped it across the lower front of the helmet in front of my mouth. I had this big gash on my mouth, and they gave me 15 stitches, but I wanted to play." Graham completed nine of 10 passes in the second half to lead Cleveland

Never Mind the Buttocks

Known as the Punky QB, **Jim McMahon** got nailed with a $5,000 fine by NFL commissioner Pete Rozelle for donning an Adidas headband during a 1985 playoff game, a violation of the league's "no logo or personal message" dress code. So McMahon showed up for his next game wearing a headband with the word "ROZELLE" hand-written on it. Rozelle wrote him a note to express his genuine amusement, and by the way, the fine still stands.

McMahon and the wild Super Bowl–Shuffling Bears would go down to New Orleans—yes, God does have a sense of humor—for the big game. That week, McMahon mooned a television news helicopter hovering over the practice field. When he wasn't practicing, he could be found getting drunk with teammates on Bourbon Street or else having his personal acupuncturist, Hiroshi Shiriashi, stick pins in his sore buttocks.

to a 23–21 comeback victory. "You better believe that was satisfying," said Graham. After commissioner Bert Bell defended the vicious late hit, Graham became one of the first people to speak out publicly against the level of NFL violence. Recalled his wife: "Otto took a lot of flak from the league for claiming professional football was dirty." Of course, today the NFL has rules to protect the quarterback such as the roughing-the-passer penalty.

Graham was also probably the first football player to be involved in a high-profile murder case—sorry, O.J. The case, which reportedly became the basis for *The Fugitive* television show and movie, involved Sam Sheppard, a doctor who was accused of murdering his wife, Marilyn, in their bedroom but who claimed the real culprit was a "bushy-haired" intruder. The Grahams lived next door to the Sheppards, and the two wives were best friends. Amazingly, the police let Graham inspect Sheppard's bedroom shortly after the murder. Graham later described to the *Saturday Evening Post* what he saw when he looked inside the room: "Oh, my God. It looks like someone stood in the middle of the room with a great big can of red paint and a brush and flicked it all around. This wasn't a couple of blows. Oh no. Whoever did it, they had to be out of their mind." Graham's wife, Beverly, recalled her disbelief that Otto had been allowed to view the crime scene: "Had he been involved, his access would have tainted the evidence, and for a while, he actually was a suspect because he had no alibi. We had gone to a party the night of the murder, and while there, Otto split the seat of his pants. Saying he'd be right back, Otto drove home and turned on the TV while he changed. Caught up in a show, he stayed awhile before returning. That was the exact time Marilyn was killed—and Otto had bushy hair." Cops even suspected that while Graham was off racking up victories on the field, Beverly was having an affair with the handsome osteopath. Earlier in the day, Graham went to the hospital to visit Sheppard, who had become the authorities' main suspect. On the way out, Graham was bum-rushed by reporters, who wanted to know if the superstar believed Sheppard's story about a "bushy-haired" killer. Graham told the media that he did, but began having doubts after his friend refused to take a lie-detector test. "And then there was the watch," Graham wrote in his 2004 autobiography *Ottomatic*, cowritten with his son Duey. Sheppard had said that his watch had gotten water-logged when he chased the intruder into a lake, but Graham knew the timepiece got soaked at the stock-car races they attended together three nights earlier. "Sure, he could have forgotten this due to the shock of the murder or soaked it further in the lake, but I began to suspect my friend might be a murderer after all." Graham was ruled out as a suspect, but his story about the watch became part of the district attorney's evidence against Sheppard, who was found guilty and served 10 years in prison. In 1966 Sheppard's new attorney, the legendary F. Lee Bailey, helped get the conviction overturned based on the circus-like publicity prejudicing the jury. "Although he was acquitted in a second trial," Graham said. "Sam's short life would never be the same."

In a 10-year career that included 105 wins to only 17 losses and four ties, "Automatic" Graham never missed a game. Perhaps his greatest big-game performance came in the twilight of his career—the 1954 championship game against the arch nemesis Detroit Lions, who had defeated them in the title showdown the previous year 17–16. His son Duey recalled how most people were betting against the veteran in what most of them believed would be his farewell game. The Browns had won eight straight before losing to the Lions in the final game of the season, played in a blizzard. "The scribes felt the loss was a bad omen going into the following Sunday's championship game against the same team in the same venue," Duey said. "Otto was frustrated that he had not thrown a touchdown against Detroit since Buddy Parker had taken over as coach, but all that changed the day after Christmas, when he threw for three touchdowns and ran for three more. The Browns broke 13 playoff records in their 56–10 rout of the Lions. The winning share per player was $2,478.57."

Paul Hornung

It was fall of 1965, and the Packers team was hunkered down at St. Norbert College for preseason training camp. Running the show: former Army assistant coach Vince Lombardi. He drove his players to the brink of existence with a bleak regiment of grueling two-a-day practices and unrelenting conditioning drills. The men ate, slept, and breathed football. Curfew was 11:00 PM. If you weren't back in your

Hunting Cowboys

What do you do when the NFL rejects your bid to acquire a franchise in their league? If you're 27-year-old Texas oil scion **Lamar Hunt**, you start your own—the AFL. And if you're the NFL, you retaliate by putting a franchise right in Hunt's backyard of Dallas, Texas—the Cowboys.

No matter. After probably shouting, "How 'bout them jerks!" Hunt built his rival league into such a successful entity that a mere six years after its launch, the NFL agreed to a merger. The news came as a major disappointment to then–AFL commissioner Al Davis, who had demanded that the NFL fold into the AFL. With the slick-haired meddler neutralized, all that was left was for the merger committee to pick a catchy name for the title contest, which had the unfortunate luck to be called the AFL-NFL Championship Game in its first two years. That was Commissioner Rozelle's choice. Others suggested the Big One. But then Lamar Hunt came to the rescue. "My daughter Sharon had a toy, a rubber ball, that was called a Super Ball," recalled Lamar Hunt. "During the meetings, we were talking about the game, and I referred to it as the 'final game,' the 'last game,' the 'Super Bowl.' It just came out of my mouth that way." When Rozelle protested that the name wasn't "dignified enough," Hunt suggested, "Why don't we add Roman numerals each year?"

Fittingly, Hunt's Kansas City Chiefs made it to the Big One that January. The same year, 1967, Hunt founded World Championship Tennis, a groundbreaking professional tennis circuit and forerunner to the ATP. Hunt stands alone as the only person to be inducted into three major Halls of Fame: the Pro Football Hall of Fame (1972), the Soccer Hall of Fame (1982), and the International Tennis Hall of Fame (1993).

bunk by then, you'd better have a good excuse: like you're dead. Otherwise, Lombardi would slap you with a stiff fine and make you run extra laps for the rest of your natural born life. How serious was Lombardi on this point? He once fined star running back Jim Taylor $25 for missing curfew. Lombardi didn't care that Taylor was sitting at the end of his bed in his shorts and socks when the clock struck 11:00. "Why aren't you in bed?" the coach barked at him.

One morning, who should come strolling in to the locker room at 10:00 AM, hungover, probably still reeking of cheap perfume (courtesy of the ladies he and his partner in crime, Max McGee, a wide receiver, had entertained at the Northland Hotel in Green Bay)? That would be

---

Major Lett Down

When, in Super Bowl XXVII, the Dallas Cowboys' **Leon Lett** gave us the ultimate example of the perils of a premature celebration, we can assume George "Mission Accomplished" Bush wasn't in Crawford, Texas, taking notes. Of course, who can forget how a showboating Lett slowed up and extended the ball out from his right hand like tasty bait, allowed a hustling Don Beebe to knock the ball out as he reached the goal line. Couldn't he hear Beebe coming up behind him? "How could I hear someone that small and that fast," said the 287-pound tackle. "I was the one making all the noise."

Here's what some people forget: in that game, the Big Cat recorded a sack and two forced fumbles, one leading to a Cowboys touchdown. The next season Lett enabled the Dolphins to win the game when he attempted to fall on a blocked field goal rather then let the clock run out, giving Miami a second chance to kick the winning field goal. "Leon was really upset about it," recalled former Dallas safety Bill Bates. "A girl from one of the schools sent him a note. She said, 'Leon, don't worry about it. Last year in the Super Bowl there was this guy who was going in to score a touchdown and had the ball ripped out of his hand right before he scored. So don't worry about it. People make mistakes all the time.'"

Paul Hornung, aka the Golden Boy. It was a nickname that perfectly suited the glamorous, golden-haired hero who'd already achieved "cover boy" status as an All-American Heisman winner at Notre Dame.

Lombardi was gathered in his office with his assistant coaches, pouring over game film, when he saw Hornung crawl in. McGee had been so frightened of Lombardi's wrath that he had already sneaked back to his room at around 5:00 AM. Lombardi came out and started cursing him out at the top of his lungs, flailing his arms, threatening him. Hornung picked up the story from there: "Finally, he hollered, 'Hornung, do you want to be a player or a playboy?' And I said, 'I want to be a playboy.'"

Hornung went back to his room and started packing his bags. "My teammates knew how hot I was," Hornung recalled. "And they chanted, 'Go, go, go,' as I packed my suitcase in the dark. There was only problem. I couldn't find my keys." Later he would learn that guard Jerry Kramer had hidden them so he couldn't leave. By that afternoon, Hornung had cooled down, as had Lombardi. The coach decided to fine him $500. ("[Max] and I could have financed a small Caribbean country with our fines," said Hornung.)

Lombardi grew to love his trouble-making star almost like a son. After Hornung, who also kicked field goals and extra points, powered the Packers to a 37–0 victory over the New York Giants in the 1961 championship game, scoring an NFL-record 19 points, Lombardi said to a reporter, "Maybe he'll give you the idea that everything is a party, but don't believe it. When I have him at practice, I take one look and can tell what he's done the night before. It's nothing, believe me. Look what he's like in a game."

Part of an unstoppable running tandem—he was "Mr. Outside," and Jim Taylor was "Mr. Inside"—the graceful Hornung could do it all: cut through the defense like a "lawnmower running through grass" or deliver a gigantic block to open up a running lane. And this was a man who had won the Heisman Trophy in 1956...*as a quarterback.* He used his effortless versatility and his uncanny "nose for the end-zone" to lead the league in scoring three consecutive years—1959 to 1961—and his 176 points in 1960 remained an NFL record until 2006, even though they only played 12 games back then. A four-time champion, Hornung was awarded the NFL's Most Valuable Player in 1961, culminating in a record-smashing 19-point scoring-spree as Green Bay rolled over the New York Giants in the championship game 37–0.

Dick Schaap, a then-27-year-old *Newsweek* editor recalled his first trip to Green Bay, trailing the Golden Boy. "Each morning Paul would get up about quarter to nine and be on the field by 9:00. They would practice until 12:00, and there would be meetings to 3:00. At 3:00 he'd come home, mix a pitcher of martinis, and drink martinis until 6:00 with Kramer and the others. Then they'd go out to dinner, a group of players. Scotch before dinner. Wine with dinner. Brandy after dinner. Then back on scotch. Every day. I lost count by the time it had reached more than 60 just how many drinks he had in that week leading up to the Browns game. Also, he never went to bed before 4:00 in the morning, he never went to bed alone, and he never repeated himself." Hornung never stopped getting into trouble—he was suspended in 1963 for gambling on football games—but it was hard to stay mad at the guy. He was too charming. What's more, "Look what he's like in a game."

Bart Starr

When Bart Starr joined the lowly Green Bay Packers in 1956—a 17th-round pick from Alabama—the chance of him earning the starting quarterback job was equal to Packers fans enjoying bikini weather in Lambeau Field. The fact that Starr became a two-time Super Bowl MVP and Hall of Fame player is one of the most surprising stories in NFL history.

Born in Montgomery, Alabama, Starr rode the bench for most of high school and college.

His military father, Bert, viewed him as weak and indecisive, someone who could never live up to the unfulfilled promise of his athletically superior older brother, Bubba, who died tragically at the age of 13. Bart finally decided, the heck with it. Maybe everyone was right. Maybe he was a loser. One day after practice he came home and told his dad he was quitting the football team. His dad didn't say anything at first. Then, very calmly, he looked at Bart and said, "All right, it's your decision. I'm glad you'll be home in the afternoons. I want you to weed the garden and cut the cornstalks. I want the garden cleaned up for fall." Bart showed up to practice the next day. In fact, he was the first one there. It's true that Bert instilled his son with zero self-belief—but he also knew how much he hated farm work.

Starr's first few years in Green Bay were a disaster. "He was not loud, he was not funny, he was not full of enthusiasm," recalled Packers teammate Jerry Kramer. "Bart was like methane gas—colorless, odorless, tasteless—virtually invisible." He became so despondent over his lack of playing time that he went out drinking at a bar with Kramer, "a sighting," according to writer David Maraniss, "as rare as a giraffe striding down Fifth Avenue." He downed a total of four Miller High Lifes: it was probably the most bombed the clean-cut athlete had ever gotten…or would ever get again.

One of the NFL's greatest odd couples was Bart Starr and Vince Lombardi. Gruff and bombastic, Lombardi ruled over his players with the intimidating authority of a four-star general. When Lombardi showed up in 1959, he took one look at Starr and determined the kid lacked the mettle to be an NFL quarterback. Once at practice, after watching Starr sail an errant pass right into the arms of a defensive player, the coach bellowed, "Starr! You could see the ball was going to be intercepted when you threw it. One more like that, and you're gone." He wasn't kidding, and Starr knew it. During an exhibition game, Lombardi pulled Starr before the end of the first half, a sure sign that you were getting the axe. Starr sat on the bench, choking back tears.

Then a funny thing happened. While looking over film tape, Lombardi noticed that Starr's mechanics were strong, his decisions with the ball smart. Still, it was only after starter Lamar McHan got injured and second-stringer Joe Francis didn't pan out that Starr, already in his fourth year, got his chance during a game against the 49ers. Trying to take control of the huddle, he told the talkative Max McGee to shut his trap. "The order had a delayed effect," David Maraniss explained. "It seemed so out of character, Jim Ringo called a timeout so that the offensive lineman could stop laughing."

Then, in a game against the Chicago Bears in 1961, Starr took a vicious hit from Chicago middle linebacker Bill George that left him with blood-stained teeth. Sportswriter Ed Gruver explained what happened next: "Standing over the fallen quarterback, George growled, 'That'll take care of you, Starr, you sissy.' Starr jumped up, and through cracked lips, said, 'Screw you, Bill George, we're coming after you.' That game proved to be one of the defining points of Starr's career, since his steely response inspired his teammates. They looked at him and saw what Kramer called 'a gentle manliness — an iron in him.'"

Taking on a monstrous linebacker was courageous, challenging Vince Lombardi was suicidal. But the pivotal moment came in the locker room after a bad loss, as Packers center Bill Curry recalled:

Angels in the End Zone

When in 2007 the Falls Creek Baptist Church in Indianapolis tried to hold their annual Super Bowl party, they received a letter from the NFL threatening legal action. "The league prohibits 'mass out-of-home' gatherings in front of a television larger than 55 inches," explained Allen St. John in *The Billion Dollar Game*. But Pastor John Newland wasn't ready to let the league sack their good times. "We're not going to let the NFL stop us from doing what God called us to do," he said. "Satan can throw up obstacles, but with God's spirit we can't be stopped."

"Standing face to face with us in his white, insulated V-neck shirt, his khaki coaching pants, and his black riffle soled shoes, [Lombardi] started by speaking evenly, 'You guys don't care. You don't want to do what's required to win the right way. You aren't responsible enough to take on your share. Why, right here in this room there is only one man who publicly took the blame for the poor performance. Willie Davis is the one leader we have here. He's the only one who told the truth to the press and the public!' But before he could continue, a voice boomed out from the back of the room. 'That's not true!' barked Bart Starr. 'If you're going to say stuff like that, get it right.' You could have heard a proverbial pin drop. The oxygen was sucked out of the room as we waited for the counter, the next eruption. The unthinkable happened. Lombardi backed down. Even more, he was actually subdued the remainder of the day."

From 1960 through 1967, Starr led the Packers to a record of 82–24–4, as well as six division titles, five NFL championships, and two Super Bowls. He was named MVP for both title games. Mr. Virtually Invincible had become virtually unstoppable.

Joe Montana

Joe Montana's legendary poise under pressure earned him the nickname Joe Cool. But to hear of the quarterback's fondness for punking his teammates, perhaps it should be Joe Goofball. There's a story about when the eventual three-time Super Bowl MVP was at 49ers training camp at Sierra College in Rocklin. The players, who rode back and forth from the dorms to the practice field on mountain bikes, would commonly emerge from practice exhausted, only to find their bikes missing. The next 20 odd minutes would be spent searching in the dark for their bikes until they finally found them—*stuck up in a tree*. "Thank you, Joe Montana," Bill Romanowski said, recalling the time that he and the rest of the defensive unit looked up to see their bikes "hanging in the top of the maple trees, like they were Christmas ornaments." Meanwhile, the devious culprit would be relaxing back at his dorm room—the door bolted shut, of course. Another time Montana tied all his teammates' bikes to a motorcycle, as he explained: "We had a big, thick chain we had bought and put it through all the tires and back through the motorcycle tire, and then locked it. So when everybody came out from their meeting at night, no one could get on their bikes, and the guy couldn't ride his motorcycle." Knowing that his teammates would be most worn-out at the end of camp, he waited until then for his ultimate stealing spree. "On the last training camp," recalled receiver Mike Wilson, "There must have been 10 bikes up there." How did he get them all up there? "Joe had help from Steve Young," said Wilson.

Over his stellar 15-year career, Montana was a late-game assassin. No less than 31 times during his career did he rally his team to a comeback victory. Some of his most unbelievable late-game feats include his end zone pass to Dwight Clark with 51 seconds left to beat Dallas and earn a spot in the 1981 Super Bowl. Then there was his 92-yard drive with time running out to defeat Cincinnati in Super Bowl XXIII. While he was usually the one brutalizing his opponents, on a few occasions it was Montana who was on the receiving end of the pain. Who can forget New York Giant Leonard Marshall's vicious hit on Montana in the fourth quarter of the 1990 NFC Championship? "As he compressed me, he broke my hand," Joe Montana recalled. "And my whole chest hurt so bad that I had no idea my hand was broken for a good 15 to 20 minutes. I couldn't breathe. I thought I was going to die." In addition to the broken hand, Montana suffered a bruised sternum, a bruised stomach, and cracked ribs. In 2008 Marshall talked to a reporter about what he felt was probably the greatest football play ever made in a crucial game: "When the call came in from the sideline from Bill Belichick [Giants defensive coordinator], I knew I'd be in position on the weak side of cover 2 man to make a play.... I dove and left my feet with the intent to strip the ball and have [Mark] Collins or [Lawrence] Taylor run it in the end zone, similar to a play L.T. made in the 1986 playoff game in New York when Jim Burt knocked Joe out of that game. As we both collapsed, Montana winced, and I knew it was the end of an era for them. I knew he was hurt bad and that it was likely he wouldn't return." Indeed, Montana never returned to the 49ers, not as a starter anyway. By the time he recovered, after missing the entire 1991 season, Steve Young had taken his place, forcing the man who had led his team to four Super Bowls to leave for the Kansas City Chiefs.

So who delivered the biggest hit ever on Joe Montana? If you guessed Leonard Marshall, you would be wrong. It was actually a costar

Quarterback Joe Montana won three of his four Super Bowl titles under 49ers head coach Bill Walsh before retiring in 1994.

of Nicolas Cage. "The hardest hit I ever took in my life wasn't delivered by Jim Burt, or Leonard Marshall, or Bruce Smith to knock me out of a playoff game," Montana said. "It was one time running the option in practice at Notre Dame, when I got nailed by a guy who later worked in Hollywood in the movie *The Rock*, he was the marine who got crushed by an enormous block of metal that fell from the ceiling. When I saw him recently, I told him it was about time he found out how that felt."

Montana was involved with Steve Young in one of the all-time classic quarterback controversies. Ten years earlier, he had almost found himself in a similar battle with Steve DeBerg. But in 1981, just before the start of the season, Walsh left no doubt that Montana was the man in charge, trading DeBerg to the Denver Broncos. After his glorious decade-long run in San Francisco, Montana went to the Chiefs, where coincidentally DeBerg had been quarterback the previous two seasons. When Montana went to his locker, he found his shoes missing. In their place was a pair of size 15s. "Stop following in my footsteps," read the note attached. Who knows what Montana did next, but it probably involved hiding Steve DeBerg's bike up in a tree.

John Elway

After 14 years of postseason heartbreak, including three Super Bowl defeats, John Elway proved that it's never too late to become one of the most recognized big-game players in NFL history. All it took were a pair of clutch performances in back-to-back Super Bowls in 1997 and 1998. Following the second one, for which he garnered an MVP award, he rode off triumphantly into the western range. Over his final four years, he posted his highest quarterback rating of his career, 17 points higher than his first four years in the league, while throwing for 101 touchdowns.

Following in the tradition of Sammy Baugh, Elway was a laser-armed third baseman on his high school team, Granada Hills in Los Angeles. He also had a nice fastball, which according to Elway, he developed by constantly throwing stuff: "In Montana, I threw snowballs at telephone poles. In California, I threw oranges." One year Granada Hills faced off against huge favorite Crenshaw in the city championship at Dodger Stadium. Clinging to a 2–0 lead in the third inning, Granada Hills coach Darryl Stroh decided to bring in a reliever. The coach initially dismissed Elway, who had not pitched in six weeks. "John was so heavily involved in football, getting ready to go off to Stanford to play, that we weren't really working with him," Stroh told writer Michael Sokolove. "It wasn't really fair to ask him to pitch." But at the last second, he looked back over at his third baseman, who was staring blankly into the outfield, and decided that if anyone had the guts to pull this off, it was John. Two innings later, Granada leading 3–2 with two men on and no outs, Elway looked in at the next Crenshaw batter, a powerful left-handed slugger. His name: Darryl Strawberry. Having already smashed a ball that barely stayed in the park, everyone expected Strawberry to swing for the fences but, inexplicably, the Crenshaw coach had Strawberry bunt—which he did—right to Elway, who easily threw out the lead runner on a force-out. Strawberry never forgot the painful incident, as he later wrote in his autobiography, "I would have to wait for my revenge against John Elway for another six years, when the Mets beat Boston in the very same season that my New York Giants beat Denver."

Not many rookies need a police escort to get a haircut. But Elway was not your typical rookie. From the moment the Stanford standout arrived in Denver, he was afforded the kind of attention usually reserved for Hollywood A-listers. Before Elway headed off to his first training camp in Greeley, he made an off-handed remark to a few reporters that he planned to get a haircut. This set off a feeding frenzy among the local Greeley press intent on capturing the historic occasion. In order to evade the press, Jim Saccomano, VP of public relations, arranged for Elway to get his hair snipped at the home of a local barber. The only problem was that everyone knew what kind of car Elway drove. Which is when Saccomano came up with a "hair-brained" solution. "I got a Greeley police officer who was willing to take John to his appointment," he said. The next day the press was shocked to see the freshly shorn quarterback throwing on the practice field. Maybe that's the real reason Troy Aikman and Joe Buck got armed U.S. marshalls to escort them to the Super Bowl—they had to make a pit stop at Supercuts.

As Denver's only Hall of Fame player, not to mention the all-time winningest quarterback in NFL history with 148, he has provided Broncos fans with plenty to cheer about. There are many stories to illustrate Elway's mythic stature among his Rocky Mountain disciples, such as Mandi George, who is such a big Broncos fan that she won the 2005 Most Valuable Tailgater award. "I've known my husband forever," she said. "When we started dating, he asked who my favorite football team was. It was part of him proposing. He then asked, 'If you were going to have an affair, who would it be with?' I said, 'John Elway.' He said, 'You're the woman for me.'"

As beloved as Elway is in Denver, that's how much he's despised in Cleveland. Just the mere utterance of his name causes Browns fans the same indigestion that Red Sox fans suffer when they hear the words Bucky Dent. But to inflict maximum pain, you don't need to bring up

Pay Day

Two-time Super Bowl–winning quarterback **Ben Roethlisberger** drew the NFL's largest paycheck in 2008, earning more than $27.7 million. When, on November 12, 1892, the Allegheny Athletic Association wanted to persuade former All-America Yale tackle **"Pudge" Heffelfinger** to play in a football game against the Pittsburgh Athletic Club, they paid him $500. As a result of this payment of service, Pudge became the first professional football player.

all of his 47 career late-game rallies, just the one known simply as The Drive. It refers to the time that Elway, with just over five minutes left in the game, and Cleveland's old stadium vibrating with 80,000 red-faced fans hollering like a bunch of crazed hyenas, led his team 98 yards down the field to send the 1986 AFC Championship Game into an improbable overtime, where a second drive resulted in a game-winning field goal. Legend has it that just before Elway started the drive on his own 2-yard line, Keith Bishop said to the Browns, "We got 'em right where we want 'em." Bishop's confidence evaporated momentarily after Elway took a sack to put the Broncos in a nerve-wracking third-and-very-long. Bishop recalled the conversation in the huddle: "John said to us, 'Do whatever it takes, and something good is going to happen.' He hit a third-and-18 pass even though the snap ricocheted off Steve Watson's rear end. Steve was going in motion, and the ball was snapped too soon, and John had to reach down a foot off the ground for the ball and get it, then stand up, and then nail a 20-yard pass. That's what John Elway can do."

Browns fans aren't the only ones relieved when No. 7 finally retired in 1998. "John Elway?" said former Oakland Raiders great Howie Long. "Let me tell you about John Elway. He was the biggest pain in the neck I ever played against. I'm serious. That guy was a nightmare." Meanwhile, detractors such as former *Wall Street Journal* writer Allen Barra argue that he benefited from a unique home advantage playing in a high-altitude stadium. "Think about it this way," said Barra. "John Elway's last two seasons are what separates his career from Dave Krieg's." Other people, like former teammate Shannon Sharpe, consider him the greatest quarterback of all time. When Dan Patrick asked the tight end about what Elway was like in the huddle, he told him, "At the start of the game, he talks very fast. But we have been over and over these plays, so we know what he's saying. But at the end of the game, if we're behind, he talks so slow it's almost like his speech is slurred. You can *hear-every-word-that-is-said.*" So does that explain why he's one of the greatest practitioners of the two-minute drill? "He drinks five cups [of coffee] in a two-hour period," Sharpe said. "That might have something to do with it."

Emmitt Smith

Maybe Emmitt Smith should form a support group for pro athletes whose workmanlike consistency, durability, and lack of flash has made them ineligible for greatest-of-all-time status. Pull up a chair, Tim Duncan. You, too, Pete Sampras. Don't be shy, Hank Aaron.

Sure, it's easy to diminish Emmitt Smith's accomplishments. (As Homer Simpson once said, "Fun too!") All one has to do is argue that while he was a great rusher, he wasn't even the best running back of his day. After all, the 1990s produced human highlight reel Barry Sanders, who chewed up huge tracks of yardage on an average Lions team. Which brings us to the other big knock against Smith—that through most of his career he had one of the most dominant O-lines in history blocking for him.

Smith didn't have much money growing up in Pensacola, Florida. He couldn't even afford two *T*s in his name. The truth is that he was born with one *T*, but after getting back a school paper with the misspelling, Smith decided to keep it. As he explained, "My father is Emmit and my grandfather is Emmit, but I wanted something extra so I could separate my Emmitt from the rest of them. Even though on my birth certificate it has one *T*, I just added the extra *T* for me."

Despite his All-America career at the University of Florida, there were those who questioned his speed and size. "There were all these

What Recession?

The cost of a 30-second television commercial for Super Bowl I in 1967: $42,000. Last year, despite the troubled economy, an average spot cost $3 million.

people saying, 'He's too slow,' or, 'He's too small,'" former Cowboys coach Jimmy Johnson said. "All I know is that every time I saw a film of him, he was running 50, 60, 70, 80 yards for a touchdown. That looked pretty good to me." Good enough for the Cowboys to make him the 17th overall pick of the 1990 draft. It didn't take long for his teammates to remark on his diminutive stature, anointing him "Bushwick Bill" after the 3'8" Geto Boys rapper who survived a pre-Plaxico, self-inflicted gunshot wound (yes, he was loaded.) NASCAR star Mark Martin's little kid, Matt, had a different reaction when introduced to the gridiron legend. "Meeting Emmitt was tight. He's a pretty cool guy. He's about 5'9". That's the size I want to be, too, 5'9"." Joe Montana paid him the ultimate compliment: "Emmitt Smith is only 5'9", but he's about as tough to bring down as Larry Csonka was."

Over his 13 years with Dallas, Smith used his stout frame to rack up 17,162 of his record 18,355 career yards, leading the Cowboys to three Super Bowl victories in four years, a feat no other team had ever accomplished (later matched by New England). He also set top marks for career rushing touchdowns (153), number of 100-yard games in a career (78), and consecutive 1,000-yard seasons (11). *Not a bad draft pick.* But without question, his most impressive milestone is his all-time rushing record, made a reality with Smith's 11-yard run against Seattle on October 27, 2002. Sportswriter Rick Weinberg explained why it was voted one of ESPN's 100 Most Memorable Moments of the past 25 years: "The crowd, the TV cameras zero in on No. 22 as he displays his signature burst off left tackle, hits a small hole, squeezes his way through, cuts left, and finds a seam. There's daylight. 'Walter,' Smith says quietly to himself. 'See ya.' His thought, he later reveals, is out of respect and admiration for Payton, not cockiness or disrespect. Smith bounces off one attempted tackle. He chugs along, running low, running square. He receives a crushing block from fullback Robert Thomas. He stumbles, ever so slightly, over the arm of an opponent, yet he quickly places his right hand on the turf, enabling him to keep his balance and keep chugging along until he passes Payton. When Smith is finally brought down, 11 yards later, with the crowd in a frenzy, Smith bounces to his feet. The record is his."

Is he deserving of the record? Ask the family of the man he passed in the record book, and the answer is an emphatic yes. Payton's wife,

Connie, whom Smith included in the buildup to the record, wrote the foreword to his authorized biography, *Emmitt Smith: Run to History* by Rudy Klancik. "In September 2001 she [Connie Payton] was in Dallas for a news conference about Smith's pursuit of the rushing record," said Klancik. "On the morning of the September 11 terrorist attacks, Payton was in a Dallas hotel room. She was supposed to catch a flight that morning, but air travel was suspended, and she was stranded. Smith called her and told her to stay with his family. Like so many Americans unsure of what the next hours and days would bring, Payton and Smith's wife, Pat, went to the grocery store to buy food and water. 'I spent the whole day with Emmitt and Pat, all of his family,' Connie Payton said. 'We were glued to the television set.' In the middle of the night, two of Payton's friends made the 14-hour drive from Chicago to pick her up and take her home so she could be with her family. But her time in Dallas was revealing. She decided to stay in contact with Smith, who has taken an interest in the Payton children. In July Payton selected Smith to receive the Spirit of Sweetness Award from the Walter Payton Cancer Fund, one of two foundations she runs. During his acceptance speech in Aurora, Illinois, Smith started to cry as he talked about his pride in being associated with Walter Payton and in chasing his record."

Growing up in Pensacola, Florida, Smith so idolized Payton, he hung a picture of Walter Payton in his high school locker. Another person who deemed Smith worthy of his rarified status was none other than the man whose all-time rushing record Smith broke in 2002. Days before Payton's untimely death from liver disease, he told his son Jarrett, then a running back at the University of Miami, that he should try to follow Smith's example as a player and a person. His brother Eddie told ESPN's *SportsCentury*, "[Walter] once said that if anybody breaks his record, he hopes it is Emmitt because he would do it with the class and the dignity that the record represents."

Smith might not have been the fastest or the biggest player, but he never lacked for confidence. Back in school, he used to keep a piece of paper with his modest goals: *Lead NFL in rushing, NFL rookie of the year, Hall of Fame, NFL's all-time leading rusher, greatest running back ever!!!* With that said, he was the first person to give credit for his storied career to his linemen. In 1992, six hours before the Monday night opener against the Redskins, Smith snuck into the Cowboys locker room, took out a bunch of $7,500 Rolexes, and put them in the locker of every offensive lineman. The inscription on the back of the watches read: THANKS FOR THE 1,563 RUSHING YARDS: NFL RUSHING TITLE. EMMITT SMITH. His thankful teammates opened up lanes for Smith, who ran for 140 yards in a 23–10 victory.

How much credit Smith deserves versus his offensive linemen is unknowable. One thing is for sure: Smith's tenacious, hard-driving running style has unquestionably earned him status as one of the greatest big-game running backs of the Super Bowl era. It's a short list that includes Larry Csonka, Franco Harris, Marcus Allen, John Riggins, O.J. Anderson, and Terrell Davis. What do all these men share besides a never-die attitude? Besides Smith, they are the only seven running backs to win the Super Bowl MVP. In the last 15 years, only Smith and Davis have achieved the prestigious honor.

Scoring two second-half touchdowns to seal Super Bowl XXVIII in 1994 might be his most clutch performance, but his gutsiest came during the finale of the regular season, a battle for home-field advantage against their hated rivals, the New York Giants. Despite suffering a dislocated shoulder, Smith carried the ball 32 times for 168 yards as

Exposed Offense

It was the "wardrobe malfunction" seen around the world—unless you were hiding in a cave in Afghanistan. The incident occurred on the MTV-produced live halftime show at the 2004 Super Bowl. Justin "Rock Your Body" Timberlake ripped away the front of Janet Jackson's costume after singing to her, "I'm going to make you naked by the end of this song." The nation got a glimpse of Ms. Jackson's left ta-ta, with the national outcry somehow eclipsing anything seen during Bush's entire first term.

As a result of the media storm, the FCC fined CBS stations a record $550,000 despite the broadcaster's argument that it was "accidental" rather than "willful." CBS said that they were originally going to book another "performer" whom the NFL objected to "because of a prior incident in which the performer unexpectedly removed her clothes during a national telecast of an NFL event." Britney? Xtina? In the end, CBS selected Timberlake and Jackson to perform the show, in their words, "to minimize the possibility of the unexpected."

the visiting Cowboys triumphed 16–13 on Eddie Murray's game-winning field goal in overtime. "I heard bones cracking around me all day long," Smith said after the game. A few plays before the decisive kick, Cowboys coach Jimmy Johnson had sent Lincoln Coleman to replace Smith. "Jimmy told me to go in," Coleman recalled. "But Emmitt told me to get out." Emmitt gained 42 yards to single-handedly put Murray in range. "Emmitt was hurting real bad," Cowboys guard Nate Newton said. "Most guys at any position would have come out for good after that. Not Emmitt. And the thing was, he came to us and told us that he wasn't coming out. No way."

There's a story about Jerry Jones calling Emmitt Smith into his office midway through the 1992 season to offer him a new contract. "By giving you this contract, the Dallas Cowboys are saying to the world that Emmitt Smith is every bit the running back of Barry Sanders," said a grinning Jones. The owner knew that Smith worshipped Sanders. He also knew that Sanders had one of the worst contracts in the league—five years for $5.9 million. Not surprisingly, Smith walked out fuming. So began a contract war of epic proportions between two Texas-sized egos content to wait until the other one blinked. By the time the next season rolled around, the disgruntled Smith was a holdout, and the stubbornly proud Jones had replaced him with some rookie named Derrick Lassic. After starting the season with losses to the Redskins and Bills, it was clear that nobody could fill Smith's shoes; they didn't just miss his running ability, they missed his first-one-into-battle spirit.

All hell finally broke loose in the Cowboys' locker room following the Bills loss, as Jeff Pearlman recounted in the excellent *Boys Will Be Boys: The Glory Days and Party Nights of the Dallas Cowboys Dynasty*: "Immediately after the game [Charles] Haley had stormed into the room, tears streaming down his cheeks. He fumed aloud, 'We're never gonna win with that fucking rookie!' When Jones entered, Haley picked up his helmet by the face mask and whizzed it 10 feet through the air, past the owner, and through a wall. *Thud!* 'You need to sign that motherfucker now!' he screamed. The silence was deafening. 'I thought that thing was going to kill me,' says Jones.... A bawling Haley proceeded to approach Jones, lean into his ear, and whisper, 'Sign Emmitt! I don't care how you do it. Cut me. Take the money out of my check. Just sign

> ## By the Number...
> Redskins quarterback **Jason Campbell** wears No. 17 in honor of Doug Williams, the first black QB to win the Super Bowl.

Emmitt!' It was a new kind of crazy for Haley, who—in a career chock-full of nutty moments—had never before whipped a helmet at the man signing his paychecks." Jones got the message. Four days later he signed Smith to the largest contract for any running back in the league—four years, $13.6 million. With Smith back, the Cowboys went on to become the first team to start 0–2 and go on to win the Super Bowl.

Currently an ESPN analyst, Smith has stayed busy since retiring from football, even campaigning for Barack Obama during the elections. "I saw Emmitt Smith and former Dallas mayor Ron Kirk introduce Obama at his campaign rally in February in Dallas," recalled one audience member. "Emmitt was a strong, magnetic presence and really fired them up for Obama. Definitely one of the more rhetorically and oratorically gifted pro athletes out there. Obama was very admiring when he came on stage. 'Emmitt, is there anything you can't do?' he asked. 'I'm glad [Emmitt Smith] isn't running for president,' he added." It was clear from Smith's remarks that day that the admiration was mutual: "As a young man, people told me I was too small and not fast enough to do the things that I wanted to do in terms of football. Well, you know what, I did not allow them to keep me down. Barack Obama is not going to allow them to keep him down."

Smith might have a future in politics, but the chances of joining the PGA are less likely. Craig Neal, an NBA player who shared the same agent, recalled hitting the links with Smith and spending the round searching in the woods for Smith's errant shots: "I wound up getting a poison ivy shot." On the other hand, he surprised many with his dancing ability, taking home the Disco Ball trophy on the TV show *Dancing with the Stars* in 2007. "It's funny to see how people, especially couples, react to me. The woman will ask her boyfriend or husband, 'Hey, isn't that the dancer?' And the guy will say, 'Nah, that's the famous football player.' I get a chuckle out of it."

Tom Brady

Days before Super Bowl XLII, Michael Strahan was asked his opinion of the quarterback he'd be facing that Sunday. "I love Tom Brady," he said. "I'm jealous that I'm not Tom Brady." He's not alone. After all, the Patriots' two-time Super Bowl MVP has been named to *Forbes'* Top 100 Celebrities, landed on *People's* Most Beautiful People list, and took home *SI's* Man of the Year in 2005. He earns around $10 million in endorsement deals—he could earn twice that amount, but he's too classy to over-saturate himself. Oh, and did we mention he's married to Brazilian supermodel Giselle Bundchen? But you knew that. What you might not know about Brady is that he has shit luck.

Back when he was just "another" student at the University of Michigan, he couldn't get laid to save his life. Maybe that's an exaggeration—he was on the football team, after all. Still, Brady had a crush on this cute girl who wouldn't give him the time of day. He would drive by her house, hoping to get a glimpse of her, maybe even work up the courage to strike up a conversation. When the chance arose for actual human interaction—like at a local club—he blew it. She just wasn't interested. Brady explains his Peter Parker–like personality. "I'm very confident as a football player; I have no problems. I'm not natural with cameras and pictures. Put me in a room with my family, and I'm the one cracking jokes. Put me in a room with people I don't know, I'll be a little shy for a while until I can figure out what to say. What it comes down to is that I just want to be a great football player."

So, let's get to that bad luck. The string of unfortunate incidents began when the coach who recruited him to Michigan left for Stanford. "This is a month after he signed, and the two people who wanted him there are gone," recalled his father. "And he's screwed, but he didn't know how screwed he was."

Next came the attack of appendicitis. He lost 30 pounds his freshman year. Desperate to get his life together, he went to see a counselor in the athletics department, Greg Hardin. "So he tells me that he's going to be the starting quarterback at Michigan," said Hardin, "and I'm looking at him, and I'm thinking, *Okay, I'm not going to rain on his parade.* But he's all broke down and emotionally worn out." Only one other Michigan player, recalled Hardin, had ever committed himself to the psychological-based program—Desmond Howard, the receiver and kick-off returner who won the Heisman Trophy at Michigan in 1991.

Brady worked his way back into shape and even outperformed Brian Griese during training camp. It was a foregone conclusion that Brady would start the season, especially after Griese got suspended for throwing a barstool through a saloon window. Yet the son of the Hall of Fame Miami Dolphins quarterback got the job, leaving Brady relegated to the sideline. Brady remained calm. He kept working and working, and he always kept his sense of humor. "He'd do an imitation of Al Pacino's Tony Montana that sounded like Donald Duck, and he'd laugh at himself as loudly as they would," explained Charles P. Pierce in *Moving the Chains*. "This guy, they thought, better make it to the NFL because he'd never get work as an actor."

Having climbed his way up from seventh on the depth chart, and with Griese graduated, it was finally Brady's time to shine as a starter. But like a plot straight out of an episode of *Friday Night Lights*, the local boosters pressured coach Lloyd Carr to start incoming freshman and local son Drew Henson. So in Carr's infinite wisdom, he decided he'd have Brady play the first quarter and Henson the second one, and the quarterback who performed better would start the rest of the game. Once again, Brady hung tough, earning vindication late in his senior year, breaking several Orange Bowl passing records in a pressure-filled overtime victory over Alabama in 2000.

Then came draft day. The 49ers had shown strong interest in the California golden boy. Dwight Clark, one of Brady's childhood heroes, was working in the front office and liked what he saw from him. In the third round, the 49ers picked Giovanni Carmazzi, a quarterback out of Hofstra. "Dwight Clark—unbelievable," recalled his father. "It just killed us. Tommy was sitting there, and he was like, 'I don't understand this. I do *not* understand this.'"

In the living room, where his family had gathered around the television, all eyes turned to Tommy as he calmly walked out the door. His mom, Nancy, recalled, "He just wanted to take a walk, and he grabbed a bat." Brady proceeded to demolish the backyard, clobbering toys, whatever he could hit. While Brady was going postal, the phone rang. It was the Patriots. "You don't want to say, 'Well, he's not around,'" said

Vinatieri's Last Stands

Adam Vinatieri's road to Super Bowl glory started with a trip to Wal-Mart. After not getting drafted, he bought $20 worth of blank videotapes at the store, went home, and made a homemade pre-YouTube audition tape. He mailed out the video to teams around the NFL, but nobody was interested. Soon after, he got an unexpected offer from the Amsterdam Admirals of the NFL's World League in Europe, who had got a hold of the tape. After watching it, they asked if he would come and play for them.

Later, Bill Parcells discovered Vinatieri, presumably not on a recruiting trip, where he and the kicker hit the coffee shops and red light district. Patriots fans can rejoice that Vinatieri decided, years earlier, not to accept an appointment at West Point. If only his family ancestor, a military bandmaster, had decided not to follow his military leader, Colonel Custer, into battle.

It's poetic justice that Vinatieri had the two most successful last stands in Super Bowl history. The first came with seven seconds left in Super Bowl XXXVI in the Louisiana Superdome when he kicked a 48-yarder to lift the 14-point underdog Patriots over the Rams for their first title crown. When, two years later in Houston's Reliant Stadium, Vinatieri kicked another last-gasp field goal, this time to beat the Carolina Panthers in Super Bowl XXXVIII, he became the first player to be the deciding factor in two different Super Bowl wins.

his father. "I'm trying to cover this thing as fast as I can, so I said, 'Well, he's in the shower.' And they say, 'Well, Coach Belichick would like to talk to him for a second.'" New England made Brady their sixth-round selection. The 199th pick. As for the six QBs picked ahead of him, only Chad Pennington and Marc Bulger remained in the NFL by 2005 (Chris Redman resurfaced in 2007 after being out of the league for three seasons). Giovanni Carmazzi ended up never playing a down in the NFL. Guess Brady was one "catch" Clark failed to make.

When Brady joined the Patriots, he was once again stuck at the bottom of the depth chart. He soon became the leader...of the practice squad! Still, Belichick and offensive coordinator Charlie Weis noticed how the subs rallied around the NFL newbie like he was a seasoned veteran—this was a man whom other men followed into battle. "I'm always reminded of my mother's dictum—pride and arrogance come before the fall. Numerous times in my life, when we kind of had things going, it would all get knocked out from under me. Pride goeth before the fall. It's as true in life as it is in religion as it is in sports," Brady said. When Drew Bledsoe got knocked out of a game in 2001, Brady stepped in and led New England all the way to the Super Bowl, where they faced the high-powered St. Louis Rams, who were favored by 14-points.

Brady once again proved that he wasn't much for paying attention to odds. With 90 seconds left in a tie game, Brady started on his 17-yard line with zero timeouts. In those 90 seconds, he delivered pin-point passes as he drove his team into field-goal position, where Adam Vinatieri then delivered the game-winning kick as time expired. In those 90 seconds, he had joined entry into the most elite club of Big Gamers. Joe Montana was there to unclick the velvet rope, then Joe Namath ushered him into the VIP room, where Sid Luckman was there to hand him the Lombardi Trophy (and a glass of champagne). The patrons in the club were so in awe of his golden smile, they didn't see the gritty determination in his eyes. Same mistake they had all made since he was a kid.

Then Frank Gifford Said...

As the NFL's most glamorous and popular player of his era, Frank Gifford moved back and forth between two completely different worlds. On Sunday, it was grass stains, mud, blood, and bruises. At night, dry martinis, French cuffs, well-shaven men, and beautifully fragrant women. But it didn't matter if he was on the football field or the Manhattan cocktail circuit, nobody could keep their eyes off him. That especially holds true for defenders assigned to stop the rusher, who was as elusive as he was fast. Over his 12 seasons with the New York Giants, he was named to eight Pro Bowls—*at three different positions, including defensive cornerback*. He also won the league's MVP honor in 1956 as he led the Giants to a championship crown. After he retired from the game, the Hall of Famer entered yet another completely new world, television, where he became one of the first athletes to conquer the broadcasting booth. The NFL's one-time "golden boy" told us about playing in the Greatest Game Ever Played, hanging with the Rat Pack, and why the infamous Bednarik hit has been seriously overblown.

Before Vince Lombardi became the legendary coach of the Green Bay Packers, he was your offensive coordinator in New York. How does he compare to the great coaches of this era, for instance, Bill Belichick?

Comparing Lombardi to Belichick is ridiculous because they coached in different atmospheres. Had Lombardi coached in this era and started yelling at some of these guys, they would go run home to momma. Had Belichick coached then, who knows? They were both right for their time.

There seemed to be a rivalry on those great Giants teams of the late 1950s between the offense, coached by Lombardi, and the defense, coached by future Cowboys coaching legend Tom Landry.

Sam Huff and I were the probably the most visible people on offense and defense, but more than anything we were team players on our specific unit. Our defensive team didn't think much of our offensive team, and our offensive team didn't think much of our defensive team. But we got along.

Some people might not know that you almost chose to be an actor instead of playing in the NFL?

Even though I was drafted No. 1 by the Giants, I wasn't sure I was going to play. Back then, it wasn't that big of a deal. A lot of players got drafted and didn't play, period. I needed another semester at USC to graduate, and I wanted to get my degree. I had already started taking acting classes, and I was much more interested in working in film than football. After I got drafted by the Giants, I talked to my wife, Maxine, who I had married my senior year in college. She was an artist, a very talented lady in her own right. And we thought, it's four months out of our life. Let's do it. We could go see the sights and scenes of New York. We could go to Broadway shows, go to museums. So that's what we did and we had a great time.

Every era in New York has its place-to-be. When you played, that was Toots Shor's saloon. There, you and other New York sports stars such as Joe DiMaggio, Mickey Mantle, and Joe Namath rubbed shoulders with the likes of Ernest Hemingway, Frank Sinatra, Chief Justice Earl Warren, and Jimmy Hoffa. Did you bring your Giants teammates there?

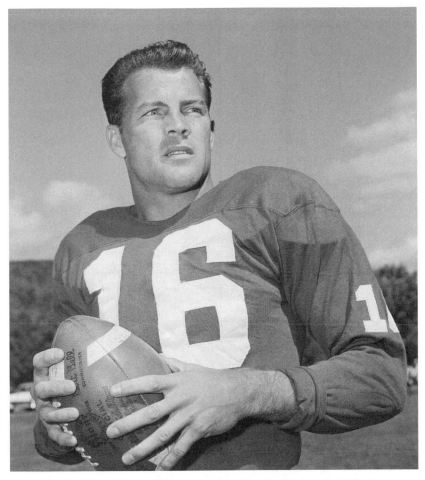

Long before he became a household name as a broadcaster, Frank Gifford was an eight-time Pro Bowl selection with the New York Giants.

Yeah, we all started hanging out there. And then we started developing into a football team. The guys started wearing jackets and ties. Nineteen fifty-six is really when things started turning around for us. By 1958 national television brought us into the forefront, but we were already recognizable in New York.

I read that one night at Toots' you spilled your drink on the Chairman of the Board?

I think it might have been the other way around. *(laughs)* Frank was a nice guy. Very shy. The first time I met him was at the bar at Toots', and he was much more impressed with me, I think, than I was with him. He was kind of on the downside of his career [his record label dropped him in 1952] and hadn't yet reemerged, which he would in 1953.

Did you know any of the other members of the Rat Rack? Dino?

Dean Martin and I were acquaintances for several years. He was a lot of fun. I was one of several football players brought in as extras [on the 1951 Martin/Lewis comedy *That's My Boy*] to make it look like real football. Jerry Lewis was more worried about the movie, but Dean was just hanging out with guys. He was terrific.

You were also friends with president Richard Nixon, a huge football fan. What did you think of *Frost/Nixon*?

Not much.

How accurate do you think was Langella's portrayal of Nixon?

I'm not going to get into this. He [Nixon] was a big fan and later became an acquaintance of mine. But every time I talk about it, somebody twists and turns it around. He was a friend of mine. He loved football. And when he was out of office, he came up to New York, and I spent a lot of time with him. He would come up to the house after the game. I would get him tickets to the game. He was a terrific guy.

Mike Stand

Forget Mike Martz or Kurt Warner. Rams fans should thank Al Davis for their thrilling Super Bowl victory over the Titans on January 30, 2000. It was the controversial Raiders owner who converted Missouri running back **Mike Jones** to linebacker after signing him as a rookie free agent in 1991. That's the same Mike Jones, of course, who made "the Tackle" that secured the Rams' first Super Bowl title. With the Rams leading 23–16 in Super Bowl XXXIV and Steve McNair engineering a last-ditch drive for the tie, Jones wrapped up Kevin Dyson one yard shy of the end zone as time expired. Before his teammates called him Super Bowl Hero, they had another name for him: Hands of Stone Jones. He picked up the nickname after teammates noted his knack for dropping interceptions in practice.

Before the 1956 NFL Championship Game, Giants linebacker Andy Robustelli famously handed out sneakers from his Connecticut sporting goods shop, which ended up giving you a major advantage as you crushed the Bears 47–7. Did anyone on the Giants not want to wear them?

If I recall, I wasn't too fond about wearing sneakers. But then I went out on the field. It was frozen as solid as concrete and slippery in spots. I remember J.C. Caroline was covering me on our first drive, and we needed 12 or 13 yards for a first down. I took the ball and broke it to outside. Caroline tried to reverse field and he fell on his ass. I thought, *This is going to be a long day for the Bears.*

In your recent book, *The Glory Game*, you reflect on the 1958 NFL Championship Game, or as it's often referred to, the Greatest Game Ever Played. Are you amazed at how its memory has endured?

Well, you're talking about something that happened over 50 years ago. And people still remember specific parts of the game. It really is interesting. I guess it's partly because of the people who played in it. They stayed alive in our world of imagination. Fifty years later Johnny Unitas is still a legendary name. People still talk about Raymond Berry, Sam Huff, myself. It's hard to find two teams that had such an impact of the NFL.

Apart from its other historical significance, it was also the first overtime game in the history of the NFL.

Sam Huff and I have become really good friends over the years. He remembers coming up to me on the sideline after regulation and saying, "What the hell are we going to do now?" We did actually play an overtime game that year—in preseason. They were just testing it. We played Chicago up in Boston and we went into an overtime period, and I remember being pissed off because we were all trying to catch a shuttle plane back to New York—we had the weekend off—and we missed the damn thing.

In the last game of the 1958 season, against the Cleveland Browns, the Giants needed Pat Summerall's game-winning last-second miracle field goal to even get into the playoffs. Come on, how far was it, really?

Depends on how big of a Giants fan you are. It can get up as far as 60 yards. But most of the guys I talked to for my book said it was about 50 yards. Maybe 51 or 52. But Pat was a hell of a kicker. You had to have a lot of respect for a guy who could kick it 50 yards in a snowstorm. And we didn't kick in the style they kick today. I was actually a field-goal kicker myself when I first came into the league, and we kicked straightaway.

As it turned out, you got your start at halfback because legendary Texas college player, Kyle Rote, got injured in training camp of his rookie year.

I was in my senior year at USC when Rote was a rookie, and he tore up his knee stepping in a gopher hole on some really bad practice field out in Oklahoma or Texas. Wellington Mara, who scouted me, didn't know what to do because, if Kyle could play, then he was going to play. So that's why I started my Giants career playing both ways. Sometimes Kyle would play half a game, sometimes not at all. I actually started at defensive cornerback up until 1956.

How hard was it pulling double duty back in those days?

I almost quit because it was exhausting at times. A couple of games in 1953 I didn't come out of. And I also kicked off and filled in kicking field goals. I remember losing a lot of weight.

I can see why you seriously considered becoming a full-time actor after college.

The year I graduated from USC I had made a couple of screen tests. In retrospect, they were pretty awful, but at the time I felt good about them. There were a lot of things I could have done other than play in the Polo Grounds, both ways, where I figured sooner or later I'd get killed.

Speaking of which, many consider the hit you took from the Eagles' Chuck Bednarik on a frozen Yankee Stadium field in 1960 to be one of the most brutal in NFL history.

That's been so distorted. He hit me in the chest, and I flipped over backward, and my head snapped back. They didn't have a CAT scan back then, so they X-rayed my head. I had a spinal concussion, was what it was. The doctor prescribed rest. But I was okay the next day, actually. I was in the hospital, and they made me stay there a week, where I read every magazine they had. My wife and friends came to see me, and I was fine. And then over the years, people started writing about it, and it became this mythological thing.

How did that play get, in your words, so distorted?

Mainly because of Chuck and his bullshit, pardon my expression. Bednarik was a great player. He certainly didn't need to do that to enhance his reputation. He's rightfully in the Hall of Fame.

So, contrary to popular belief, that injury was not the reason you decided to retire?

Over the years people wrote that I retired because of my head and my neck. But that had nothing to do with it. During the year that I was off, I would go up and work out with the guys. I even ran pass patterns against the scout team and I could still beat them, which felt good. I decided that off-season that I could do radio and television and film work all my life, but if I stay out one more year, I'm not going to be able to play football anymore. I wanted to get it out of my system, so I played three more years.

So why did you finally hang up your cleats?

Part of it was that I had already played nine years. And then the people at CBS came to me and said, "We'd like you to do sports on the local news station. And we'll give you your own radio show." It was a heck of an offer. It was the direction I wanted to go and it was something I could do the rest of my life, so I said, "Why not?"

Did you ever have any lingering effects from the injury?

I had some tingling in my arm about seven or eight years ago. I went to a hospital in New York to see a specialist. I came into his office after he had done a CAT scan, and he asked me, "Have you ever been in an auto accident?" I had never been in a car accident.

You think it was the Bednarik hit?

That's the only thing I can think of.

chapter 4

The Playmakers

Frank Gifford

In 1957 the Soviets launched the first satellite, *Sputnik*, into orbit. Also soaring into the stratosphere in the late 1950s: Madison Avenue (tail fins!), rock 'n' roll (Elvis swings!), and cold-war paranoia (nuclear annihilation!). Pro football's popularity also skyrocketed after the epic 1958 NFL Championship Game, the first nationally televised game (Colts win!). The game would not have been historic if the team Baltimore defeated had been none other than the New York Giants, who in the late '50s became the hottest sensation in the league, boasting two marquee names—Sam Huff, the intimidating linebacker who brought star power to a heretofore anonymous defensive unit, and Frank Gifford, the nimble halfback who paired his athletic grace and movie-star face to become the toast of the town.

Every Sunday, thousands of people poured into Yankee Stadium to see the man known affectionately as Giff unleash his eye-popping moves on the much larger defenders. In a way, he was the NFL's version of Don Draper, the dashing ad exec on *Mad Men*, a TV show which casts Manhattan as a vibrant, gin-soaked city swirling in cigarette smoke and cha-cha music. Epitomizing the glamour of Madison Avenue and the cool style of the Rat Pack (he downed martinis with Sinatra and Dino), Gifford was more than just the versatile runner who appeared in five NFL Championship Games. Before Broadway Joe wore pantyhose or Tom Brady vaulted up the *Forbes* "Power Couple" list, Frank Gifford was the prototype for the NFL player as modern-day celebrity.

Halfback, Bon Vivant, Spy

When you think of New York's sophisticated upper crust, beefed-up football players don't usually leap to mind. But during the 1930s, **John "Shipwreck" Kelly**, a Giants halfback who led the league in receptions one year, hobnobbed with the crème de la crème of society. Born to a wealthy Kentucky family who made their fortune in the dairy farm business, Kelly moved into an 18-room mansion on terribly exclusive Long Island Sound, mythologized by F. Scott Fitzgerald in *The Great Gatsby*. He golfed with the Duke of Windsor, attended a bullfight in Spain with Picasso, hunted in Africa with Ernest Hemingway, and killed a mountain lion in Idaho with Clark Gable. A night-clubbing ladies' man, he dated many of Manhattan's most glamorous beauties, from Broadway star Tallulah Bankhead to filthy-rich socialite Brenda Frazier, whom he ultimately married.

On the field he looked like any other young talent; but not too many 23-year-old guys can buy an NFL franchise, which he did, buying the Brooklyn Dodgers with his business partner, Chris Cagle, who also happened to be his backfield partner on the Giants. When Cagle wanted out, he sold his half to the wife of future New York Yankees part-owner Dan Topping, ice skating legend Sonja Henie.

Called the "Fastest Man in the South" after running the 100 in 9.8 seconds, he tried out for the 1936 Olympics. "I lost to Jesse Owens," Kelly told writer Richard Whittingham. After he retired, the FBI tapped him to use his jet-set status as a cover to gather information about the enemy. "I went to Europe, to Cuba, then to Mexico, to Peru, to Chile, and when we got in the war, I spent a lot of time in Argentina," said Kelly. "I could meet people at parties and things, the big shots there because of my connections. An ordinary person didn't have access to them. But I did. There were loads of rich Germans in Argentina and high-ranking officers, all in the same international society. I would try to find about ships, the submarines, things like that, that were off our coasts. And there were a lot of them."

In 1956 the team moved into the most famous sporting venue in the world, Yankee Stadium, home of former heroes like Babe Ruth and Joe DiMaggio, as well as current stars like Mickey Mantle and Yogi Berra. Gifford said he had Mickey Mantle's locker; defensive star Sam Huff claimed he did—this argument typified the nasty rift between the defense, run by some guy named Tom Landry, and the offense, run by some other guy named Vince Lombardi. In *What It Takes To Be #1*, the Emperor of Titletown's son, Vince Lombardi Jr. (yikes, no pressure there) wrote: "Jim Lee Howell, the Giants coach who rode herd on his assistants Vince Lombardi and Tom Landry, used to joke that the main job as head coach was to make sure the footballs were inflated to the right pressure. This was exaggeration to a purpose, of course—Howell was very much in charge of that team—but he was also acknowledging that he did not have the personalities of his two assistants. Nor did he *need* to."

The 1956 season was also the first to feature televised Giants home games, which meant that for the first time ever fans across the nation could see the big-market attraction. That year, Gifford took home the NFL's MVP award as the Giants claimed their first championship in 18 years. Before the game, defensive end Andy Robustelli, who owned a sporting goods shop in Connecticut, supplied his teammates with four dozen pairs of rubber-soled basketball sneakers, all different sizes, to wear on a Yankee Stadium field frozen by a minus-20 wind chill. The shoes gave the home team some traction on the rock-solid turf, an advantage that helped them to achieve a final score of 47–7. After the game, Bears coach Paddy Driscoll muttered, "I don't know where they got theirs, but those sneakers were better than ours. The soles were thicker than the soles on our shoes." Not to mention considerably less expensive than a pair of Nike Air Zoom Apocalypses.

Fifty years before Derek Jeter was prince of the city, it was Frank Gifford who held that title. "This was the postgame routine," Gifford said, recalling the fun atmosphere of those heady days, when most of the team lived in a hotel across from Yankee Stadium. "We'd make our way back to our various apartments at the hotel—or cramped rooms. Depending on the number of guests we'd invited to our cocktail party, and the ice bags on bruised and battered bodies—as well as the need for drinks—we'd spend a couple of hours getting ready to hit the town. After a few cocktails at the Concourse Plaza, we'd walk the three blocks down 161st Street and up the stairs to the elevated subway, wait on the wooden-planked platform with its view of the empty field beneath as the December wind whipped over our overcoats, and head for downtown. The subway was our 1958 limo, the D Train our stretch car." In 1971 president Richard Nixon showed up to a preseason game in Canton, Ohio, which Gifford was announcing.

Before the game, the president, talking to Roone Arledge, head of ABC Sports, said: "I think Frank will remember me, I used to go to his apartment in New York."

It was no wonder Gifford was a darling of Madison Avenue, endorsing everything from orange juice to contact lenses. After graduating from USC, he seriously considered quitting football to become a full-time Hollywood actor. For anyone who has seen his performances in *Darby's Rangers* or *Up Periscope*, it's obvious that Gifford made a wise move choosing to play professional football. One of the brands he endorsed was Lucky Strike cigarettes. "Back then," Gifford said, "our whole backfield smoked. Kyle [Rote] was a heavy smoker. And [Alex] Webster. Alex would smoke on the bench, during games. You'd see the smoke curling out from under the hood of his cape. [Don] Heinrich, too; we had a very nervous backfield."

Gifford hobnobbed with eventual presidents, Broadway stars, and famous writers, including Ernest Hemingway, whom he was introduced to at Madison Square Garden. But the football field is where he cemented his place as a pop-culture icon. Rarely was Gifford not the best all-around athlete on the field: he was an elusive runner, a sharp passer, a sure-handed receiver, and in 1956 even kicked a field goal. Early in his career, he also lined up on the defensive side, once getting named to the Pro Bowl as a defensive back. "When I first came to the Giants in 1952," Gifford recalled, "Tom Landry and I played defense together. He played safety and was actually a player/coach. I played the cornerback."

It was the 1958 title match between the Giants and the Colts that would finally launch the NFL into the forefront of the national consciousness. Often called the Greatest Game Ever Played, it featured 12 future Hall of Famers, including Johnny Unitas, Raymond Berry, and Gifford. While no one will forget Gifford's two fumbles in the second period of the game—least of whom, Gifford—it was, in part, the combined star power of Giff and Johnny U. that elevated the game to its mythic stature. Besides, he had plenty of big plays that season to help them reach the championship game, including his famous surprise lateral to quarterback Charlie Conerly, who scampered into the end zone in the classic 1958 Eastern Conference title game against archrival Cleveland Browns. Gifford recalled what his best friend, the crusty

37-year-old Conerly, said to him after the victory: "Next time I give you the fucking ball, you keep it."

Returning to football in 1962 after sustaining a cringe-inducing shot from "Concrete" Chuck Bednarik, which forced him to spend a week recovering in the hospital, he was given an entirely new role, that of flanker, where he earned his eighth Pro Bowl at his third position. He gained almost 10,000 all-purpose yards during his 12-year Hall of Fame career before moving up full-time to the broadcasting booth.

In 1971 he joined Howard Cosell and Don Meredith as part of the announcing crew on ABC's groundbreaking *Monday Night Football*. Quite a few announcers have been rotated in and out of the *MNF* lineup, with many, like O.J. Simpson and Dennis Miller, flaming out faster than Ryan Leaf's career. Gifford's 27-year tenure on the show is, thus, a notable achievement. ESPN's blogger extraordinaire Bill Simmons recalled when Al Michaels was paired with Gifford in 1986: "We all liked Giff. Great guy. Even when he married Kathie Lee, we didn't hold it against him. With that said, he wasn't breaking down plays or anything, and he lacked Cosell's charisma to carry a telecast. So 1986 became an entire season of Giff saying things like, 'Walter Payton…for so many years…such an inspiration…what a runner…the complete package,' and then Michaels would wait for a long enough pause so he could jump in and announce the next play." If only he knew him back when he was prince of the city. Then there was the tabloid headlines, the blonde tart, the hotel room, the media feeding frenzy, the humiliation, the remorse. If only they knew him back when he was prince of the city. If only they knew how much love and affection he once received from his teammates and from his fans. If only our princes could stay princes.

Dick "Night Train" Lane

When players from the '50s and '60s talk about the first big impact cornerback, the name that they mention is Dick "Night Train" Lane. During his 14 outstanding seasons with the Rams, Cardinals, and Lions, the 6'2", 210-pound defender defined the term "ballhawk": disrupting receivers off the line of scrimmage (what came to be known as bump-and-run coverage), breaking explosively on passes to intercept them, swooping out of nowhere to deliver a jarring tackle. Packaging deadly closing speed with raw aggression, Night Train intimidated offenses to the point where they feared throwing it his way. While one of the meanest hombres to ever put on an NFL jersey, he was known as a cheerful, good-natured soul off the battlefield. People can debate if this jazzy giant was the greatest player at his position ever—that he was the prototype for the modern NFL cornerback is an undeniable fact.

The Night Train's unlikely journey to Canton, Ohio, began in Austin, Texas, in 1928. One day, Ella Lane heard what she thought was a cat meowing in the dumpster. When she looked inside, she discovered a three-month-old baby wrapped in newspapers. Dick's parents, a prostitute and a pimp known as Texas Slim, had abandoned him in the trash. Although Ella had her hands full as a widow caring for two children, she took Dick into her home, not only giving him her last name, but something far more precious, the love of a mother.

Life was a struggle for Lane, who grew up on the gritty and dangerous streets of his poor neighborhood. Long before becoming known to millions as "Night Train," he went by the nickname "Cueball." Dick got the name because of an incident he had with a kid who tried to run out on a 10-cent pool bet he'd lost. As the boy dashed off, Dick picked up the cue ball and threw it at the cheat, striking him in the head and knocking him to the ground. "It was a curveball," Lane, speaking in his thick-as-molasses southern accent, told Rick Cantu of the *Statesman* in 2001. "I'd never seen a cue ball thrown like a curve."

At 19, Dick joined the Army, serving in both World War II and the Korean War. While stationed at the Fort Ord training base in California, he joined a recreational football league, never imagining he would play professionally. One evening in 1963, the esteemed writer George Plimpton, who had joined the Detroit Lions training camp in a quixotic attempt to make the team as a quarterback, found Night Train sitting in his room, listening to the famous jazz singer Dinah Washington. As it turned out, Lane was more than just a fan of the Queen of Blues; he was also her eighth husband. As they sat in the room, the dreamy, aching voice drifting in their ears, Night Train told Plimpton about how he earned a football scholarship to college, only to learn while packing his bags that the college dropped the football program. Lacking a whole lot of career options, he took a job at an aircraft factory in California, hoisting heavy sheets of oil-covered metal into bins.

One day in 1952, desperate to escape his grimy, backbreaking job, Lane stepped off the bus in front of the offices of the defending NFL champion Los Angeles Rams. He walked inside. "I said, 'If you please I want to see the head coach.' So they let me in," Lane told Plimpton. With only a scrapbook of football clippings from high school and one year of junior college, he tried to convince Rams coach Joe Stydahar, or "Jumbo Joe" as he was known, to give him a tryout. Afterward, the coach offered him a $4,500 contract. Good money in those days. But Night Train didn't jump at the offer. Instead, as he told it, he looked at the coach and said, "'Joe, before I sign and waste your time, do I get a fair shake at my position?' He says, 'Yes, if you can beat out Elroy "Crazy Legs" Hirsch and Tom Fears.' Well, that was something. Crazy Legs is going to be in the Hall of Fame, and Fears, he wasn't the slightest slouch, neither." For the record, both ended up in the Hall of Fame.

So the undrafted rookie, who had never played more than a year of junior college, showed up at camp that summer to try and earn a spot as a wide receiver. From the start, Lane was a total disaster. He ran the wrong routes. He dropped pass after pass. His coaches yelled at him until they were hoarse. Lane was sinking fast, but once again a virtual stranger came to his rescue—amazingly, it was Tom Fears, the same man

Dance Party

The NFL has seen its fair share of unforgettable hip-shaking moves—and a few we'd just as soon forget. There's been Ickey's Shuffle, Jamal Anderson's Dirty Bird, T.O.'s Pom-Pom Cheer, and Ocho Cinco's Riverdance. But the NFL's original dancing fool was **Billy "White Shoes" Johnson**, who got his nickname in high school because he wore white cleats instead of black ones. In response to a rival team's dare while playing for a tiny Division III college, White Shoes broke out his "Funky Chicken" dance for the first time. He brought his end zone celebration to the NFL three years later as a speedy 5'9" punt returner for the Houston Oilers. In the fourth game of the 1974 season against the Steelers, after the rookie scampered in for a touchdown on a 47-yard reverse, he shocked fans by flapping his wings and swinging his knees to the imaginary beat of Rufus Thomas' hit song. Recalled writer Bill Shefski, "The end zone became Apollo Theater."

whom he was competing against. Fears began tutoring him in his dorm room at night. For a white player, let alone one of the stars on the team, to help a black player (and there weren't too many to be found in locker rooms around the league at that time) was a rare act of nobility in a racially divided America. "Is that you again?" Fears would jokingly ask each night when Lane popped in; the other players would make cracks as they walked by. Fears loved to listen to jazz on his phonograph, and his favorite song was Buddy Morrow's "Night Train." "Every day I'd be going in his room, and he'd be playing it," said Lane. "He roomed with a guy named Ben Sheets, and whenever I'd walk into the room, Sheets would say, 'Here comes Night Train.' He started calling me that, and it stuck."

One night, the Rams had a big intrasquad game, with the local press in attendance. The receivers coach Red Hickey couldn't watch any more of Lane screwing up on offense. "Play defensive end!" he barked at him. "Me?" he recalled. "Weighing 185 soaking wet!" That was also a disaster, as Night Train recalled: "And so Hickey banish me out as a defensive halfback." Later in the same game, the fullback was running an end around when, with all eyes on the ball carrier, Lane crushed him. "Well, Jumbo Joe Stydahar, he come rushing out of nowhere and he says, 'That's the type of ballplayer I want.'" The next morning Lane awoke with a bruised, swollen face from the collision. "My roommate, Willie Davis, rustled the newspapers at me.... 'Say, Star, wake up, hey, Star, read 'bout the star,' I say to him, 'Oh, you read it, Willie Davis, I'm too sore to read it.'"

Lane would make an immediate impact his rookie season, intercepting an incredible 14 passes, a record that remains to this day. While the rules back then allowed for much more grabbing and holding of receivers, that's still an otherworldly number of picks, particularly when you consider it was set over a 12-game season. "I probably dropped 10 passes the year I caught 14," Lane recalled at the age of 72. "But I kept getting hit in the head by the ball."

Despite a performance ESPN named one of the 10 greatest seasons in football history, the Rams traded him two years later to the Chicago Cardinals. That would be the same Cardinals who in 1948 won the last championship in franchise history (nice try, Kurt Warner). Six years later, in 1954, the Cardinals played a game against the Washington Redskins,

Comeback of a Lifetime

It's one of the great medical mysteries in sports history—not that **Kevin Everett** is complaining. During the 2007 season opener against Denver, Bills tight end Kevin Everett sustained a fracture dislocation of the third and fourth vertebrae of his spine while making a tackle on Dominic Hixon. All eyes inside Buffalo Stadium were trained anxiously on Everett, who lay motionless on the field, paralyzed from the neck down.

As the ambulance rushed him to the hospital, the first question was if he would he survive. Inside the emergency vehicle, Dr. Andy Cappuccino, the Bills' spine specialist, chose to use an untested and unproven technique on Everett. Known as cold therapy, cool saline is injected into the bloodstream to lower the core temperature, or in Cappuccino's words, "use the body as an ice bag around the spinal cord." Everett's family was told that the odds of him ever regaining use of his arms and legs were slim.

Five months later, he was walking onto the stage of *The Oprah Winfrey Show*. His miraculous recovery spawned controversy within the medical community, some crediting Dr. Cappuccino's cooling methods, others arguing his treatment went too far, and in the end, contributed little to the shocking comeback.

"They call it human experience," Cappuccino told ABC News' James Hill and Jaime Hennessey. "I want them to talk to Kevin Everett. And if Kevin Everett is unhappy with the job I've done for him, then I'll feel bad." Talk to Everett, and there's no mystery over the fight he showed from day one. "The rest of this story is about Kevin Everett and the warrior that he is," said Cappuccino. "I have never seen one come this far, this fast."

who were led by running back Charlie "Choo Choo" Justice. With Night Train Lane shutting down their star player, the Cardinals won 38–16. The headline in the local Chicago paper the next day read: "Night Train Derails Choo Choo." The name gained instant notoriety with fans across the country to the delight of Lane, who had always worried that perhaps the name had demeaning racial undertones. "I thought it was pretty good to be mentioned in a big paper, so I decided to keep the nickname," he said.

To receivers of his era, Night Train Lane was a human wrecking ball, dislodging them from the ball in one crackling collision. Alex Hawkins recalled, "Night Train and Dick Butkus—they'd hurt you when they hit you." When the *Sporting News* listed him the 19th greatest football player of all time, the top-rated cornerback, they noted that, "He was one of the NFL's original ball-strippers, and his reputation for dishing out pain was almost legendary." He became especially known around the league for his arm-around-the-throat tackle, known as the Night Train Necktie. His head-ripping, face-mask yanking tactics were so vicious that the NFL banned them. "I told him once, 'Night Train, you need to tackle a little lower—for my health,'" Hall of Fame wide receiver Tommy McDonald told the *Chicago Tribune*. Lane remained unapologetic about his rough tactics, "I'd grab him by the eyebrows, if that's the way I can get him down," he said.

What makes Lane's story so amazing is the amount of tragedy he had to overcome in his life to become what Vince Lombardi called "the best cornerback I'd ever seen." The saddest event in his life was the unexpected death of his wife, Dinah Washington. Writer Jeff Davis recounted how fate intervened on the eve of the 1963 season finale against the rival Bears, causing Lane to miss the game. "Shortly before 5:00 AM...[he] had leaned over to kiss her good-bye before he left to catch the team's charter to Chicago. When she didn't stir, he called the fire department, whose emergency crew could not revive her. She was 39. Night Train Lane, a long time Chicago favorite from his days with the Cardinals, went into seclusion." It turned out the troubled singer had died from an overdose of sleeping pills, just months after Night Train, with George Plimpton in his dorm room, listened to her sing on the phonograph, a big smile on his face.

From the time he burst onto the professional scene in 1952, Lane's approach to the cornerback position was cutting-edge: *You throw the ball my way, I'm taking it from you and I'm running it back for a touchdown. Or I'll hit you so hard the ball will be knocked free. And if by some fluke you should manage to survive the impact, I'll strip the ball from you by any means necessary. And I mean by any means necessary.* What allowed him to play with this aggressive big-play mentality was his unique combination of closing speed, cat-like reflexes, and risk-taking bravado. "I tried a few in the flat against Lane," Giants Pro Bowl quarterback Y.A. Tittle told *SI* in 1958. "This guy has arms two feet longer than most—or they look that way. He makes a small mistake and recovers so fast he's got an interception on you."

Over his 14-year Hall of Fame career, the first eight played with the Rams and the Cardinals, the last six played with the Lions, Lane intercepted 68 passes, fourth all-time behind Paul Krause (81), Emlen Tunnell (79), and Rod Woodson (71). By adding this dimension as a threat to intercept the ball and even score on a return—he gained 1,207 yards and five touchdowns—he made the cornerback a person not only to watch, but seriously fear. And with his ferocious hit-man style of tackling—coming in and sticking running backs as well as rocking receivers off their feet—it's clear to see Lane's influence on how the position evolved. According to Hall of Famer Lem Barney, "Guys like Herb Adderley, Mel Blount, Mel Renfro, Willie Brown, and myself [all of whom played in the 1960s and 1970s] called him the 'Godfather of the Cornerbacks.'" His more recent ballhawk heirs, including Ronnie Lott, Rod Woodson, Ed Reed, Bob Sanders, and Troy Polamalu, owe Lane a debt of gratitude for showing them that while the best defense is a good offense, it's also true sometimes that the best offense is a good defense.

After Lane retired from the game, he worked a brief stint as comedian Redd Foxx's road manager. Lane dreamed of coaching in the NFL, perhaps to win the championship that eluded him as a player, but his overtures were rebuffed, not surprising given the social climate. He went on to run a police youth football league in Detroit, working with underprivileged kids from the same kind of hardscrabble neighborhood he'd grown up in. In 2002, nearly 40 years after Dinah Washington's premature death, Night Train suffered a heart attack and joined his wife in the hereafter. Terry Yates, the care worker who was there when he passed, recalled that he was listening to jazz the night he died. "A musician's got to have a style—maybe it's a way of holding the horn or playing a phrase," Lane once remarked. "That's what I was always after. I wanted to create my own style of playing."

Gale Sayers

Football is a violent game. It has the power to reduce strong, almost invincible-looking men into crippled spectators long before that first gray hair is ever plucked. But one man's interrupted greatness overshadows all the others whose flame burned out prematurely. "His days at the top of his game were numbered, but there was a magic about him that

In 1977 Gale Sayers became the youngest man ever inducted into the Pro Football Hall of Fame. Photo courtesy of Getty Images.

still sets him apart from the other great running backs in pro football." This was Pulitzer Prize–winning sportswriter Red Smith writing about the most explosive offensive threat in NFL history, Gale Sayers. As a Pro Bowl halfback and kick returner for the Chicago Bears in the mid- to late '60s, he used his lightning-fast bursts of speed to leave would-be tacklers in the dust. He would only play five full seasons, but the dazzling show he put on every Sunday guaranteed that, at age 34, he would become the youngest player ever to be inducted into the Hall of Fame.

Some rookies fly under the radar, not Gale Sayers. When the "Kansas Comet" arrived in Chicago in 1965, he caught the eye of his coaches and teammates, not just for his natural agility, but his all-out approach to everything he did. As soon as he stepped onto the practice field, they saw he was cut from a different cloth. Normally, when a team ran a play in practice, it ended as soon as the running back broke through the first wave of defenders. If each play wasn't cut short, if it was allowed to finish, players would be sucking wind after 20 minutes. "I remember one Bears practice in particular from my rookie year," said Sayers in 2007's *Sayers: My Life and Times*. "The ball was on the 50-yard line and I took the hand-off and ran all the way to the goal line. Coach Halas stopped practice when he saw me do that. He said: 'If Gale Sayers can run all the way to the goal line, we all can run to the goal line.' So for the next 20 minutes or so, everyone had to run hard in practice, all the way to the goal line. Some of the players were pissed off at me, but I'm sorry, that's me. That's the way I had to get in shape, because I knew I was going to be keyed on during the games. That's the way I did it in college at Kansas. That was the only way I knew. Coach Halas appreciated it, but a lot of the veterans didn't."

What the veterans did appreciate was the way Sayers would soon be leaving defenders flailing all over the field. In only his second game, a tilt against the Rams, he turned a simple screen pass into an 80-yard gain, as Hall of Fame Rosey Grier recalled, "I hit him so hard. I thought my shoulder must have busted him in two. I heard a roar from the crowd and figured he fumbled. Then there he was, 15 yards away and going for the score." In another game, on December 12, 1965, Sayers scored a record-setting six touchdowns against the 49ers at wet, muddy Wrigley Field. After he set the mark on an 85-yard punt return, the announcer shouted, "Here he is. Galloping Gale carrying the mail. This is his sixth touchdown of the game. He adds his name to the record book besides Ernie Nevers and Dub Jones. The Bears crush San Francisco 61 to 20, and revenge is soooo swcct!" Almost exactly 23 years to the date, Gale Sayers told Chicago radio personality Mike Murphy the secret of what George Halas called the greatest performance he had ever seen on a football field: "When I ran on a muddy field, I kind of ran flat-footed. It enabled me to cut a little better." After scoring 22 touchdowns, a single-season record for a rookie that has stood for 44 years, Sayers capped off his spectacular inaugural campaign by taking home the Rookie of the Year award. "He is the man who splits himself in half and leaves the half without the football with the tackler," Bill Cosby once proclaimed.

The story of Gale Sayers and Brian Piccolo is as moving as any in sports. The two Chicago Bears running backs—one black, one white—competed for the starting job in the late 1960s, but the rivalry brought the two men from divergent backgrounds closer. In 1967 the teammates caused a stir by rooming together. Never before in the league's history had men of different races been roommates. "One time a writer came into our room to interview us about being interracial roommates. 'What do you fellas talk about?' the writer asked. 'Mostly race relations,' I answered. Then Pick chimed in, 'Nothing but the normal racist stuff.' Then the writer asked, 'If you had your choice, who would you want as your roommate?' I looked him in the eye and said, 'If you're asking me what white, Italian fullback from Wake Forest, I'd say Pick.'"

The teammates developed such a tight bond that after the naturally gifted Sayers suffered a career-threatening knee injury in 1968, it was the undrafted, overachieving Piccolo who helped work him back into shape. Before Piccolo started training his teammate, he told him, "I'm gonna whip you, Sayers, but you got to be at your best, or it won't mean a thing." Many doubted Sayers would ever return to form, but Sayers honored his friend, coming back and winning the NFL rushing title the next year. Meanwhile, Piccolo's story took a tragic turn; he was diagnosed with lung cancer. When Sayers was invited to the Professional Football Writer's Banquet in New York to accept the George S. Halas Award, given to the most courageous player of the year, he asked Piccolo and his wife to accompany him and his wife. Piccolo's wife attended alone; Pick was too sick to leave the hospital that night. When Sayers stepped forward to receive the award, the audience exploded with applause. With tears streaming down his cheeks, he said, "You flatter me by giving me this award. But I accept it for Brian Piccolo. Brian is the man who should receive the award. I love Brian, and I'd like you to love him, too. Tonight when you hit your knees, please ask God to love him, too."

Piccolo would lose his struggle at just 26. The moving story of friendship was turned into *Brian's Song*, the most watched TV movie in history when it came out in 1971. It also caused a record number of grown men to cry. The made-for-TV flick created such a sensation that it was actually released in movie theaters; some inspired souls even named their kid after Sayers. Here's what you might not know about *Brian's Song*: Gale

Sayers initially had someone else in mind to play him other than the future Lando Calrissian. "I was flattered that the directors would choose Billy Dee Williams," he said, "but I must admit that I had some reservations at first because he was very slightly built and he did not look all that athletic to me. I would have preferred to play my role myself, but the fact the movie was filmed during training camp made it impossible for me to pull that off." But he wasn't the only NFL player who almost had the role. "Most people don't know that [49ers receiver] Bernie Casey, who played my former teammate, J.C. Caroline, actually wanted to play my part in the movie," Sayers said. "But the directors decided he was too tall at 6'4" to resemble me, so they stuck with their decision to have Billy Dee play my part." Those who weren't around back then might know Casey better for his role as U.N. Jefferson, the head of the fraternal organization, Lambda Lambda Lambda, in the movie *The Revenge of the Nerds*.

Sayers' career ended tragically short after a pair of serious knee injuries forced him to retire before the 1972 season. While he only played a total of 68 career games, never once making it to the postseason, his impact on the game is immeasurable. His teammate Mike Ditka provided this analysis in 2008: "Let me tell you something, if he would have played 100 [games]—*100*—nobody would ever have beat his records. I was there in 1965 when he came into the league, and I saw his greatness. He'll never talk about it. Sixty-eight games. He made me look good as a blocker, and I couldn't block anybody."

His career might have been cut short, but Sayers' influence has reached far beyond football, as Oscar-winning actor Denzel Washington wrote in his autobiography: "He was like Michael Jordan or Tiger Woods or Muhammad Ali to my friends and me. He was the standard, and where I grew up, when I grew up, there weren't a whole lot of African Americans out there for me to look up to. I suppose if I'd had an interest in drama as a kid, I might have looked to someone like Sidney Poitier, but athletics was what got me going. All my friends wanted to be Jim Brown, but I wanted to be Gale Sayers. He was my idol on the football field, which is why I was so pumped when Gale Sayers came to see me, when I was doing *Julius Caesar* on Broadway. He came backstage after the show and he gave me a couple T-shirts, which he signed, and I was like a nine-year-old kid all over again."

Jerry Rice

Jerry Rice has caught more touchdowns than any other player in NFL history. But growing up in Oktibbeha County, Mississippi, he spent his time catching bricks, not footballs. "My brothers and I would bring the bricks to a worksite and pass them from one to another until handing them to my dad for placing," Rice remembered. "Often, when my father had moved to the second floor of a structure, I would balance myself on the scaffolding two stories up and catch the bricks my brothers would throw to me from the ground." However, the idea that his great hands as a receiver came from his brick-laying days is a myth, as Rice told John Brenkus of FSN's "Sports Science:" "Brick-laying requires hard hands and an aggressive approach; catching a football requires soft hands to cradle." All that didn't matter to his dad, who depended on his son to help him run the business: "He handled bricks better than any worker I ever had. I was sorry to see him go."

Rice might still be working on some construction crew had he not played hooky from East Oktibbeha County High School. One day in 1978 Rice, a sophomore, and his friend decided to sneak off campus during the middle of the day. While making their getaway, they were spotted by their principal, Ezell Wickes. Rice and his accomplice high-tailed it down the hallway. "Mr. Wickes never caught up to us, but seeing that it was a small school, he easily recognized my face and clothing," recalled Rice. "Suffice to say, I knew what I had coming when I returned. He had a big old leather strap in his office, and he gave me five hard hits with it. It was painful. But Mr. Wickes witnessed how fast I had sprinted away from him, and realized my speed could be put to good use to keep me out of trouble."

After meeting with Rice, the head coach told him to come out and try to make the varsity team. Rice made the team, despite, in his words, "running the wrong route, dropping easy balls, and even putting on my pads the wrong way." Rice knew that he could not match the skills of his more experienced opponents, but like the U.S. Olympic Hockey Team that two years later would upset the veteran Soviet squad in Lake Placid, he was determined to be the superiorly conditioned athlete. That meant running 10 miles home after a grueling practice. It meant running up and down hills in the Mississippi heat long after his teammates had packed up their gear and left. It even meant running across the dusty pasture, chasing down untamed horses with his brothers. "I ran with no real purpose or goal. I just enjoyed running," said Rice. "If the movie [*Forrest Gump*] had come out when I was a kid, they would have nicknamed me Forrest.... Run, Forrest, run!"

When he first arrived in San Francisco, the workout freak met his match in running back Roger Craig. "When I did decide to join him for a run up a two-and-a-half-mile hill, I could barely keep up," Rice said. He was in no rush to join Craig for another run up the Hill. "I had to look for him for two to three weeks to try to convince him to try again," recalled Craig. Eventually the Hill became part of his famous grueling off-season regiment—one that helped him to become one of the most durable players in history. "I dare anyone to come out and hang with me," he told *Sky Magazine* in 1996. "Full-out, no holding back."

It's hard to believe, but Jerry Rice dropped around 15 passes his rookie season. "That year, I didn't know what was happening," he remembered. "I even resorted to wearing gloves, something I never did." The problem was nerves, which the small-town kid had suffered from since the very first trip to San Francisco, which also happened to be his first airplane flight ever. "The reality was that I was more scared to board the airplane to San Francisco than I was to play with the Super Bowl champions."

No one can question Rice's amazing stamina or desire, but plenty questioned his speed after he ran a 40-yard dash in the months before the draft. "That's not an incredible time," explained Timothy James Gay who has a PhD in physics. "It's fairly typical for a wide receiver. What separates Rice from the pack of his peers is his ability to get open, and that has to do with quickness, only one aspect of that 40-yard time." In other words it was his burst—his force of acceleration—that made him

The NFL School of Business

Through a program launched in 2005, the NFL has sent more than 350 active and retired players to four of the country's top business schools: Harvard Business School, Stanford's Graduate School of Business, Penn's Wharton School, and Northwestern's Kellogg School of Management. Another league program, started in 2002, reimburses players up to $15,000 per year in college or university tuition.

so dangerous. "Jerry's got game speed," San Francisco safety Ronnie Lott told *SI's* Ralph Wiley in 1987. "He's 4.2 in games. Hard to explain, but nobody outruns Jerry in a game." Or as former teammate Terrell Owens put it: he could "get off the line faster than any player in the history of the game. He shot out of his stance quicker than anyone and was impossible to cover one and one." So how quick did Rice get off the line of scrimmage? The average human reaction time is .19 seconds. Rice's was clocked by the *Sports Science* team at .13 seconds—an incredible 31.6 percent better. "The average bolt of lightning is .15 seconds," said the show's narrator. "So in fact Jerry Rice can get off the line faster than a bolt of lightning."

Rice didn't like being called slow, but he was called worse by his 49ers teammates, like "Fifi." How did he earn this nickname? It was his poodle cut—buzzed on the sides, high on top. "I didn't like the nickname," said Rice. "I especially hated it when they called me Fifi during meetings." Perhaps he preferred his other nickname: Bert from *Sesame Street.*

Rice managed to snag runner-up on the *Dancing with the Stars* competition, but Craig recalled that the 6'1", 200-pound receiver wasn't taking home any trophies with the touchdown dance he performed early in his career: "His one routine was 'The Cabbage Patch,' which was a popular dance move in the mid-1980s. We didn't embrace Jerry's dance too well, but he was in the end zone so often, we got to the point where we didn't mind him doing it."

Barry Sanders

The only thing more elusive than Barry Sanders, who spent his entire career whirling, spinning, and cutting on a dime for the Detroit Lions, is Barry Sanders the man. Here's a guy who walked away from the game in 1998 with plenty left in the tank and Walter Payton's all-time rushing record all but in his grasp. He's perhaps the most dynamic and electrifying running back to ever wear an NFL uniform, yet one of the most unassuming and humble superstars you will ever meet. Which is not to say that Barry Sanders is dull or apathetic—in fact, he has a sharp sense of humor and a deep passion for his faith. Beneath his quiet exterior, Sanders possessed a fierce competitive streak, something that was not

Getcha Painkillers Ready

The amount of drama on *Gossip Girl* looks modest compared to the career of **Terrell Owens**. A few vintage T.O. episodes: in a 2002 *Monday Night Football* game in Seattle, Owens celebrated a touchdown by pulling a hidden Sharpie from his sock, signing the football, and then bestowing it upon his financial advisor, who was watching from an end zone luxury suite. The owner of the suite: Shawn Springs, the cornerback he had just burned on the play.

Then on November 3, 2005, he set a new standard for how much drama you could fit into one day. He kicked off that Thursday with a locker-room fight with Eagles teammate Hugh Douglas that one eyewitness described as "a WWE Smackdown." After fists flew, Owens dared anyone else on the team to step up and fight him, a challenge that many in the room believed was directed at quarterback Donovan McNabb. Later in the day, he dissed his main foil in an ESPN interview, comparing him unfavorably to Brett Favre. Two days later, the Eagles suspended him for four games, effectively ending his rocky tenure in Philadelphia.

But perhaps his craziest incident came in Dallas, where he once overdosed on a mixture of painkillers and supplements. Authorities claimed it was an attempted suicide after his publicist Kim Etheredge, who made the panicky 9-1-1 call, told them her client was "depressed." In the ensuing press conference, Etheredge was suddenly in the odd position of convincing the public that the suicide rumors were bogus; that Owens simply had an allergic reaction to the drug combo. Her inarguable defense: "Terrell has 25 million reasons to be alive," referring to his high-priced salary. The Cowboys canceled the "soap opera" in March 2009 by cutting the world-class wide receiver. He's now starring in a sitcom set in Ralph Wilson Stadium.

overlooked by the many defenders left grasping at air as he vanished from sight.

In high school, Sanders had an unusual way of getting stronger. He and his older brother, Byron, hopped up the countless rows of stadium steps at Wichita State. When he got to Oklahoma, he measured a 40-inch vertical jump from a stand still. "I know I got my leaping ability from my first love—basketball—but mostly from hopping up those stadium stairs at Wichita State," he said.

Barry Sanders' claim that his hardcourt game was good enough for the NBA has been a running joke to those who know him well, including his former Lions teammate Herman Moore. "He's pretty jealous of

Barry Sanders was one of the most electrifying players in NFL history during his 10 years in Detroit.

my game, I'm not surprised," Sanders told writer Paula Pasche in 1998. "All he can do is dunk, and he can't even do that halfway good." Dunking the basketball was a talent the 5'8" Sanders had even back in high school. "If I was a lot taller and a lot better, I probably could have had a career in basketball," said Sanders. "I've played with David Robinson; you may have heard of him. Also, A.C. Green, Bobby Jones.

I didn't go up to him and say, 'Dave, were you impressed with my game?'—I'm sure he was, though. Any day, I could get a call from Pat Riley or somebody like that."

Because of his height and size, few colleges aggressively recruited him. According to Sanders, "Oklahoma State took a gamble." Early on at OSU, Sanders backed up another future NFL standout—Thurman Thomas—but strength coach Jerry Schmidt marveled at his performance in the weight room. "Barry can squat nearly triple his body weight—556 pounds!" Still, Schmidt was very happy that Sanders was getting his degree in four years, as he said at the time. "I told Barry that was really great," Schmidt said, "because he'd need a degree to get a job right away. Obviously, pro football was out because he was too small. Barry immediately laughed. It was a confident laugh, but Barry is also aware of the odds. He answered my challenge, 'I've been told all my life that I'm too small to play at any level. I don't listen too hard. What's important is that I give my best effort at all times. If the pros think I'm too small, I'll use my degree to get a job. I want to play pro football. It'd be nice.'"

After winning the Heisman Trophy his junior year, the Lions took a chance on Sanders, making him the third overall pick in the 1989 draft. It did not take long for him to prove people wrong, or to let them know what he thought about personal accolades. On the final game of his rookie season in 1989, Barry needed a total of 11 yards to surpass Christian "the Nigerian Nightmare" Okoye of the Kansas City Chiefs for the NFL rushing title. With a few minutes left in the game, Coach Wayne Fontes asked Barry if he wanted to come off the bench to become the rushing leader. Barry Sanders declined. "Let's just win it and go home," he said. Like it or not, his 1,470 yards, 5.3 average, and 14 touchdowns earned him Rookie of the Year honors.

Barry Sanders credits his father, William, for always believing he could play. At the same time, his father always reminded him that he wasn't in the same ballpark as Jim Brown, as he once told Dan Patrick: "No matter what topic you're talking about. You can walk in and say, 'Daddy, how are you doing today?' And he'll say, 'You'll never be as good as Jim Brown.'"

In 1997 Barry Sanders juked and jived his way to 2,053 yards, earning him the NFL's co-MVP honor with Brett Favre. He was only the third player to ever break the 2,000-yard barrier, after O.J. Simpson in 1973 and Eric Dickerson in 1984. (Since that time, Terrell Davis and Jamal Lewis have joined the elite club.) But his own selflessness almost kept him from the record. On the final game of the season, Sanders needed 131 yards to break the 2,000-yard barrier. Sanders accomplished the feat late in the fourth quarter. Coach Bobby Ross wanted to bring in a sub, knowing that a tackle for a loss could jeopardize the record. Sanders told Ross that he was staying in the game. On the next play, he tore off a 53-yard run. Sanders had completed one of the all-time best seasons in NFL history, which included a record 14-consecutive 100-yard games.

After the game, Sanders was anything but a show-off, as Detroit sports columnist Terry Foster recalled: "He even refused to accept the game ball after his 2,000-yard season unless his linemen were with him." This was no surprise to Foster. While the 10-time Pro Bowler thrived on game day, he shunned media attention throughout his career. He almost didn't show up to the Heisman Award ceremony, and after he won he declined an invitation to the White House. Later, he quietly donated a 10th of his $2.1 million signing bonus to Paradise Baptist Church in Wichita, Kansas, and made it a point to gift 10 percent of his salary to charity throughout his career. "Sanders was as spectacular as any athlete," remarked Foster. "Yet when he scored, he simply flipped the ball to the official and ran back to play another day. Who doesn't want a guy like that on your team?"

For all his accomplishments in 1997, the one that was most improbable was changing his father's mind about who was better between him and Jim Brown. After his remarkable season, the old man started telling his friends that his son was now at the top off his list—not that Sanders was any the wiser. "He never told me then," Sanders said. "He told other people. He told me later."

In spite of a record-setting 10 straight 1,000-yard rushing seasons, and being named NFL Player of the Year in 1991 and 1997, his Lions team never went far in the postseason. The late Reggie White once told a story about how his rival Packers team held Barry Sanders for minus one yard on 13 carries in a wild-card game on December 11, 1994. "What we did," White said, "we pushed their linemen into the backfield and didn't give Barry a chance to get going. Once he gets a chance to get going, he's going to kill you." It makes sense then why Sanders told Dan Patrick that if he could play defense and deliver a hit on one player, it would be the Minister of Defense: "I'd like to have him play running back. I'd like to be able to deliver some blows on him. He's gotten his share on me." To which Patrick asked, "Do you think you could hurt Reggie White if he was running the football?" Barry Sanders retorted, "Probably not."

Lions fan Barry Schumer recalled one time being on the putting green when he looking up, and to his surprise, seeing Barry Sanders. It turned out Sanders was an avid golfer. "I told him I met Lawrence Taylor at a golf tournament and couldn't believe how big he was," said Schumer. "I said to Barry, 'How could you survive a hit from a guy that big?' He answered, 'Now you know why I ran so fast!'" Sanders remarked to Dan Patrick what L.T. said to him after his first start in the pros: "He came up to me and said, 'If they get you a fullback and a tight end, you'll be unstoppable.'" To which Patrick responded, "You're still waiting for that fullback and tight end, aren't you? So I guess you're stoppable." Sanders deadpanned, "That's pretty funny." Patrick smiled back, "I can say that kind of thing. You can't."

Prime Time

One of the most dominant cornerbacks in NFL history, **Deion Sanders** never worried much about getting burned downfield. The more pressing concern in his life was to produce enough wild moments to keep Prime Time in primetime. Not a problem, as a glimpse back at his playing days shows: in 1989 Sanders wowed NFL scouts by allegedly running a 4.27 in the 40-yard dash, a mark beaten in 1999 when current record-holder Rondel Menendez of Eastern Kentucky ran a 4.24, according to NFLDraftScout.com.

One Sunday afternoon in 1991 Sanders played for the Atlanta Falcons, then hopped on a helicopter that flew him to his Atlanta Braves team, who had an NL playoff game that night. Already infamous for his high-stepping dance across the goal line, he showed up in his pal MC Hammer's 1994 music video "Too Legit to Quit." Sanders, not about to set his clock to Hammer Time, released his own full-length rap album called—what else—*Prime Time*. He once again made headlines, renouncing his brash, selfish ways and becoming a born-again Christian, saying, "Prime time is God's time now."

While Barry Sanders was a human highlight reel on the field, he was rather subdued on the sideline. How subdued? Sanders admitted to Dan Patrick that he had fallen asleep a couple of times on the bench, only to be woken up by Herman Moore: "We didn't have a very exciting defense." Come on, you can come up with a better excuse than that. "Oh, man. I was dreaming about the next series."

Barry Sanders was one sleeping giant you didn't want to awake. Just ask Michael Strahan. "I once made the mistake of talking trash to the great Barry Sanders," Strahan recalled. The towering lineman had just leveled the compact running back. Standing over him, Strahan yelled, "That's right, Barry! All day, all day! What are you going to do?" Strahan recalled what happened next: "He sat there silently like he always did, because the man never said a word out there, then stood up and said to me, 'I'll be back.' That was his form of talking smack, and you know what? It scared the shit out of me. I actually wanted to apologize right there on the spot. 'Hey, man. I'm sorry. I didn't mean that, sir. Really, sir, can I get a mulligan on the trash talking? Please, sir, Mr., um, Sanders, sir?'"

With more gravity-defying moves than Beyoncé, nobody made tacklers miss like Sanders. "There are times when I'm watching Barry Sanders, and I think the bottom is just going to fall out of that guy," Hall of Fame Cowboys running back Tony Dorsett said. "The way he springs forward and stops, backs up and takes off—I sit back and say to myself, 'How long are those knees going to take that kind of beating on that turf?' But it doesn't seem to bother him. He just keeps going. The man can contort his body more than anybody I've ever seen." Apparently, superior body control and vision runs in the family. A video of high school freshman Barry Sanders Jr. slashing and cutting his way through an impossibly tight squeeze for a 64-yard touchdown run in the Oklahoma state high school playoffs became a YouTube sensation in 2008.

Sanders is often compared to a pair of Chicago Bears running backs from different eras. The first one is Gale Sayers, the only other player to be elected to the Hall of Fame before age 40. "I never played against Gale Sayers, but I saw him on film," said former Raiders defender Howie Long. "Sanders does the same things he used to do. He puts a move on a defender, and you see the guy's knees buckle." Before the 1997 season,

Gale Sayers said, "People talk about whether Barry can gain 2,000 yards in a season. Well, if he had Dallas' line, we'd be asking how many years he'd be gaining 2,000 yards."

Sanders shocked his fans when he abruptly announced his retirement in 1999. Everyone thought he would at least play until he gained the 1,457 yards to break Walter Payton's historic mark. "I never valued [the record] so much that I thought it was worth my dignity or Walter's dignity to pursue it amid so much media and marketing attention," he said. With that said, many believe that Sanders is the best NFL running back in history, regardless of the record books, as Allen Barra pointed out, "Sanders averaged more than half a yard per carry more than Payton, and nearly 12 more yards per game." But, as writer Joseph Weisbach pointed out, the records didn't matter half as much as competing his hardest to win: "After what would be his last game, against the Ravens in 1998…he sat weeping at his locker after a 19–10 loss closed a 5–11 season."

Then Jerry Rice Said...

The NFL has been a showcase for many great athletes over the past 100 years. But few have been as good as Jerry Rice. Over his 20-year career with the San Francisco 49ers, Oakland Raiders, and Seattle Seahawks, he redefined the wide receiver position, breaking some of the biggest records in the game, including the vaunted mark for most career touchdowns. We asked the man known to many as the greatest receiver of all time to tell us the difference between Montana and Young, what he's learned from Tiger Woods, and his insane runs up the Hill.

You were arguably the greatest playmaker in NFL history. What do you think all the great playmakers have in common? Do you need a certain makeup?

I think we have to be selfish, in a way. But you also have to put team first. The majority of playmakers are the guys who want the ball when the game is on the line. They're willing to stick their neck out, and know that if they don't make the play, there's going to be negativity. You're going to have to be able to deal with that.

Rushing to Excellence

A 1,000-yard rushing season in the NFL. It might have lost a little bit of its luster with players stretching up toward the 2,000 plateau since 1978, when the season was expanded from 14 to 16 games, but it remains a benchmark of excellence. In 1934 rookie running back **Beattie Feathers** of the Chicago Bears became the first player in NFL history to accomplish the feat with 1,004 rushing yards on just 119 carries. With backfield partner Bronko Nagurski, he averaged 8.44 yards per attempt, still all-time best among running backs, although 72 years later, in 2006, quarterback Michael Vick edged him with an 8.45 YPA, compiling 1,039 yards on 123 attempts. It's no wonder that Vick's return to the NFL in 2009 after his two-year prison sentence has people speculating that he will be converted to a running back.

Is there another athlete besides yourself who excelled at that?

Michael Jordan was the same way toward the end of the basketball game. During all those championships, he wanted the ball in his hands. And if he didn't make the play, they criticized him—but he was willing to take that chance.

I had the opportunity to go and watch his last championship run. I remember watching him do his thing—controlling the game, making unbelievable shots. The day afterward we went and played golf. We just talked about the love of the game, the great time he had on the basketball court and that I had on the football field.

Do you see any other similarities between the way you and he competed in your sports?

You know, we both played the game with passion. Sure, there's a lot of money involved, but Michael—he enjoyed going out there and entertaining. And I feel like he represented the NBA the way it should be represented. It was the same thing for me in the NFL—I wanted to be the best player I could possibly be. And, yes, I had to sacrifice. The first 10 years, I didn't take a vacation because I was so focused in on doing my job. And I wanted people to enjoy coming to the ballgame, to walk away feeling, *Wow. I just watched something really special.*

You and Joe Montana certainly gave fans their money's worth. Where would you rank Montana among the all-time great QBs?

(Laughs) Well, I may be a little biased. I believe he was the best quarterback who ever played in the NFL. I think Joe was just magical. The way he could break a defense down. The way he knew where his primary, secondary, and third receiver were on the field. Everyone talks about him not having a very strong arm, but he compensated by releasing the ball early. And you have to have confidence to release that ball early. Whenever I ran my route and turned my head around, the ball was right there. So he made life easy for me.

There's the famous story of how, during his pressure-packed last-minute Super Bowl drive, he said, "Hey, look. There's John Candy in the stands." Do you remember that?

I didn't hear that. I was so zoned out and so focused. But you know what, every football game Joe was that cool. The defensive opponent could be hitting him all day, and he never showed any emotion. He would never lose it. He was always cool.

But I heard off the field Montana was quite the prankster.

He once decided to sneak into the locker room and put Tiger Balm in some of the players' jocks. We're all out at practice, and all of a sudden you notice that some of the players clearly have some burning sensation going on.

I heard that when the 49ers were training up at Sierra College in Sacramento the players would ride bikes back and forth from the practice facility to the dorm a good distance away, and that Joe Montana would steal players' bikes and put them in trees.

Oh, he was a professional thief. The rookies would come outside after practice to ride their bikes back to the dorm, which was a good walk, and it was, like, 112, 115 degrees everyday. They'd be looking around everywhere for their bikes. They learned real fast. You better lock your bike up with Joe around.

Many would be surprised to learn that Montana didn't throw you your first completion but rather Matt Cavanaugh. What do you remember about that play?

Cavanaugh and I had pretty good chemistry, but to be honest, I don't remember that play. The first touchdown I ever caught was thrown by Joe Montana against the Atlanta Falcons—that was the one I remembered. It was incredible because I felt like, okay, I belong now.

You felt like you didn't belong before that?

As a rookie, you want to come in and impress that quarterback. We're talking about Joe Montana. You want the quarterback to have confidence in you to make those plays. Because you're going to get opportunities. But I had some problems during preseason with too many drops. After going through so much adversity, I remember Joe throwing me that ball in Atlanta. When I made that catch for my first touchdown, I felt, *I have arrived. I'm ready to go.*

Joe Montana said that you added five to six years to his career. What did he mean?

The 49ers were more of a finesse team. The thing about playing quarterback in that system, if you could get the ball out of your hand quickly, you weren't going to take as many hits. But they didn't have anyone who could run that slant route, so there were times that Joe was taking a lot of punishment. But I could run those five-yard slants, those quick outs, those three-step routes which allowed him to get the ball out of his hands. And we receivers were known to turn those short routes into big plays. I think that really helped his career out.

Do you still have that first touchdown ball?

Of course I do. I try not to collect everything but have a lot of memorabilia in my office. The stuff that's real special to me. The ball when I passed Steve Largent and then Jim Brown. The Super Bowl MVP. You hold on to stuff like that so you can pass it down to your kids.

Do you have anything from *Dancing with the Stars*?

I have a couple of the outfits I competed in.

You never know. Your son Jerry Jr., who is a high school football star, may want to borrow one of them for a date.

Jerry Rice retired in 2004 with more receptions, yards, and touchdowns than any other receiver in NFL history.

(Laughs) Nah. He's too hip for that.

What made those Super Bowl champion 49ers teams so successful?

We played with a lot of heart and determination. We wanted to go out there and destroy. We wanted to win. We wanted to win championships. And we did that.

How did hard-hitting 49ers defensive back Ronnie Lott symbolize that spirit you're talking about?

Ronnie was just nasty. His leadership on the field, his determination, the way he set the tempo. It was seek and destroy. He was going to hit somebody and, believe me, it was going to be heard around the world. I remember Super Bowl XXIII. He hit [Bengals running back] Ickey Woods, and Ickey was pretty much done for the rest of the game.

Are there any other incidents that stand out?

I remember he had the tip of his finger amputated so he could return faster to the field. That was unbelievable. He had a fracture in his finger, and that was going to put him down maybe for the year. So he opted to have his finger cut off so he could play. You don't get anymore incredible than that. It sent chills down my body.

What's your favorite memory of those glory days with the 49ers?

I think just to be able to be part of something that went down in history. When they go back and show the Super Bowl XXIII, XXIV, XXIX. You look at yourself and you say, *Wow, I was part of that. That's amazing. I had a chance to live a dream.*

Steve Young was your second Hall of Fame quarterback. Was it hard to adapt to his style after so many years catching passes from Montana?

Steve was a lefty. I had never caught a ball from a guy who threw left-handed. There's a whole different spin on the ball—a whole different

---

Plaxidents Will Happen

Things that don't end well: carrying a loaded gun. In the waistband of your sweatpants. In a nightclub. (To up the ante, add alcohol to the mix.) While this might sound obvious, it wasn't to former New York Giants star receiver **Plaxico Burress**. On November 29, 2008, Burress accidentally shot himself in a Manhattan nightclub with his Glock semiautomatic. Burress was arrested—not for accidentally lodging a slug in his thigh, but for allegedly possessing a loaded gun without a proper license.

Not surprisingly, this past off-season, the Giants released the talented but troubled wideout, who hauled in the game-winning touchdown pass for the G-Men in the 2008 Super Bowl. As for the question: does Plax have a future in the NFL? It remains unclear. But he probably shouldn't count on too many of his ex-teammates to provide positive referrals. To be sure, former Big Blue backup QB Tim Hasselbeck, who said on ESPN's *NFL Live,* "If you want to wait for a guy to show up to meetings. If you want to have to beg a guy to run full-speed in practice, if you want a guy that would disappear in games because he doesn't get the ball early—then look, Plaxico Burress is your guy."

rotation. Also, when he came into the league, he was known more as a running quarterback. So I'm running my route and I'm used to having a little extra time to beat my defender, and I hear the crowd start cheering, and Steve is up my back! He's running right next to me.

As a receiver, how important was it for you to build the same kind of chemistry with Young that you had with Montana?

You've got to be able to build a relationship if you're going to have success on the football field. This guy has to know your body language. Know when you're ready to come out of a route. How do you build that chemistry? It's out there on the football field. It's staying after practice to run a few more routes, or to go over different situations, whatever it takes to make sure you're on the same page. Once Steve Young and I were able to do that, we were able to do great things. I actually caught more passes from him than I did with Joe Montana. I've had the best of both worlds. I've had two Hall of Famers. We were all on the same page. We were willing to do whatever we had to do so that we could go out on the field and give our best performance.

Did you and the team have any unusual ways of preparing for game day?

We were pretty open to try things that could give our team an extra advantage. We had chiropractors because, as a football player, you could get seriously out of whack. We even had a trainer who would warm us up before games by having us do karate chops. As a receiver, you have to use your hands. They have to be active when you come off the line of scrimmage. So warming up with this guy helped with that. If there had been yoga, you probably would have had some players doing yoga. It was all about winning football games and championships.

What is the key to going out and performing at the level that you did?

Repetition is everything. You do something for a long time, and it's going to become instinctual. You're just going to react. It's like golf. You repeat the swing over and over again. Lots of amateur guys want to be good golfers, but they don't put the time in to be professionals.

Has the greatest wide receiver in NFL history ever met the greatest golfer of all time, Tiger Woods?

I met Tiger Woods when he was at Stanford, before he turned pro. I had just picked the game of golf up. He asked me to go out with him, and I told him, "Look, man I would love to play with you, but I just started playing and I don't want to torture you like that." I've got my handicap down, so I'm looking forward to teeing it up with him down the road. But look at Tiger. From 7:00 to 9:00 he's lifting weight. From 9:00 to 11:00 he's pounding golf balls. From 11:00 to around noon he's playing nine holes. Has lunch. Then he comes back and putts for an hour or two. After that he play's nine more holes. Then he works on his short game. That's incredible and that's why he's so good. Repetition. You have to work at your craft to be the best.

You were known as a workout beast when you played. Is that why?

I wanted to be in the best shape I could possibly be in, knowing it's going to give me longevity. That I would be able to recuperate faster. I felt I had to wear my opponent down. I wanted the fourth quarter to feel just like the first quarter to me. I knew that would give me an advantage, so I was willing to sacrifice in the off-season. Everybody thought I was crazy. But all that training allowed me to do some great things.

Talk to me about the legendary Hill that you'd run up to get into such incredible shape.

It's in Redwood City, right off Route 280. The Hill is about a mile and a half to two miles up. There's a few areas that are flat, but the last 800 meters are a steep incline.

I was a rookie the first time I ran the Hill with a bunch of the guys. I thought I was in great shape. This hill isn't going to do anything to me. That thing ate me up. You know, I stayed away for a couple of days. But then I said, I have to go back and conquer this. Because I never wanted to be a quitter. I went back, and the Hill has been a part of my life ever since.

I did it three times a week. And every time I got off that 280 exit, I knew what I had to do. I had to go into the zone. I had to say, I will not let this hill conquer me today. I'm going to conquer this hill.

How did training on the Hill help you on the field as a football player?

The Hill is going to make you or break you. You have guys who try it once and never come back. You have other guys who want to be the best, so they come back to conquer it. But it's always that last 800 meters where you see who can gut it out. You had guys throwing up and just completely quit. It can sink your confidence. I never wanted that to happen, even if I was running alone. You have these thoughts in your head: *I can quit. There's nobody around. Why don't you just walk those last 100 meters?* But you do that, and then you start quitting in other phases of your life. The true warrior is going to be able to endure and somehow get up it.

I knew if I could conquer the Hill I'd able to put my body through torture in the fourth quarter. I'd never give in to being tired. I'd still be able to focus and make plays. A lot of guys can't do that. They get tired in the fourth quarter and give up.

Did you ever take any teammates up the Hill with you?

I remember Ricky Watters came out once. We had just started going up the Hill, and he thought, *Oh, this is a piece of cake.* He was keeping up with me so he thought that he was fine. Then we got to that last 800 meters, and all of a sudden my trainer told me to go. And Ricky is thinking, *Oh my God. What do you mean 'go'? I'm dying.* He couldn't believe I had so much left that I could finish the way I did. It took away his ego. But a lot of guys weren't able to finish. It takes a true warrior to be able to endure and somehow get up it. But you can't imagine the feeling when you get to the top and you look down. *Wow, I made it.*

Now that you've retired, do you still run up the Hill?

Yeah. Sometimes I'll take people up with me. Sometimes I'll go myself. But I still want to finish. It's always a challenge to me.

chapter 5

The Punishers: Defense

Throughout NFL history, hard-hitters have sparked great passion. But the elite punishers have inspired lore. Stories of ice-breathing gladiators bearing down on foes with their blazing speed and brute strength, filling the air with the sound of bodies colliding and men grunting in pain. The crowd erupts into a frenzied chant of "De-fense! De-fense! De-fense!" As the torch is passed down from one generation of punisher to the next, the savagery and splendor with which they rip out the heart of the offense once again arouses a raucous cheer from the crowd. In the frigid cold or the baking heat, their attack on the enemy is relentless, as if fueled by the anger of Zeus. It's only after the offense had been demolished and demoralized, only after victory has been secured and the locker room celebration has expired, that the punisher lays his battered body down, wincing as pain reverberates through his cracked ribs. It's a pain that will stay with him many years after his reign of wrath is over. But while he might not live on forever, the stories about his 60 minutes of mayhem will.

Sam Huff

The middle linebacker has long been thought of as the captain of the defensive unit. He roams the field with reckless abandon, pouncing on those who dare trespass his territory like a hungry, vicious mountain cat. Each era has produced those guys who fans of collisions love and ball-carriers fear, but the original dominator was New York Giants linebacker Sam Huff. Anchoring Tom Landry's revolutionary 4-3 defense, he defined the linebacker position for future generations, ferocious hunters like Mike Singletary, Lawrence Taylor, Junior Seau, Brian Urlacher, and Ray Lewis. What's more, thanks to the growing power of television to bring every one of his savage hits into the living room, Huff became the first defensive player to achieve a level of stardom equal to the guys on the other side of the ball.

At the height of his popularity, Huff would be immortalized in the CBS documentary *The Violent World of Sam Huff*. A year earlier, in 1959, he graced the cover of *Time* magazine, which hailed football a "Man's Game." For them to put an NFL player on the cover of their magazine in 1959 was almost unthinkable, and for it to be a defender was beyond belief. The article's author, Jim Atwater, told a story illustrating Huff's brute force: "After San Francisco's Hugh McElhenny took a screen pass and set out behind two 250-pound blockers, Huff knocked all three out of bounds with one grizzly-like shove."

Sam Huff didn't just tackle ballcarriers, he left them with battle scars. For that reason, people often overlook the way he used his intelligence to patrol the field from sideline to sideline. In that famous *Time* magazine feature, Huff revealed how he relied on his astute power of observation to reveal his rival's intentions. "A back like Paul Hornung of the Packers—if he's coming straight ahead on a hand-off, he'll have more weight on his hand and be more in a sprinter's position, so he can really blow into the line. So if I see that, I cheat over a little bit so that I can be right in front of him when he gets the ball. Ollie Matson, when he's going to run straight ahead, he has his feet cocked, and when he's going to the outside, he has both feet even and no weight on his hands," he said.

If it wasn't for Vince Lombardi, Sam Huff might not have played a single season of pro football, let alone become a national hero. In 1956 Huff, a third-round draft choice out of West Virginia, was attending his first Giants training camp in Vermont. Hampered by a bad knee and a bullying head coach, Huff longed desperately to return to his small-town life back in the small mining town of Edna Gas, West Virginia, where he could be reunited with high school sweetheart Mary Fletcher, who he married at 17. "One morning as Sam Huff and another uneasy rookie, kicker Don Chandler, were resting on the beds in their dorm room listening to a country-western station," recalled David Maraniss in *When Pride Still Mattered*, "Huff said that if a homesick song called 'Detroit

City' came on, they should just pack up and leave training camp. 'Damn if it didn't come on the radio right after I said that,' Huff recalled. 'And I said, "Let's go." Chandler was quiet and lonesome and ready to go with me." The two rookies went downstairs to turn in their playbooks and found Lombardi taking a catnap in his first-floor room. "We walk in and say, 'Coach,' and he jumps out of bed and starts screaming, 'What the hell do you want!'" Huff said later. "Jesus. We held out our playbooks. 'We're quitting.' He goes off on us. He says, 'We've got two weeks invested in you guys. You may not make the ballclub, but you're sure as hell not quitting on me!'" When Lombardi found out that the two men had left for the airport in a teammate's station wagon, he rushed after them. They were sitting in the airport lounge an hour later when Lombardi drove up like a truant officer, announced that he would not allow them to leave and escorted them back to training camp. Even though Lombardi would go on to Green Bay, where he would become Huff's opponent, Huff would forever be thankful to his old coach for saving his career.

Few men can stay they shut down Jim Brown. But on a December afternoon in 1958, on a hard, frozen Yankee Stadium field, Sam Huff struck a major blow in the public war the two men had violently waged against each other for years. "I like to play angry, I was an angry player, at linebacker you had to be. He would psych you, he would get up and pat you on the back and say, 'That was a nice tackle, Big Sam.' I would say, 'Leave me alone, don't talk to me.'"

The stakes couldn't have been higher that clear, crisp day in the Bronx before 61,174 cheering fans: a spot in the championship game against Johnny Unitas and the Baltimore Colts. The Giants were facing an unstoppable force in Brown, and history was not on their side: no NFL team had ever beaten another three times in one season. And while the Giants had won the first two meetings, Brown had rushed for 113 yards and 148 yards, respectively, in those games, and it was only the miracle of Pat Summerall's last-second 49-yard kick in a blizzard that forced a third and deciding game.

On that day, the Giants defense had done, in the words of Huff, what "no other defense had ever done," namely stuff the league's rushing king. And stuff they did: Brown was held to a career-low eight yards, and the Giants triumphed 10–0, giving Cleveland only its second shutout since joining the NFL in 1950. (If not for a 20-yard gain in the third quarter, Brown's total would have been in the negative column.) While the defense was ferocious as a whole, it was Huff's relentless effort against Brown that made the difference. "I don't know that anyone ever hit me harder than Sam Huff," Brown said. "Especially in that playoff game, he had my number on a couple of plays." One of those plays occurred at the pitcher's mound of the converted baseball park. "Dick Modzelewski hit him low," Huff recalled, "and Jim Brown was trying to shake him off, and I came in and drilled him and hit him and dinged him. He said he wasn't knocked out, I said, 'You might as well have been.'"

"That game made Sam Huff," said Browns tackle Jimmy Ray Smith. Not bad for a guy who, a week later, would play in the game that made the NFL.

Ray Nitschke

Ray Nitschke was to football what the Hulk was to comic books: a bald, mild-mannered businessman in horn-rimmed glasses who, when made angry, would transform into a crazed, yelling monster. Once unleashed, this middle linebacker's blindside licks, in the words of ex-Bears running back Ronnie Bull, felt "like a two-ton truck." While he showed no mercy on the football field, off it he was as gentle as a daisy. "He was a classic example of Dr. Jekyll and Mr. Hyde," said Green Bay teammate Bart Starr. "Off the field, you hardly would have identified Ray as being a middle linebacker. He was meek and mild and easygoing, very respectful of others. When they met him, people couldn't believe that here was the wildman linebacker they had been watching all these years."

Nitschke's visage—the mud-covered jersey, the blood-stained pads, the black eye paint smeared under his eyes—came to symbolize the rough-and-tumble, lunchpail image of the NFL in the '60s. "Probably one of the most ugliest and frightening sights was Ray Nitschke lined up in front of you," former Dallas center Dave Manders recounted. "No teeth, sweating hard, breathing hard, talking a lot of rough BS. And he didn't have any teeth to keep the saliva in his mouth. Just a real weird picture." Those missing upper front teeth, which added so much to his fearsome, foaming-at-the-mouth mystique, were knocked out during a loss his Illinois Fighting Illini suffered to the Ohio State Buckeyes on October 13, 1956. "Hustling down the field in his face-maskless helmet," recounted Edward Gruver in his biography *Nitschke*. "Nitschke caught a Buckeye helmet in the mouth. The collision caused two of his teeth to break off and go flying; the other two were dangling by their roots. A teammate shoved a wad of cotton in Nitschke's mouth to slow the flow of blood, and Ray played on—played the whole 60 minutes while spitting blood all over the field. At game's end, Nitschke headed back to the deserted field and began scouring the scarred field for his missing teeth. 'How am I going to look with no teeth,' he thought. His thoughts were interrupted when someone approached and asked Nitschke what he wanted the missing teeth for. 'Because they're mine,' he said growling through blood-caked gums. Nitschke never did find them, and eventually he replaced the missing teeth with a false plate. In future years, his toothless face terrorized NFL opponents, and on occasion, he would startle unsuspecting Ohio State alums by suddenly yanking his bridgework out upon introduction. 'That's what your school did to me,' he would say, then issue a gummy grin."

Teeth were guaranteed to rattle when Mike Ditka, one of the great offensive punishers, and Ray Nitschke, one of the great defensive punishers, faced off on opposites sides of NFL's fiercest rivalry—the Packers and Bears. "I had been thinking about No. 89, that I owed this guy somethin'," Nitschke recalled. "He caught the ball right in front of me, and I hit him pretty good. I thought I killed him. It was some experience. You got this I'm-going-to-get-this-guy attitude, and then all of a sudden, you say, 'Man, I saw the whites of this guy's eyes and I thought I killed him.' I knocked him out, and they had to carry him off the field." After reassembling the pieces of his brain, Ditka returned in the second quarter. "I continued to play," said Ditka. "But I had no recollection of anything until I saw the films."

While Nitschke became a kind, respected family man later in life, he was not always such a nice guy. The death of his father at the age of three and his mother 10 years later brewed a rage in his heart that would result in Nitschke spending his youth lashing out at the world. Nasty scrapes were a common occurrence for Nitschke growing up—once, he got banned from the Boy Scouts as a result of getting into a fistfight at his first meeting. Early in his Packers career, if there was a barroom brawl, Nitschke was usually at the center of it. The linebacker's drunk and rowdy behavior would prove to be a bad fit with his new coach, Vince Lombardi. Guys who played for Lombardi were expected to show civic pride, less face the coach's unholy wrath. One of the cardinal sins a player could commit was to be caught sitting up at the bar—a professional athlete should drink at a table like a gentleman.

A day prior to the 1960 season finale against the Rams, a game that would decide the division crown, Lombardi walked into an L.A. restaurant with a couple of his coaches. As Lombardi walked to a booth in the back, he passed a couple of players sitting at tables. Further along, he peered into a lounge, where he spotted Ray Nitschke bellied up to the bar, throwing back a tall glass of beer. Lombardi sat down in the back room with his coaches and started cracking open peanuts with a fuming scowl. A waiter appeared at the table with a round of drinks. Lombardi asked him, "Who ordered these drinks? We didn't order any drinks. Who bought these?"

"That gentleman at the bar," said the waiter, gesturing over to Nitschke.

"And Jesus," recalled coach Norb Hecker, "Vince's hand dove into the bowl of peanuts, I'll never forget it, and he started to crunch the shells, and I could see the blood starting to flow, and he got redder and redder."

Donald Phillips, author of *Run to Win*, recounts what happened next:

> "Let's get out of here!" shouted Lombardi as he bolted away from the table toward the front entrance.
>
> With his eyes blinking furiously and his neck turning red—"and getting redder and redder," as Hecker noted—Vince kept staring straight ahead as he walked by the bar. "You're all done!" he thundered at Nitschke. "You're through! Get out of town!"
>
> Lombardi exited the establishment and walked quickly down the street with Bengston at his heels and Hecker a distant third. Bengston, who was the coach of the defense, began

pleading with Lombardi to let Nitschke stay. "We have no extra linebackers," said Phil. "And we've got to win Sunday. We've got to beat the Rams. We need him."

"He's all through!" screamed Lombardi. "Get him out of town! He's done! I can't stand that!"

The men finally spotted another restaurant and ducked inside. And all through their meal, Bengston kept begging Vince to change his mind. "What are we going to do?"

"I don't care!" snapped a still-angry Lombardi. "Get rid of him. I don't want him around here."

After some time had passed, though, and he had finished his meal, Vince began to cool down, but he would not back down. When Bengston asked one more time to let Nitschke stay, Vince at last said: "Tell you what. We'll leave it up to the players to decide." The next morning, the Packers voted 39–0 to keep Ray Nitschke on the team.

Not the most surprising outcome. I don't think you wanted Nitschke to find out you were the one guy who voted against him.

Earlier that year in training camp, Nitschke faced his toughest opponent: a 25-foot steel tower that stood between the practice fields. As Gruver recounted, "Nitschke hustled back to the base of the steel tower where he had put his equipment and began putting his pads on to protect them from getting wet. He put his helmet on too, and the instant he pulled the hard plastic shell down over his head, a strong gust of wind caught the tower and tipped it over. A thousand pounds of steel scaffolding collapsed on top of Nitschke, sending him sprawling to the ground. A steel bolt drove through his yellow-gold helmet, four inches above his temple. NFL helmets in 1960 were constructed of plastic with a web of suspension that provided and inch of space between the top of the helmet and the head. The bolt that punched through Nitschke's helmet stopped just short of his skull. 'I put my helmet on to protect this,' Nitschke said later, pointing to his bald head. 'If I hadn't, I might have spent the rest of the season in the cemetery.' After Lombardi saw that Nitschke was the player being pulled out of the rubble, he said, 'Oh, him. He's all right. Everybody back to practice.'"

Gossip Guy

As the leader of the fearsome "New York Sack Exchange" defense of the 1980s, Jets defensive end **Mark Gastineau** was one of the most outlandish players in NFL history. His crazy sack dance almost single-handedly led the league to enact a no-taunt rule in 1984. Meanwhile, his love affair with Brigitte Nielsen, aka ex–Mrs. Stallone, became such hot gossip fodder in 1988 that the pair landed on the cover of *People* magazine. The skyscraping lovebirds gazed into each other's eyes next to the title, "The Hot & the Heavy: Is the world ready for this clash of the titans?" Explaining the instant sparks that flew between the still-married sack king and herself, the future *Celebrity Rehab* star said, "When we met in the gym, it just said 'bang' for both of us." Still, at least one person accurately predicted their break-up. "That football player—I wish him luck," remarked noted psychic/Rocky momma Jackie Stallone. "I just hope he's not silly enough to put his income in a joint account with hers." Brigitte wasn't the only one of No. 99's ex-wives to hit reality TV paydirt: in 2004 Lisa Gastineau and aspiring model/socialite daughter Brittny debuted in *Gastineau Girls*.

Nitschke was more than just a stalwart member of the Lombardi-era Green Bay Packers, winner of five championships. He was the roaring motor of a defense that refused to lose. Among his greatest efforts: his MVP performance in the 1962 NFL Championship Game in which he deflected a pass for a Packers interception and set up the only Packers' touchdown with one of his two fumble recoveries (his career total of 20 fumble recoveries is second all-time behind Willie Davis' 21).

Perhaps Nitschke's gutsiest performance came in the classic 1967 Ice Bowl against the Dallas Cowboys, played in minus-13 temperature and minus-46 below wind chill. The sideline heaters on Lambeau's "frozen tundra" had broken down, the referee whistles had frozen solid, and six of Nitschke's toes had turned purple as he stood on the sideline, watching Bart Starr command an epic drive with time running out for a 21–17 win. "The 1967 Ice Bowl victory over Dallas was the greatest satisfaction I've ever received," said Nitschke. As the exhausted victors gathered together in the locker room after the game, in the words of David Maraniss, "glacial tears burned the cheeks of Ray Nitschke."

When trainers examined his numb feet, they discovered frostbite. "Ray Nitschke's ears, toes, and fingers were white, and the skin was falling off those guys by the yard," recalled Packers publicist Chuck Lane. But Lombardi would never admit that one of his tough players had gotten frostbite. "The Dallas Cowboys got frostbite," said Lombardi at a press conference for the upcoming Super Bowl in Miami. "Ray Nitschke just had a blister. Only a blister. That's all it was. A blister." At that exact second, Nitschke, who had also dropped eight pounds due to the flu, had an instant recovery, walking perfectly as he passed in front of a glaring Lombardi. Three days later, Nitschke was back in the Packers' locker room, getting his injured toes bandaged. As the trainer advised him to skip practice because of the 5-degree temperature outside, Lombardi came over and said to him, "Just go out and work up a good sweat." Just as Nitschke was about to ask the coach how the hell you do that in 5-degree weather, he just exhaled, "Aw, forget it, man."

Blocking out the pain of his feet and head cold, Nitschke came up with nine tackles to lead the Packers to a 31–14 triumph over the Oakland Raiders in Super Bowl II in Miami. Green Bay's public relations director at the time, Lee Remmel, recalled how Nitschke established a mood of invincibility in that game with his stinging blows on Raiders running back Hewritt Dixon on the first two plays: "Hewritt was quivering like a tuning fork, Ray hit him with such ferocity. That seemed to neutralize him for the rest of the day."

Nitschke's mythic stature is perhaps best illustrated in this final tale. George Halas' son-in-law, Ed McCaskey, went to visit Brian Piccolo as he lay in the hospital on his deathbed. The sight of the dying Piccolo caused McCaskey to burst into tears. Piccolo, gasping for every breath, said, "Don't worry, Big Ed, I'm not afraid of anything—only Nitschke."

Gino Marchetti

Great rampages in history: King Kong in New York City. Genghis Khan in Persia. Jason Voorhees at Crystal Lake. But this list isn't complete without Gino "the Giant" in Memorial Stadium. Every great team has an enforcer, and for the epic Baltimore Colts teams of the 1950s and '60s, that man was Gino Marchetti. To any quarterback who ever looked up and saw the 6'4", 244-pound defensive end tearing through the blanket of protection and charging full tilt at him, it's three seconds of helpless terror that would stay etched in his mind forever.

A rambunctious kid from a big Italian family, Gino Marchetti got into big trouble his senior year in high school. Facing expulsion, school officials gave him an option: join the service and automatically get his diploma. It wasn't until he was on the front line, taking heavy fire from Hitler's massive and relentless German offensive in Belgium while enduring hypothermia temperatures and blinding snow, that Marchetti realized just what kind of deep shit he had stepped into. "I'll never forget, artillery shells going pssssssst, whistling. Me and this guy McKinney hitting the mud. Me looking at him, he looking at me. You know, 'Get us out of here,'" he remembered. It turned out the 18-year-old had landed himself smack dab in the middle of the Battle of the Bulge—the biggest and bloodiest single fight in American history. In the end, Allied forces were able to drive back the Nazis, but not before more than 65,000 U.S. soldiers were either killed, injured, or captured. Marchetti returned in the summer of '46—one of the lucky ones.

In his first two years of professional football, Marchetti was signed to three different teams. Two days after Marchetti was drafted in 1952 by the New York Yankees football franchise, the team became the Dallas Texans, who folded a year later to become the Baltimore Colts. Marchetti remembered one payday, during the Texans' latter days in Dallas. Coach Jimmy Phelan called the players in before the day's workout began. "He said, 'I'm not telling you these checks aren't any good,'" Marchetti recalled. "'But what I'm going to do is cancel practice right now.'"

"You want to see 33 guys hustle? No showers. No anything. Straight to the bank," said Marchetti.

If George Halas was a genius for switching Mike Ditka from defense to offense, Baltimore coach Weeb Ewbank was equally smart for moving Gino Marchetti in the exact opposite direction. "Gino, play defensive end," was all Weeb Ewbank said to Marchetti, an offensive tackle on the undefeated 1951 University of San Francisco team.

Ever since Marchetti slipped on a football jersey, his father Ernest Marchetti was petrified that he would be badly injured. He refused to watch him play—not even on the television. If Ernest had watched, he would have seen that Marchetti was the one who was usually dishing out the pain.

As much as Marchetti loved hitting quarterbacks is how much he hated getting fancied up for special occasions. "We had a hard time getting a neck tie on him," recalled his Colts coach, Weeb Ewbank. "He didn't want to come to banquets because he didn't like to dress up." The fact was, Marchetti wasn't full of himself despite his almost mythic stature throughout the Midwest. "Fame?" Marchetti once said. "It's a game. One time a guy says, 'Jesus Christ, you're talking to me.' He was an electrician. I said, 'I don't know anything about electricity. You don't know how to play football. So we're even.'"

The NFL title game has witnessed its fair share of epic tackles—the Cowboys' Bob Lilly sacking Miami quarterback Bob Griese for a record 29-yard loss in Super Bowl VI, Jack Tatum knocking the helmet off Vikings running back Sammy White in Super Bowl XI, and Mike Jones wrapping up Kevin Dyson on the 1-yard line as time expired in Super Bowl XXXIV. But none of them paid the price that Gino Marchetti did in what might be the biggest tackle of them all—stopping Frank Gifford inches short of a first down in the fourth quarter of the 1958 championship, the key defensive play in the Greatest Game Ever Played. After Marchetti knocked Gifford to the ground, everybody dived onto the pile. Crashing down on Marchetti was 290-pound Colts tackle Eugene "Big Daddy" Lipscomb. Marchetti let out a horrific scream. "Everyone started to yell, 'Get off him! Get off him!'" recalled Gifford. "It was chaos." When the pile broke up, Marchetti was lying on the ground with his ankle broken in two places. Marchetti later told Gifford, "Some Giant said to me, 'You can get up now, Gino—the play is over.' I could have cared less. I was in so much pain, if I wasn't a grown man, I'd have cried."

Once Marchetti was carried off the field, he had three guys, including moving van operator and professional wrestling referee Vince DePaula, shuttle him up and down the field on his stretcher so he could continue to follow the action. "Marchetti sat up on a stretcher, still in uniform, legs bundled under blankets on the sideline, looking like some vet shot down on the battlefield," recounted Michael MacCambridge in *America's Game*. "The makeshift tourniquet around Marchetti's just broken ankle was the only concession he'd make to the injury. As the Colts' medical staff tried to transport him to the locker room, he barked that he was going to stay right there until he game was over."

While Marchetti stubbornly refused to leave his teammates, after Steve Myhra's field goal forced the first overtime game in NFL history, medical staff forced him inside. Back in the empty locker room, he laid on a gurney in excruciating pain, trying to gather clues on how his teammates were doing from the faint crowd noise in the distance. Marchetti recalled, "Finally, Pellington opened the door, and lets out a shout: 'We're the world champs!' Then my leg felt better."

To this day, Gifford and other Giants players swear that all the yelling and confusion caused the referee to mistakenly spot the ball short of the first down marker. "It turned out that the best play Big Daddy made that day, on a day when he made the biggest plays of his career, was on a late hit of his own man," Gifford said. "I know he didn't plan it that way, but breaking his teammate's leg won his team a championship."

What did Colts defender Artie Donovan make of Gifford's claim that Marchetti hadn't stopped him, that he had got the first down: "Hell, he didn't even get back to the line of scrimmage."

Marchetti went on to make a total of 11 straight Pro Bowls. An All-Pro at 37 years old, he even convinced his dad to come watch him play the last home game of his career. "That was really the greatest day I ever had because he was there," recalled Marchetti. "When the game was almost over, I sat by him on the bench. He said, 'Gino, maybe you did know how to play this a little bit.' The last game he says this."

As for a life after football, Marchetti gave it little thought. That was until Carroll Rosenbloom, the Colts owner, called him into his private suite and told him to get into business. Marchetti responded that he didn't know the first thing about business (remember, you had to hold him down to get a suit and tie on his gigantic frame), but Rosenbloom still staked him $100,000 so he could join fullback Alan Ameche and two others in running a fast-food franchise. Gino the Giant suddenly doubled as the name for their restaurant's trademark burger. In 1982 Marchetti sold his 43 KFC outlets and 113 Rustler Steaks to Marriott for $48.6 million, after which, Marriott renamed them Roy Rogers. (When all was said and done, Marchetti had gone from one battle of the bulge to another, albeit on opposing sides of the fight.)

When Johnny Unitas was asked what made Marchetti one of the best defensive ends of all time, he responded, "Well, he had the ability.

And again, he was a guy who would probably play for nothing. He just loved it. He loved the competition and he loved the camaraderie of the people we played with…. To this day, when he sees me, he calls me 'kid.'"

Dick Butkus

For NFL teams of the late 1960s and early '70s, knocking off the Chicago Bears wasn't the real challenge. (A 13-year playoff drought will attest to this.) The challenge was getting off the field before Dick Butkus separated your head from the rest of your body. Over nine seasons, Butkus unofficially racked up 1,020 tackles and 489 assists (for a ridiculous 12.7 average per game), but the numbers only tell part of the story. They don't measure the vicious impact of each of those takedowns. "If I had a choice, I'd sooner go one-on-one with a grizzly bear," said running back MacArthur Lane of the Green Bay Packers. "I pray that I can get up every time Butkus hits me." Saints wideout Dan Abramowicz said of him, "Dick wasn't satisfied with just an ordinary tackle. He had to hit you. Pick you up. Drive you and grind you into the ground." And as Rams enforcer Deacon Jones explained, "Dick was an animal. I call him a maniac. A stone cold maniac. And every time he hit you, he tried to put you in the cemetery, not the hospital." Or as the late John Facenda of NFL Films once said in his deep and powerful baritone, "He was Moby Dick in a goldfish bowl. His nine-year career stands apart as the single-most sustained work of devastation ever committed on a football field by anyone, anywhere, anytime."

Although Butkus wreaked havoc as a two-time All-American at Illinois, opponents couldn't fathom the magnitude of the tornado-like fury and destruction he would unleash in Chicago. Preparing to play the rookie middle linebacker for the first time in 1965, Lombardi confidently told his troops during a film session, "I want you to take a look at this Butkus. He's a big, sloppy-looking kid. Forrest, you'll be able to kick his ass. He plays way too deep. Jerry and Fuzzy, when we go up the middle, you should have a field day blocking." In the game, Butkus was a one-man wrecking crew, holding the potent running attack of Paul Hornung and Jim Taylor to 85 yards on 24 carries while racking up a slew of unassisted tackles. Recalled Hornung, "As we were reviewing the films after the game, Lombardi finally shut off the projector and said,

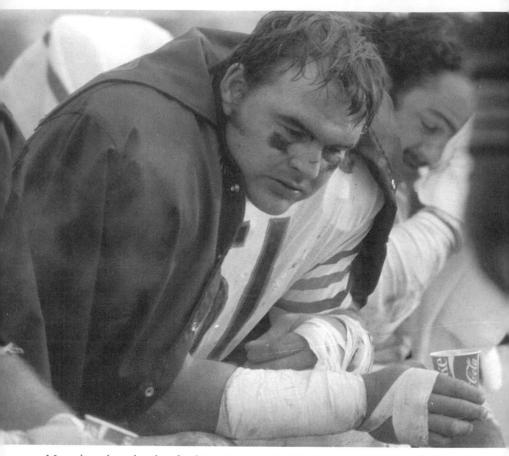

More than three decades after his retirement, Dick Butkus remains the standard by which all middle linebackers are measured.

'I'm sorry, boys, but this Butkus may be something special.' It was the first time I ever heard him apologize." Such was the respect Lombardi had for Butkus, he later altered his trademark Packers Sweep when facing him. "Dick was so good and so fast," recalled Packers quarterback Don Horn. "We had to change our blocking schemes because he was that good." Reflecting Butkus' misfortunes in the Windy City, for all of the platitudes the Packers bestowed upon him, his Bears would go 2–8 against them in his first five years.

Many young quarterbacks crumbled at the very sight of a foaming, growling Butkus fixing his wild-eyed gaze at them from behind the line.

"He reminded me of the way a mongoose stares at his prey and hypno-
tizes it," Terry Bradshaw recalled. "That was Butkus and me. I think he
hypnotized me. I had the football, and I just said, 'Here. You take it, sir.'
And he did. He intercepted two of my passes. It wasn't tough, I threw
them right to him. I felt terrible about it, but there was something
thrilling about having two passes intercepted."

Butkus used personal slights—big and small, real and imagined—to
fuel his weekly binge of violence. "I remember Butkus had written a
book, and sportswriters asked me what I thought of him writing a
book," recalled Lions linebacker Mike Lucci. "I said, 'He wrote a book?
Hell, I didn't even know he could even read.' Just a comment like
that.... We go out there, and instead of shaking hands with me, he steps
back. So we don't shake hands." The animosity Butkus had for Lucci
extended to the entire Detroit team. In one game between the rivals, the
referee flipped the coin to decide possession. Steve Sabol of NFL Films
recalled the conversation picked up by the microphone: "The refs says,
'Captain [Dick] LeBeau, what are you going to do?' And he said, 'We'll
receive.' And then the ref said, 'Captain Butkus, what are you going to
do?' And he points at LeBeau and says, 'We're going to kick your ass all
over the field.'"

Once Butkus chased Lions rookie running back Altie Taylor, who
had made the mistake of calling him overrated in a postgame interview
earlier that season, off the field and almost right out of Wrigley Field.
"That guy's crazy!" declared Taylor, when he returned to the huddle,
after leaping over the ballpark wall to escape a charging Butkus. Said
Butkus, "I wouldn't ever set out to hurt anybody deliberately unless it
was, you know, important, like a league game or something."

Knee injuries would cut short his great career. In 1973 Butkus went
to see the nation's top orthopedic surgeons. "The surgeon reportedly
called it the 'worst-looking knee I've ever seen,'" said media and sports
professor Michael Real, "and told Butkus, 'I don't know how a man in
your shape can play football or why you would even want to.'" But what
the doctor didn't know is that this was the same guy who once became
despondent when a scrimmage was canceled due to nasty weather.
According to Real, "The doctor advised Butkus that, if he must play, he
should spend all of his time from the end of one game until 10 minutes

before kickoff of the next either in bed or on crutches. The surgeon thought there was no danger of ruining the knee further by playing, because there wasn't that much left to ruin. Butkus, needless to say, finished the season and was reportedly considering the installation of a metal knee after his playing days were over." Butkus ended up suing the Bears over their handling of his injuries.

Once he retired from the game, the former Maestro of Mayhem became one of the most popular pop-culture figures of the late '70s, bringing his macho image to police shows and B-movies but also playing shrewdly against-type in sitcoms and commercials. He also appeared in *Gus*, a movie about a field-goal kicking mule from Yugoslavia, and *Mother, Jugs & Speed*, starring Bill Cosby, Harvey Keitel, and Raquel Welch, as a bumbling ambulance crew. (Oh, the '70s...) His most famous spot had him teaming up with another ex-player, Bubba Smith, to argue if Miller Lite was great because it was "Less Filling!" or because it "Tastes Great!" For a brief moment in time, the odd couple emerged as a hot buddy duo, even landing their own television show on ABC, *Blue Thunder*. His work on such fine shows as *The Love Boat, Fantasy Island, The Greatest American Hero, Magnum P.I.*, and *MacGyver* almost makes up for his appearance on *My Two Dads*. On second thought, the man with 25 fumble recoveries, third all-time in NFL history, is allowed a few fumbles of his own.

Believe it or not, he wasn't the most successful Butkus in Hollywood. Butkus Stallone, Sylvester Stallone's 125-pound bullmastiff scored big roles in *Rocky* and *Rocky II* (Yo, Butkus!). The four-legged thespian got his shot at stardom because producers lacked the money to rent a professional canine for the first movie, so Stallone brought flatulent-inflicted Butkus ("I was gassed to death," said the Italian Stallion) with him on his three-day train ride from Hollywood to the film set in Philadelphia. "We got him when he was about six weeks old," explained Stallone. "He was a ferocious-looking little devil, and when he ate his security blanket, we decided to name him after Dick Butkus, possibly the fiercest football player in history. We became very well acquainted, because in addition to me, there was my wife, Sasha, and another giant dog all living in the third tiniest apartment in New York." After Butkus died, Stallone had a sculpture of him erected in the hall of his Beverly Hills home.

While Chicago residents haven't got around yet to building a statue of Dick Butkus, one thing is for sure: he would smash it to pieces if they ever tried. To him, football wasn't about accolades, it was about the fight in the trenches. It was about hitting anything in sight as hard as humanly possible, even his own teammates. "I've said many times that my teammate Dick Butkus had hit me as hard in practice as anybody in a game," said Gale Sayers, who joined the Bears in 1965, the same year as Butkus. "He was a tremendous practice player, and if you want to be good on Sunday, you had to do it in practice, and he didn't let up in practice."

That was Butkus. He'd come at you in your sleep.

Deacon Jones

When Deacon Jones took the field, he had a simple mission: search and destroy. His target had approximately four seconds to pray for mercy before Jones came charging into the backfield, tossing aside the poor bastard assigned to stop him, as well as the other big fella trying to hold him back, and rocked him into another orbit.

The world Jones came from was about a million miles from the NFL stadiums were he would slash and thrash his way to glory. His was a tough childhood, spent picking watermelons in the blazing Florida heat. "If you're the pitcher, you've got a problem," Deacon said of loading up the 50-pound melons. "After about four hours of that, it was like you were picking up the Empire State Building and throwing it up on the truck." If the work wasn't enough to break your spirit, the virulent racism of the Deep South would. Once a young Jones was standing outside a church when a group of white teenagers came hollering by in a yellow convertible. Jones shouted a warning as a watermelon flew toward the crowd. It struck an old woman in the head. She bled to death. As for the investigation, it was over before it even got started. "My uncle ran the police force in Eatonville, but he couldn't do nothing about it," said Jones. "A black man couldn't arrest a white guy."

Deacon Jones might have unleashed his anger at society through violent crime if he hadn't made a trip one day to the ballpark in Orlando to watch his boyhood idol, Jackie Robinson, play ball. "During the game, Robinson slid into second base," said Ron Pollack telling the story in *Pro Football Weekly*. "And the white second baseman for the opposing team intentionally ground his cleats into Robinson's hand, smiled at what he had done, and then got away with it when the white umpire chose to do nothing about it. Deacon and half a dozen friends, sitting in the blacks-only section in the outfield of the segregated ballpark, watched in anger. After the game, Deacon, a brash kid even then, went up to Robinson near the dressing room. Deacon wanted to know if Robinson, whose hand was bandaged, was angry. 'He didn't have any animosity in his heart,' Deacon says. 'Or he didn't show any. I know he had to be pissed off. I know I would have been.'" Robinson's words may have been spoken quietly, but don't confuse that with acceptance of the situation. Deacon said to Robinson, "I guess you get used to it." Robinson responded, "No, son, you don't ever get used to it."

Jones would need every bit of that self-control and discipline when the unknown 14th-round draft choice joined the Rams in 1961. He and his black teammates had to stay in smaller hotel rooms. Meanwhile, a couple of his white teammates thought it would be a gas to haze the rookie by rushing into his room one night dressed in white Ku Klux Klan sheets. "These guys never gave any consideration to where I came from and what my life was like," said Jones. "I had chills. Cold sweat."

Jones used his pent-up aggression every bit as much as his sprinter speed and rock-solid body to become an unstoppable pass rusher. "This was the get-even process," he said. "All I thought about was kicking some ass and not going to jail. I was at the height of my anger period." Coaches were forced to employ double teams to try and contain Jones, who turned the pass rush into the sideline-to-sideline glamour position later played by Lawrence Taylor and Reggie White. "One of them wouldn't do against me," an animated Jones said. "You should be asking me who were the toughest 'two' linemen or what was the toughest combination or the toughest team—because you'd definitely have to bring more than one when you come at me. If you just bring one, I'm going to kill somebody."

If you ever wondered how the headslap came to be outlawed in the NFL, the answer is Deacon Jones. From his rookie season in 1961 until he retired in 1975, the 6'5", 255-pound defensive end rattled the brains of the league's best linemen, using his giant, padded meat-hook hands to deliver a ferocious lick across their helmets. As 49ers tight end Bob Windsor recalled, "Our right tackle, Cas Banaszek, had ice bags on his head after every game

> ## Too Good to Be True?
>
> Has there ever been such thing as a "nice" punisher? If so, his name has to be **Merlin Olsen**. Ironically, he was part of a legendary defensive front called the Fearsome Foursome. At 6'5", 270 pounds, quarterbacks and blockers had good reason to fear the Rams' tackle. More frightening than that, he also possessed uncanny mobility for a big man, not to mention Phi Beta Kappa smarts. Did we mention that over his 15-year career he also never missed a game after his rookie season? (No player matched his record streak of 14 straight Pro Bowls until former Tennessee Titans offensive lineman Bruce Matthews in 2001.)
>
> But because of his affable nature off the field, his toughness on the field is too often overlooked, at least compared to his bruising brothers, Deacon Jones and Jack Youngblood. For instance, people still talk about how Youngblood fractured his leg in the first round of the 1979 playoffs but still played every defensive down in that year's Super Bowl. But ask Youngblood who taught him the meaning of grit and determination, and he would almost certainly tell you it was Merlin Olsen. "I remember one time when a guy stepped on Merlin's hand with those nylon cleats. Ripped it wide open," said the future Hall of Famer. "He came back to the huddle holding it. I looked over, and I could see all the bones. I almost fainted. Merlin said, 'Aw, it's all right.' He held it together and stopped the bleeding a little bit. That was first down. He stayed out there two more plays before he went to the sideline."
>
> Pa Ingalls' gentle buddy on TV's *Little House on the Prairie*—yep, same guy.

against the Rams. His head was swollen by inches of pounding, Deacon hit him so hard." Then he came after the quarterback. "He smacked John Brodie as hard as you could ever smack him. John got up with blood caked all over his helmet and up his nose. On his way back, Deacon said to me, 'I'll do that the next play, too.'" At least one lineman, Hall of Famer Bob Brown, figured a way to exact revenge. "Bob Brown had a thing where he would unscrew the corners of his face mask," Steve Sabol of NFL Films told Rich Eisen. "So Deacon Jones or somebody would come up with the head slap and go right into the screws of Bob Brown's helmets." Three years after Jones retired, the headslap was banned for good.

Deciding that his birth name, David, didn't suit his larger-than-life personality, Jones added a new nickname to the NFL lexicon. "I picked out 'Deacon' because it has a religious connotation and it would be remembered in the violent pro football world," he said. "When the Rams sent out my player questionnaire, I simply listed my name as Deacon

Jones. From then on, that's what I was." But his biggest linguistic contri-
bution to the league was the term "sack," which he coined with the Rams.
"Sacking the quarterback is like you devastate (sack) a city," he explained.
"Or you cream a multitude of people. It's like you put all the offensive
players in the same bag, and I just take a baseball bat and beat on the bag."
Sacks didn't become an NFL statistical category until 1982, meaning that
the same man who invented the term would never get official credit for
any of the ones he made. "I had 26 sacks in 14 games and six in the postseason [in 1967]," said Jones, referring to the personal tally he recorded in
notebooks at the time. "And in 1968 I had 24 sacks. Uh-uh! I can't let that
go! I will never let that go!" In 2000 researcher John Turney used old game
summaries and film to prove that Jones had 173.5 sacks, which puts him
third in NFL history behind Bruce Smith's 200 and Reggie White's 198.

During his 14-year career with the Rams, Chargers, and Redskins,
Jones was as quick with a brash, often hilarious quip as he was chasing
down quarterbacks. "I'm the best defensive end around," he once said.
"I'd hate to have to play against me." He also claimed once he could
"outrun daylight." His dislike of quarterbacks was so intense that it was
a prerequisite for marriage. "When Deacon and I first met," said
Elizabeth Jones, "he made it very pointed to me that I was no longer to
love Joe Montana." The eight-time Pro Bowler didn't just set the standard for pass rushers to come but for all future trash-talkers. "I was the
originator of smack," declared Jones. "Some guys rattle with smack; with
other guys it rolls right off their shoulders like nothing."

When it comes to the list of most vaunted defensive duos of all-time,
Deacon Jones and Merlin Olsen are at or are very near the top. From
1962 to 1966, they, along with Rosey Grier and Lamar Lundy, made up
the Fearsome Foursome—or in the words of Dick Butkus, "the most
dominant line in football history." A successful on-field partnership
between Olsen, the white Mormon from national powerhouse Utah
State (picked third overall) and Jones, the dirt-poor black kid from
Mississippi Vocational and later South Carolina State (picked 186th
overall), forged a race-transcending bond that was rare for the times.

"The Fearsome Foursome was one of the few situations on a football
team where there was a majority of black and a minority of white
[players]," recalled Jones. "At the defensive line position there were three

starting brothers and one white guy. So we chose the democratic route in building our relationship. And we did everything by vote. Majority rules. And Merlin fell right into it, and Merlin abides by it to this day. And our relationships were built on a firm foundation, because it still lasts to this very minute. He was a great person to work with. He's been a great friend."

Despite the way the Fearsome Foursome dominated, like in 1968 when they set a 14-game NFL record for the fewest yards allowed, they never played in an NFL title game. What they did do was bring a sophisticated approach to the defensive line, such as perfecting the stunt, or loop, move. "Against Detroit in their fifth game [in 1963]," wrote Karen Donnelly in *Deacon Jones*, "Merlin Olsen suggested that Jones hesitate for a split second after the snap, letting Olsen cross over and cut down Jones' opponent. This "stunt" opened a hole in Detroit's offensive line. Both Olsen and Jones were free to run through the hole into the backfield, throwing Detroit for a huge loss." Long before the Super Bowl Shuffle, the exciting L.A. product became one of the first sports units to become crossover celebrities, even developing a singing and dancing nightclub show. "We worked with Bob Hope, we worked with Big Crosby, we worked with Jimmy Durante," recalled Jones. "We sang and danced on the first *Shindig*. So there was a lot to the Fearsome Foursome."

After retiring from the game in 1975, the high-wire defender proved there was a lot more to him than pummeling quarterbacks. He went on to appear in movies and television shows, including *Bewitched* and *The Odd Couple*. And *Brady Bunch* fans can argue if his guest appearance was better than Joe Namath's. But it's through his Deacon Jones Foundation that he's made the biggest impact. His work providing academic scholarships to underprivileged kids has brought out the emotional and kindhearted man lurking under the mad-dog persona. While he smiled about giving kids the chance to succeed that he was denied in the segregated South, he shed tears when he couldn't provide one of the finalists a scholarship. In March of 2003 he visited soldiers fighting in Iraq. "It was very gratifying," he says, "but I have to admit that I've never been more scared in my life than I was in Baghdad. And only a few hours after we left, a bomb went off in the Sheraton Hotel across the street from where we had been hosted in a feast the night before."

Later, he visited the Walter Reed Army Medical Center, where, spur-of-the-moment, he invited six of the amputees to come with him and his wife to Hall of Fame weekend in Canton. (One assumes that the only pre-condition was that they all had to agree to hate quarterbacks.) But for all his work away from football, in his heart, he will forever be a pass rusher. As a 70-year-old Jones told NFL Films, "I'd like to see if I could get up off my death bed and still whip a NFL tackle."

Then Greg Cosell Said...

A 30-year veteran of NFL Films, few people have analyzed as much game footage as Greg Cosell. Originally, he produced those famous documentary films, which turned gridiron battles into glorious Shakespearean epics about glory, failure, and survival. "I'm a sucker for the *Sturm und Drang* of an NFL Films production," said *Newsweek*'s Mark Starr. (He's not the only dude to be rendered "teary" by the poetic images of bravery during brutal warfare.) Cosell was actually the last man to work with the iconic voice of NFL Films, John "the Frozen Tundra of Lambeau Field" Facenda. Since 1984 Cosell has served as the executive producer of *NFL Matchup*, an oasis for diehards craving nitty-gritty analysis of game plans and strategy. He spoke with us about famous relatives, offensive masterminds, and how Len Dawson's victory in Super Bowl IV was more important than Joe Namath's in Super Bowl III.

Steve Sabol said that when he hired you at NFL Films that "you never mentioned Howard [Cosell] and, frankly, we never checked." So, in your daily life, do people ever talk to you about your famous uncle?
No. They don't come in, sit down, and say, "Gee, let's talk about Howard Cosell." Because it's almost not important. He just happened to be my uncle. He's a famous guy. But from the time I was born, he was just my father's brother.

That's interesting. So you weren't really that close with him as a kid?
He wasn't really a factor in my life growing up. His family and my family lived far away [from one another], so it wasn't like he came over on weekends or even on holidays. Howard was in California. And I was

in Michigan, going to college, living in my own world. Of course, he was so big at the time that everyone I knew would ask me if I was related.

Do you have any memories you can share?

Well, I remember going out to his beach house in West Hampton on Long Island with my cousins, his grandchildren. Those were fun times. He wasn't Howard Cosell, the broadcaster. He was Howard Cosell, the grandfather. The way he talked was the way he talked all the time. But he was a different guy—just somebody who loved his grandchildren so much. You know, when somebody is in your family, all that other stuff doesn't matter. The way people saw him, it had no bearing on my existence. People could view him any way they wanted. It didn't matter to me.

How did you first get involved with NFL Films?

Well, actually, my first year out of college, I was a teacher at a private high school outside of Detroit, Michigan. And I also coached baseball and basketball. I knew after six months that it wasn't what I wanted to do, so I applied to many different companies. From there, NFL Films offered me a job. That goes back to 1979. It was a much smaller company then; probably only 50 people. So back then you really had a chance to sit, watch, and learn. In my first 10 years, I did a ton of the well-known documentary films. That's how I cut my teeth. Then in 1984 Steve Sabol and I created the *NFL Matchup* show concept. Basically, since then I've been working on that program and dealing with the game more from an Xs-and-Os level.

You have access to the same game film that NFL coaches have. How much does an average person miss just viewing what they see on their television screen?

When you watch football on TV, you're probably seeing about 20 percent of the game.

Only 20 percent?

Maybe. It's like the difference between reading a book and the Cliff Notes. Of course, that doesn't stop everybody from being an expert.

Give me an example of a common misconception held by your typical armchair expert.

What the average fan responds to is: if the play works, then it was a good call; if it doesn't work, it was a bad call. You hear people talk about a coach making a bad play call. Or you'll hear people say, "They blew the coverage." Number one, does the fan watching at home even know what the coverage was? Does he understand the individual responsibilities of each player within that coverage? Okay? So how can he possibly know that they blew the coverage? Because the guy seemed to be open? Don't forget. No coverage, especially zone coverage, takes care of everything. Or everybody would run the same coverage.

The biggest mystery in NFL history has to be the "Immaculate Reception" because the footage we've seen is inconclusive. Tell me that you have the equivalent of the Zapruder film, showing what really happened.

No. There's nothing hidden away here at NFL Films that would make you say, "Ooooh, that's the real shot," and we just haven't shown it all these years. When a ball takes funny bounces like that, it's difficult for the cameramen. Ultimately it had to be meshed together. It's always been cut the same way.

What do you think it means to be a "gunslinger" in the NFL?

I think it's the willingness to take chances when they throw the ball, knowing there's a risk factor and a potential reward factor. Obviously, not every quarterback is willing to make those kinds of throws. I believe, from watching tape for many years, that in order to be an elite quarterback, and I don't use that term loosely, you have to be willing to make stick throws into tight windows. You don't necessarily need to be a "gunslinger" like Brett Favre. He's an example of a guy who's made a lot of ill-advised throws. Usually, gunslingers have bigger arms, giving them an unwavering belief and confidence in their ability to make any throw. The term that's often used is "throw it through people." You rarely say that a quarterback with an average arm is a gunslinger because most of them understand their physical limitations and don't necessarily even attempt those throws.

So who's the best example of a gunslinger playing today?

I think the number one gunslinger now is [new Bears QB] Jake Cutler. He plays with an almost total lack of conscience. He has such tremendous confidence in his ability to make throws that at times he seems almost impervious to the defense. He simply believes, *I can get the ball to my receiver.*

Do you think the criticism that Cutler received in Denver [before moving to the Chicago Bears] is justified?

He's been on a team that has a very poor defense by NFL standards. So Cutler knows, before he even suits up that he needs to put up 30 points for his team to have a chance to win. Even just to compete. That's a major burden on a quarterback. Because the mandate for guys like Cutler or Carson Palmer in Cincinnati is to put up lots of points, they feel like they have to make every throw worthwhile. Every throw counts. They can't just throw the ball away, or throw a lot of check downs. In other words, take what the defense gives them. That's not going to get them 30 points.

Would you put Dan Marino in that category?

Marino was arguably the best pure passer to ever play. He was another guy who believed he could make any throw at any time. His Dolphins did not run the ball well or often. That doesn't mean you can't make plays. Clearly, Marino made lots of throws and put up huge numbers. But it's very hard for any offense to be consistent when it chooses to be one-dimensional. We saw the same thing with the Patriots in 2007. Which is why I don't think the Giants' win in that year's Super Bowl was a huge upset.

Huh. Some people argue it was the biggest upset in Super Bowl history.

The Giants defense still had to play at the level that they did or the Patriots could have put up 35 points. But it's much easier to defend an offense that chooses to be one-dimensional. As good as the Patriots were, it finally caught up to them.

Which coaches do you think had the most ingenious offenses in NFL history?

Bill Walsh comes to mind. His West Coast concept actually began in 1970 with the Cincinnati Bengals, when he lost his strong-armed quarterback, Greg Cook, and had to play Virgil Carter, who was a smart, savvy quarterback with a weak arm. Plus, they couldn't run the ball very well. So Bill Walsh devised an offensive scheme that at the time was unheard of—essentially a horizontal passing game. Back then it was the vertical game of Sid Gillman that was the dominant passing concept. But Bill Walsh, out of necessity, knew he could not move the chains without throwing these shorter, quicker passes. This was the precursor to what became his great West Coast offenses in San Francisco.

Are there any other offensive masterminds that stand out?
Head coach Sid Gillman is really the father of the modern NFL passing game. Then came Chargers coach Don Coryell, who took advantage of two big rule changes in 1978. Defensive backs could only hit a wide receiver within five yards of the line of scrimmage and then you had to let him go. The other rule change was no holding, which they had basically allowed as long as the offensive lineman's hands were inside the pass rusher. Coryell was able to see new possibilities in the passing game. For instance, he lined up tight end Kellen Winslow outside the formation, almost using him like a wide receiver. This gave him an advantage.

When people talk about the most important games in NFL history, they usually mention the 1958 championship game or Super Bowl III. Are there any big games that may have been overlooked?
Clearly Super Bowl III was a big moment because the AFL team beat the NFL team. But in an odd way you could argue the following year's Super Bowl between the Kansas City Chiefs and the Minnesota Vikings was even bigger. If the AFL's Chiefs had lost, the argument could have been made that Super Bowl III was a fluke. But when the Chiefs handily beat the Vikings, it became evident that the official merger in 1970 would take place.

So do you think that Namath's victory in Super Bowl III overshadowed the talent of that '69 Kansas City Chiefs team?

No question. When you look at the individual players, they had a better team than the Super Bowl–champion Jets. Len Dawson was the Chiefs' quarterback. Otis Taylor was a terrific, big wide receiver. Mike Garrett was their running back. They had a lot of great players on defense. They had Bobby Bell, who arguably was as good a linebacker as anyone who's ever played the game. He was somewhat ahead of his time—one of those big, fast guys who could have played today. From an athletic standpoint, he was that good. They also had Willie Lanier at middle linebacker. He's in the Hall of Fame. They had first team All-Pro Johnny Robinson at safety. Just a lot of really good players.

Who do you think was the best defensive unit in NFL history?

Two defenses come to mind. The '85 Chicago Bears and the 2000 Baltimore Ravens. The Bears were somewhat ahead of their time because of Buddy Ryan's defensive approach. His belief in pressure schemes stemmed back to his days as an assistant coach with the New York Jets. He saw how Weeb Ewbank spent so much time on offense trying to "protect" Joe Namath, he thought, *Okay, then I'm going to spend all my time trying to "get" the quarterback.* So he built his defense in Chicago around pressure schemes that broke the mold, bringing linebackers, safeties, corners. It doesn't matter who he brings. He says, *If there's a breakdown in coverage or if I leave an area exposed, that's okay because we're going to get to the quarterback, or make him throw it so quickly he won't be able to exploit that weakness in coverage.*

Jack "the Assassin" Tatum

Once Jack Tatum had you in his sights, he didn't leave you much time to kiss your ass good-bye. "I never make a tackle just to bring someone down," said the three-time Pro Bowl Raiders safety in his 1980 autobiography *They Call Me Assassin.* "I want to punish the man I'm going after. I like to believe that my best hits border on felonious assault." For all Tatum's ill-timed boasting—it came two years removed from his vicious shot on New England receiver Darryl Stingley during a preseason game that left him a quadriplegic—the truth was that he'd never be the same Assassin he was before the tragic accident. Tatum wasn't the only one to be forever altered by the events in Oakland on August 12, 1978. Other

All in a Name

When you talk about the great nicknames for a defensive unit, you have to put the **Orange Crush** near the very top of the list. They also belong on the list of most punishing defenses in NFL history. The Orange Crush, the nickname of the Denver Broncos' defensive squads of the 1970s, had their most dominant season in 1977, leading the then-moribund franchise (three winning seasons since it's birth in 1960) to the Super Bowl. They did it with one of the all-time lethal pass-rushing brigades, led by madman Lyle Alzado, blitz-master Tom Jackson, and Randy "Why Is This Dude Not in the Hall of Fame?" Gradishar. By Christmastime in 1977, the Orange Crush had put the Broncos in the playoffs and the city into a deranged frenzy. "Santa Claus took a backseat to the Denver Broncos," recalled Larry Zimmer, the former play-by-play man of the team. One Santa even appeared in an orange suit. Many toted home orange Christmas trees. Orange cars appeared in the streets. The most popular and played song in Denver was not "Silent Night," but Jon Keyworth's "Make Those Miracles Happen."

Unfortunately, the NFC's representative in the Super Bowl, the Dallas Cowboys, just happened to also have one of the best defensive units in NFL history. Known as the **Doomsday Defense**, it consisted of that Super Bowl's eventual co-MVPs, Harvey Martin and future Hall of Famer Randy White, along with Mel Renfro, another Hall of Famer, and fearsome Ed "Too Tall" Jones. In the Big Game in the Superdome on January 15, 1978, the Doomsday unit held the Broncos' offense to 10 points, while the Orange Crush surrendered 27 points to the 'Boys. Of course, the Dallas offense had a few future Hall of Famers themselves in Roger Staubach and Tony Dorsett, not to mention a Hall of Fame coach in Tom Landry.

hard-hitters around the league rethought their "put him in a body bag" shots. At the same time, the NFL began taking measures to reduce such career-ending hits. "I saw replays many, many, many times, and many times Jack Tatum was criticized. But here wasn't anything at the time that was illegal about the play," said Patriots head coach Chuck Fairbanks of the tragic slant pattern collision. "I do think probably that play was a forerunner for some of the changes in rules that exist today that are more protective of receivers, especially if there is head-to-head to contact."

While the Stingley hit dominates Tatum's résumé, he will also be remembered as a crucial cog of a defense that delivered the Oakland Raiders their long-awaited first Super Bowl title. In Pasadena, California, the NFL's bad boys of the 1970s capped a one-loss season by dominating the Vikings 32–14. The most famous image from that Super Bowl, and among the most lasting in championship history, is Tatum brutally separating the helmet from the rest of Rookie of the Year receiver Sammy White. Longtime Raiders fan Craig Parker recalled, "On the catch, Skip Thomas attacked from behind while Jack Tatum rushed in full bore and unloaded the lumber with his left shoulder into White's head. Sammy crumpled to the ground while Tatum stood over him."

People forget that, with all due respect to the Big Man upstairs, that the Steelers might never have gone from the league's perennial doormats to Super Bowl dynasty if Tatum didn't have a habit of launching his body at receivers. You may recall the play on December 23, 1972, in Three Rivers Stadium: the Raiders were clinging to a 7–6 lead over the Steelers, with 22 seconds left in the AFC playoff game. Terry Bradshaw heaved a desperate pass on fourth-and-10. It deflected off a player into the air. Franco Harris scooped the ball of his shoelaces and ran it into the end zone for the game-winning touchdown.

The Immaculate Reception was born, and with it the controversy over which player the ball deflected off: Jack Tatum or the guy whose head he was delivering a vicious forearm to at the time, Steelers halfback "Frenchy" Fuqua. "He really gave me a lick," Fuqua recalled. "He dazed me. I hadn't seen him coming. I thought I had the ball, and just then I had the accident." In the words of Tatum, "I was covering the tight end when this dude cut in front of me. I didn't know it was Fuqua. At first I thought I had a chance at the ball, but I didn't. Then I went for the man I never did hit the ball." But the referees ruled that Tatum had deflected the pass, and not Fuqua, thus it was ruled a legal pass. Of course, either way, it was the force of Tatum's hit that caused the ball to sail its magical journey through the air and down into Franco Harris' big paws. "I remember after I made that hit, we all thought the game was over," Tatum said. "I saw Franco Harris running and I thought, *Man, that guy's in a hurry to get to the locker room.* We had that game won; it was a mess."

When the Rose Bowl champion Ohio State Buckeyes were invited onto Bob Hope's television show in 1969, here's how the comedian introduced their All-America defensive back: "I became a Jack Tatum fan when I saw him play in the Rose Bowl. Jack hit O.J. [Simpson] so hard that he knocked me out of my 50-yard-line seat and into the parking lot.

Imagine how the Juice felt...squeezed." Who knows the final verdict on Jack Tatum, but these jokes reflect how his aggressive brand of hitting was once celebrated. (In some parts it still is: like at his alma mater, where in 2001 head coach Jim Tressel started rewarding the Ohio State player with the biggest game hit with the "Jack Tatum Hit of the Week Award.")

Nobody would deny that some of Tatum's past remarks and actions were insensitive, even thoughtless, but we should remember that he was part of a football legacy going back to the days of Nitshcke, a culture based on the tenant that if you had a legitimate chance to put a full-force lick on somebody, you took it. This maybe explains why Tatum could never understand why so many viewed him as a villainous thug. "It's just like for nine years I've been playing the game the wrong way," he said, "but I've made All-Pro, I've been runner-up for Rookie of the Year, I've got all the honors playing exactly the same way. So, you know, it just kind of mystified me as to why there was just all of a sudden this stuff because a guy got hurt." Two years ago Stingley passed away. Tatum would go on to have part of his foot amputated while battling diabetes. Perhaps Frank Gifford had it right when he said, "Pro football is like nuclear warfare. There are no winners, only survivors."

"Mean" Joe Greene

In 1969 37-year-old Chuck Noll took over as head coach of the Pittsburgh Steelers, a franchise that stunk for decades like the black plumes of smoke belching from a steel mill. The 1969 NFL Draft would provide the first-time coach his first opportunity to start turning around the team's fortunes. In the first round, Noll picked a 6'4", 270-pound defensive end named Joe Greene. The reaction of fans, newspaper scribes, and team veterans was almost unanimous: *What in God's name is Noll thinking? How could he waste the fourth overall pick on some relatively unknown defensive tackle from obscure North Texas State?* Famed *SI* sports writer Roy Blount Jr. revealed how Noll's own scouts were against the pick: "The last entry in the Steelers' scouting file on Greene says: 'I would question taking a boy like this in the first round, as he could turn out to be a big dog.'" (Perhaps the scout would have preferred second-pick George Kunz or third pick Leroy Keyes. The first pick was a guy named O.J. Simpson.)

You can't blame the Steelers universe for their anxiety; after all, for decades they'd been one of the league's most snake-bitten, inept organizations. Consider that from the time they entered the league in 1933 until 1972—nearly a 40-year span—the team played in a total of one playoff game (a dismal 21–0 loss to the Eagles in 1947). Want to trace the rise of the Steelers from the bowels of the NFL to perhaps the most glorious franchise: winning an unprecedented six Super Bowls—four Lombardi trophies in the '70s, two in the last four years—and appearing in 12 of the 17 playoffs since 1992? It starts on draft day in 1969 and the fourth overall pick, "Mean" Joe Greene. As for that "dog" comment in the scouting report, Blount Jr. explained, "This note was prophetic only to the extent that it might have conjured up the difficulties involved in trying to block a Doberman pinscher."

The late summer months in Florida are sometimes referred to as the "mean season" for their nasty weather; but perhaps the meanest season came in 1969, when rookie Joe Greene raged like a category-five hurricane through the Steelers' abysmal 1–13 season. Some people hate to lose; it drove Greene to the point of near-psychosis. His first enraged outburst occurred in the fourth contest against the New York Giants. Late in the game Greene vented his fury on Viking Fran Tarkenton, delivering a late hit that got him kicked out of the game. After the Giants prevailed 10–7, retired Eagles running back Steve Van Buren told *SI* that he credited the ejection of the rookie defender for the win. "The Giants would never have penetrated far enough to kick the winning field goal," Van Buren said. "If I owned the Steelers, I'd have fined Greene $2,000 for getting himself thrown out."

Other ejections followed. When Vikings lineman Jim Vellone delivered a hard clean block on Greene, he retaliated by clutching a hold of the tackle's shoulders and kicking him flush in his baby-maker. But his piece de resistance happened in Philadelphia, where, in a rage, he picked up the other team's ball and chucked it as far as he could into the crowd. As Steelers teammate Andy Russell recalled, "Everybody looked at him. *He can't be doing this,* we thought. We watched the ball spiral into the seats. It seemed like it took forever. The crowd was dead silent. And the players—there we were, we didn't have a ball, we didn't have a left tackle. It was like he was saying, 'Okay, if you won't play right, we won't play at all.' Nobody else would do such a thing. In the NFL! Anybody else would get in trouble with the league, with the coaches, Joe did it. In a moment the crowd exploded. They loved it." Russell loved it, too. "Hell," he said, "I don't know why they put him out of a game for that. They should have given him some kind of award. It might have been the best pass a guy on our club threw all year."

Here's the irony: Joe Greene considered himself, in the words of Rooney, "a teddy bear." As for his late hit on Tarkenton, Greene explained in 1975, "I kept chasing him and when I finally hit him I didn't realize he had thrown the ball five minutes before. I got flagged for it and got escorted off the field. I had been called 'Mean' Joe before, but this made it even stronger. I prefer Joe." In fact, the origins of his nickname had nothing to do with his brutal tactics. "That happened my sophomore year at North Texas," he told Blount. "We wore green, and the defense was going good, and they called us the Mean Green. Me being named Greene, it naturally rubbed off on me. I do the best I can on every play and I go hard, but I'm not mean. Sometimes I may talk to the quarterback if I get to him, but it ain't mean. Like one time I sacked somebody, I don't remember who, and when he got up, I said, 'Don't bother to run the draw, because I'm going to be sitting right there in the hole waiting for it.'"

Joe Greene was as badass as anybody to ever play the game. But at times, he was less Mr. Mean and more Mr. Sensitive. Once, the Steelers cut a friend of his from college, and a distraught Greene had to be convinced not to quit in solidarity. Then there was the time Greene landed a role in the high school play but, as he told *Sports Illustrated*'s Stan Isaacs in 1979, he became "scared to death and had to drop out in the dress rehearsal." He was also bullied constantly by a kid named Old Speedy. That is until one day Greene decided to stand up to his older aggressor. "I mopped the floor with him," recalled Greene. "I gave him a really good beating. That fight, when I was in the ninth grade, got me over the hump. I went from average football player to good player. I was able to find myself as a man after that fight."

Another time in high school, Greene became so furious over losing a football game that when he ran into the victors at a diner afterward, he nearly got into a fight—*with their entire team*. "Their quarterback had

Legendary defensive lineman "Mean" Joe Greene was one of the cornerstones of the Steelers' "Steel Curtain" defense in the 1970s. Photo courtesy of Getty Images.

an ice cream cone," he recalled. "I took it away from him and smeared it all over his face. He didn't do anything. He went back to the team bus. Then I heard somebody call my name. I turned around, and a soda bottle hit my chest, and the guy I'd done ducked back into the bus. Like a damn fool, I went at the bus. In the front door. They all went out the back door."

Greene seemed determined to change his image from a "wild man" to the poised leader who would lead his team to Super Bowl glory. He took rookie quarterback Terry Bradshaw under his wings; recalled Bradshaw, if Greene laughed, that let his teammates know his joke was funny. Tempering his emotions without losing his aggressive nature, he went on to spearhead a defensive front four that also featured L.C. Greenwood, Ernie Holmes, and Dwight White. Together, they emerged as one of the most formidable runstopping defenses in the history of the game. "While many of today's athletes have to consult horoscopes before they play, on Sunday I was always ready to kick some ass," Greene told *Cigar Aficionado.* "I wasn't worried about being penalized for cut blocks or head slaps; I'd get after a guy. When the Steelers were playing, it was like Jaws was in the water. Everyone else had to get the hell out of there."

Apart from plugging up the middle, play after play, year after year, Greene had an uncanny knack for catching fire when his teammates needed it most. A victory over Houston in the next-to-last week of the 1972 season was crucial to their pursuit of the AFC Central crown, but injuries had all but decimated the black-and-yellow crew. A tribute video to Green played at a 2003 Mel Blount Youth Home event captured the scene: "Before the game is 15 minutes old, there are more injured Steelers on the sideline than there are points on the scoreboard. Bruce Van Dyke, Gerry Mullins, Ron Shanklin, Terry Bradshaw, L.C. Greenwood, Craig Hanneman, Sam Davis, and Jim Clack are injured. That's four offensive lineman, the starting quarterback, the leading receiver, and two starting defensive linemen. Done for the day, or in the case of Mullins, so sick as to be barely able to stand."

But Greene wasn't about to let the Steelers miss the playoffs, not without at least wreaking as much havoc as possible. His five sacks and blocked field-goal attempt single-handedly kept the Steelers in the game. "With the Steelers holding a tenuous 6–3 lead in the fourth quarter and completely unable to muster any offense, Greene burst into the backfield to dump running back Fred Willis for a 12-yard loss, force a fumble, and recover it himself at the Houston 13-yard line," wrote Blount Jr. "Roy Gerela's short field goal clinched the result, and the Steelers had turned a corner. On the charter flight home that night, team captain Andy Russell made this announcement: 'After much consideration, we decided to award the game ball to a guy who is so outstanding that much of the time his play is taken for granted. We are giving the game ball to Joe Greene.'" A victory the following week clinched the first division title in team history.

In Super Bowl IX in Tulane Stadium, the Steel Curtain gave new meaning to the word *stingy*, holding the Vikings to just 17 yards on the ground. But late in the game, the Vikings were at the 5-yard line poised to score a touchdown and pull within two points. "Mean" Joe Greene once again took matters into his own hands. The hand-off went to Chuck Foreman. Greene stripped the ball and recovered it. "That was the biggest defensive play of the day," said Noll. "They tried to run a counter play, and Greene knocked the ball out of Foreman's hands. If they had scored then, they would have made it tough on us." One sportswriter remembered watching Greene trot off the field after the play, he "gestured triumphantly, shaking his fist at the Vikings, a Steeler way of saying who was the boss. It was the Steeler defense."

His four Super Bowl titles showed people his domination, but it was a commercial that made them finally see his gentle side. In May 1979 Coca-Cola introduced one of the most iconic 30-second spots in television history. A young kid sees his hero, "Mean" Joe Greene, limping grimly down the locker room tunnel after a hard-fought game. He gives the exhausted warrior his bottle of Coke, but after downing it, Greene just walks away, leaving the boy heartbroken. Suddenly, Greene shouts from down the hallway, "Catch!" and throws his jersey to the young fan to his wide-eyed amazement. "Let's have a kid and a bruiser," said the campaign's creative architect Roger Mosconi. "We've got to use 'Mean' Joe Greene." Only problem was that Greene was far less experienced than his nine-year old costar, Tommy Okon, a veteran commercial actor. Greene's first national commercial was actually for United Airlines in 1974 "The idea was that the plane was so comfortable that a mean, tough guy like me almost liked it," recalled Greene of his debut. But even with that job under his belt, Greene had to guzzle 27 bottles of Coke during an endless string of takes. His pint-sized costar recalled Greene ripping a few belches that almost knocked him over. "He's a big guy," said Okon. "You can only do that for so long before something is going to blow up on you."

For his work over the three-day 1978 shoot, filmed in a small municipal stadium in Mount Vernon, New York, Greene got $150,000. Not exactly Tom Brady numbers. But William Van Loan, then Coca-Cola's director of marketing operations said of the ex–high school play dropout, "When Joe turns around to face the kid, he looks like Othello." Young Tommy Okon grew up to become the co-owner for a stone-importing company in College Point, New York, and a father of four. As for "Mean"

Joe Greene, he retired in 1981 after 10 Pro Bowl seasons and eventually joined coaching staffs in Pittsburgh, Miami, and Arizona. In the end, he returned as a Steelers scout, which is somewhat ironic since, had Noll listened to his scouts, Greene would never have become a Steel City legend.

Jack Lambert

When James Harrison ran back a 100-yard interception for a touchdown in last year's Super Bowl, he did more than help the Pittsburgh Steelers win their record sixth Super Bowl. He also carried on the team's tradition of great linebackers—a group of men who are as responsible for the city's reputation of hard-nosed toughness as the steel factories upon which it was built. It's a tradition that started in the 1970s. It started with an unstoppable defensive unit known as the Steel Curtain. But most of all, it started with the gap-toothed snarl and take-no-prisoners attitude of middle linebacker Jack Lambert. As the fiery leader of the four-time

It's a Mad, Mad Duck

Before he punched out a horse in *Blazing Saddles* and adopted a lovable seven-year-old orphan named *Webster*, **Alex Karras** was the Mad Duck of the NFL. A four-time Pro Bowl defensive tackle for the Detroit Lions from most of 1958 to 1970, he was the toughest hombre on a famously fierce defensive line. The unit handed the storied 1962 Packers their only loss of the entire season; a game in which Karras and Co. sacked Bart Starr a team-record 11 times.

During one of the NFL's more wild and carefree eras, Karras had a reputation as one of the biggest troublemakers. In 1963 the NFL commissioner slapped him with a one-year suspension after he admitted to betting on NFL games. (Packers great Paul Hornung was also suspended.) During his time off, he agreed to take on famous wrestler Dick "the Bruiser" Afflis; but only after the Bruiser challenged him to a fight one night in Karras' Detroit bar, then proceeded to destroy "everyone and everything in the bar and on the streets outside the bar." As Chris Schramm recalled in *SLAM! Wrestling* magazine, "The match made headlines across the nation, and some 16,000 fans flocked to the Detroit Olympia on April 27, 1963. Afflis got a wide cut above his right eye during the bout, but the pain just angered Afflis more. Some 11 minutes into the match, Afflis was able to roll up Karras up for the win." That was it for "Killer Karras," who returned to the Lions in 1964. Once back, he was asked to participate in the pregame coin toss. The referee asked Karras to call it, heads or tails. He responded, "I'm sorry, sir. I'm not permitted to gamble."

Super Bowl–winning defense, and finest ambassador for its unit's mean, relentless, and dominating playing style, Lambert set the standard for all other Steelers who would come along and play the position. It's no coincidence that since his rookie season in 1974, Pittsburgh has sent at least one linebacker to the Pro Bowl in 30 of the last 35 seasons. You almost get the feeling that if a guy didn't play linebacker the way it was supposed to be played in the Steel City, Lambert would find him and straighten him out.

Eight linebackers had been picked in the 1974 draft before the Steelers surprised everyone by selecting Kent State's Jack Lambert. Switching the 6′4″, 205-pound former high school quarterback seemed like a crazy gamble. "There was some transfer from Buffalo named Bob Bender who was going to be the middle linebacker," Lambert recalled. "He was supposed to be the next Dick Butkus or something, but he quit two weeks before the season started, so they threw me in there. They had no choice. It was the greatest break of my life. Right away I loved it. Last time I heard about Bender, he was a bodyguard for the Rolling Stones." Meanwhile, Lambert went on to earn the NFL Defensive Rookie of the Year award, his clutch play-making ability helping the Steelers to win their first Super Bowl, a 16–6 defensive whipping of the Minnesota Vikings.

Of all the great Steel Curtain units, it's somewhat surprising that the 1976 incarnation is often considered to be the best—after all, that year's Pittsburgh team lost four of their first five games and, unlike the previous two years, failed to win a Super Bowl. Yet many believe that the 1976 group delivered the greatest defensive season, not just in Steelers history, but in the history of the NFL. With Terry Bradshaw sidelined with a neck injury caused by Browns defensive end "Turkey" Jones' infamous head-slam and "Mean" Joe Greene suffering chronic back pain, the dreams of a third-straight Super Bowl were quickly evaporating. In the sixth game of the season, the division-leading Cincinnati Bengals came into Three River Stadium to face a desperate Pittsburgh team led by back-up quarterback Mike Kruczek. "We were down to one quarterback, and Cincinnati knew it," recalled Lambert. "At least [Bengals linebacker] Bo Harris knew it, I guess. And Mike was scrambling and he ran out of bounds, and Harris gave him a shot. It wasn't a vicious shot, but it was a pretty good shot. So I went down the line and gave him one back."

Where's the Party?

Hall of Fame Oakland Raiders linebacker **Ted Hendricks**, nicknamed the Mad Stork, once rode a horse onto the practice field during training camp, wearing his uniform adorned with a German WWI helmet and substituting a traffic cone for a lance. "Most Raiders loved to party," said quarterback Ken Stabler. "Ted Hendricks was a party all by himself."

Seconds after Lambert angrily retaliated, players on both sides had to be held back. It was a message. A call to arms. The Steelers were done being pushed around. "What followed was the most amazing defensive streak in modern history," boomed the voice of NFL Films John Facenda. "The dimension of which offers statistical delight to even the most casual football historian."

Following the Cincinnati game, the Steelers rolled off three straight shutouts and held their opponents scoreless in five of their final eight games. Only once during that stretch did they allow the other team to score a touchdown, and that was in a 32–16 trouncing over the Houston Oilers. Carrying the team on their broad shoulder pads, Lambert and Co. allowed an amazing 9.9 points a game and 3.22 yards per rushing attempt. The Steelers made it to the AFC Championship Game against John Madden's Oakland Raiders, but the loss of both running backs, Franco Harris and war hero Rocky Bleier, proved too much to overcome, even for this resilient crew. "It was the most frustrating game I ever played in my life," Lambert said. "Give us a six pack and we'll go back out and play them again."

As one of the game's all-time toughest enforcers, it's not surprising that Lambert had one of the most memorable takedowns in Super Bowl history—what's strange is that it came after a field-goal attempt. When Steelers kicker Roy Gerela blew a three-point conversion in the third quarter of Super Bowl X, Cowboys safety Cliff Harris patted him on the helmet and mockingly "thanked" him for his miss. The next thing Harris knew, he was being lifted up from behind by a pissed-off Lambert, who then drove him into the ground. "We were getting intimidated and we're supposed to be the intimidators," Lambert said. "So I decided to do something." On the next series, a pumped-up Lambert made three tackles. From that point on, the Steelers defense took over the game. The fan site Steelers Tribute listed Lambert's slam on Harris as one of the greatest special-teams plays in team history, claiming that "it not only got the Steelers fired up in that game, but it also defined everything that was different about those two teams, and why it was so great to see the blue-collar Steelers say 'enough is enough' to the Cowboys and their cocky 'America's Team' image."

Not surprisingly, Lambert had his fair share of enemies on the Cowboys' sideline. "I don't care for the man," said Dallas linebacker Thomas "Hollywood" Henderson. "He makes more money than I do, and he don't have no teeth. He's Dracula." For others, like John Elway, who faced Pittsburgh in his first game as a pro, in 1983, the sight of a toothless Lambert standing across from him and, in his words, "slobbering all over" inspired less anger than profound regret over his career choice. "I wanted to click my heels and say, 'Auntie Em, bring me home. I'll give back the signing bonus,'" Elway remarked years later. When "Mean" Joe Greene was asked about his infamous reputation, he responded, "I'm not mean. I avoid violence. We got a lot meaner man on the team than me. Jack Lambert. He's so mean, he don't even like himself."

Lambert knew he couldn't scare anyone with his size, so he delighted any time he could frighten people with his Mad Jack reputation. The linebacker, who had his own cheering section, Lambert's Lunatics, would rile people up with comments like, "Yes, I get satisfaction out of hitting a guy and seeing him lay there awhile," and, "Quarterbacks should wear dresses." On one occasion he introduced himself on *Monday Night Football* as "Jack Lambert, Buzzard's Breath, Wyoming." Recalled Fred Paulenich, who grew up with Lambert in Mantua, Ohio, "I could see all of Mantua sitting up at that one. Howard Cosell even repeated it later, and I said, 'Oh, my God, he believed it.'"

Eventually Lambert worried his wildman image was making him a target of officials and overshadowing his tremendous technique. "His tough-guy image," said teammate Andy Russell, "throwing Cliff Harris down in the Super Bowl, fighting in Cleveland, swaggering around the field, stutter-stepping like Butkus, was a smokescreen to distract the opponent. In reality, he was a superb technician, killing them with his precision and focused intensity. The four-time Super Bowl winner and nine-time Pro Bowl selection readily admits that his scrappy determination was the quality that earned him his status as one of the all-time defensive punishers. "The Steelers drafted guys who were bigger, stronger, and faster than I," he said, "but they never found one who could take my job away from me."

Lawrence Taylor

Mix passion, will, and speed into a granite frame, leave out any trace of mercy, and you have Lawrence Taylor, the best pursuing linebacker in NFL history. Double teams. Triple teams. It seemed nothing short of a lightning bolt striking down from heaven could stop No. 56 from getting to his target. Not even while wearing a shoulder harness for a torn pectoral, as he did in 1988 game against the New Orleans Saints, could he be stopped. His line in the Giants 13–12' victory: seven tackles, three sacks, two forced fumbles.

Two years earlier his "take-over-the-game" method—he had a total of 20.5 sacks and 105 tackles—led the Giants over the Broncos for their first-ever Super Bowl (a "wide-right" victory versus the Bills would come in 1990). L.T. also became the first defender to win the NFL's MVP award since the Vikings' Alan Page in 1971.

> "I remember a game in New Orleans in 1988. His [L.T.'s] shoulder was so bad they put it in a harness, which limited his movement tremendously. He went down there and he was sacking the quarterback and making plays and causing fumbles. It was an unbelievable effort. He almost single-handedly won that game for us."
> —*Phil Simms*

Veteran quarterbacks are infamous for disguising plays in order to catch inexperienced rookies out of position. Sure enough, when Lawrence Taylor was a rookie with the Giants, offenses would dupe him regularly. On such occasions, L.T. had a rule: "If you get confused, rush and get the quarterback on his back as soon as you can." A foolish strategy unless, of course, you were L.T. Bursting forth like a human heat-seeking missile, he would drop the quarterback before his error in coverage was revealed. In fact, L.T. recorded his first-ever sack, clobbering Philadelphia quarterback Ron Jaworski, on a messed-up defensive assignment. "We lost that game," recalled L.T. "But I think the Eagles sensed the tide was going to turn, that there was a new badass sheriff in town, and he wasn't taking any prisoners. I also think it set the tone for future games against Jaworski. He'd spend the rest of his days looking over his shoulder to see if 56 was on his ass. And I usually was."

When *Entertainment Weekly*'s Dalton Ross counted down the 10 most memorable moments in the history of *Monday Night Football*, he put L.T.'s hit on Joe Theismann at the top of the list: "'That's the shot everyone remembers,' says [former] *MNF* analyst John Madden, 'where Lawrence Taylor hits him. You knew immediately that that was it for Joe Theismann.' And it was—the QB never played again. But for all those who miraculously did not vomit the first time while watching Theismann's bone snap and protrude out of his skin, ABC was kind enough to replay the image approximately…oh, 837 times. Still, there is one person who to this day has never seen the play—Theismann himself. 'I have no desire to look at it,' says the victim. 'I know what happened.'"

L.T.'s competitive drive was so relentless that when he ran out of opponents to battle, he'd turn to his own teammates. "Phil Simms and I used to get into arguments over who could do the other's job better," L.T. told the *New York Post*'s Paul Schwartz. "I said to him one day, I can throw this football farther than your ass could ever throw it.' He said, 'Give me a break.' I promptly threw that son of a bitch from the 50-yard line into the second level at Giants Stadium. Phil didn't even bother trying once he saw that. 'Take that shit, Simms,' I gloated."

Once in a while you get a player who breaks all the rules because he can. Joe Namath and Paul Hornung were the rare phenoms who could shrug off a damage-laden night of booze and beauties and go out the next day and have a stellar game. But it's hard to imagine even those party animals keeping up with L.T. in his prime. His nights out in New York City were less Tony Romo and more Tony Montana, as his pal and far more reserved teammate Phil Simms recalled, "I'm in a quarterback's meeting getting a cup of coffee, and Lawrence walks in at two minutes to 9:00, wearing leather pants, a big leather jacket, sunglasses on. He takes the sunglasses off, and I start to laugh, and he starts to laugh. I say, 'You're just coming in from the night?'"

While his teammates were recovering from an exhausting practice, L.T. was putting for birdie on some golf course. While they spent countless hours in the weight room, L.T. would stroll in and dead-lift 315 pounds on his first attempt. "That had never been done before. Never," recalled stunned teammate George Martin. "When Lawrence did that, you could have heard a rat piss on cotton. I mean, it was astonishing."

L.T. may have been a carefree dude most of the time, but not on Sundays—that's when he would become a tornado of terror, as if somebody flipped on the Terminator mode in his brain. "I caught Stump Mitchell one time at the goal line and broke that son of a bitch's back," recalled L.T. "He tried to jump in sideways, and I hit him dead in the back, and it was like he was an accordion. You bend that way, but I bent him back the other way. It was solid."

Nobody was immune from the wrath that came from awakening L.T., not even his own team. Minutes prior to a heated division battle with the Redskins, coach Bill Parcells made the mistake of asking L.T. if he was "gonna play today." In the words of Parcells, "He came right back at me, he said, 'You just worry about those other son of a bitches you're coaching.' He was almost spitting on me."

Anybody who thought that years of chasing down quarterbacks took some of the edge off of L.T. were sorely mistaken, as Steve Serby explained in *LT: Over the Edge*, "One of the offensive veterans decided to play a joke on the rookie, Derek Brown. He told him, 'You gotta hit L.T.!' Phil Simms said, 'Don't touch L.T.!' But Brown needed to make an early impression, so he hits L.T. full speed, and the guys were yelling, 'Oh, yeah!' When L.T. buckles his chin strap and ties his shoes, it's a live practice. That means he's ticked off. Ray Handley was the coach at the time. He ran over to L.T. and said, 'It's not a live practice.' L.T. didn't say a word. Phil Simms knew what was coming, and left the huddle. In stepped Kent Graham. The next snap, L.T. hit Derek Brown with some kind of head body snap and broke his nose. Brown was dazed and watched the rest of the practice. When practice was over, his football helmet had no face mask. L.T. had busted it. You don't mess with L.T."

After 10 Pro Bowl seasons, 132.5 sacks, 1,088 tackles, and 33 forced fumbles, L.T. was the one who found himself laid out on his back, sacked by drugs and alcohol. But after years battling his addictions, his

One of a Kind

It's safe to say that there's only one defensive punisher in NFL history to weigh nearly 400 pounds. Wait, I'm not done. And rush for a touchdown in a Super Bowl. Hang on. And have his own barbecue sauce. And have his own rap song. And his own GI Joe action figure. And compete in a Wrestlemania battle royale, a boxing match against 7'6" Manute Bol, and the Famous Nathan's Hot Dog Eating Contest. And star in an episode of *A-Team* with Hulk Hogan and Mr. T. And leave pro football to become a bricklayer.

Who else could it be but **William "the Refrigerator" Perry**? But don't let the bizarre life and times of the Fridge make your forget that he was blowtorching paths on both sides of the ball. As Bears linebacker Jim Morrissey once told the big fella, "Fridge, you're knocking more guys out of the league than the drug policy."

wild days seem to be behind him. Which is good news, because in the end, he should be remembered for the warrior pride he showed when the blue helmet and white cleats went on. In the words of John Madden, "He was the most dominant defensive player I've ever seen."

Ray Lewis

No player can be in on every tackle. But at times it seemed somehow that No. 52 of the Baltimore Ravens was. "Ray Lewis stands alone," said ex–Giants GM Ernie Accorsi. "I've never seen anybody better than him for flying around and disrupting an offense."

Since he arrived in Baltimore as a late first-round pick out of Miami, Lewis has been a combustible force of nature, igniting the fire in the defense, the fans, and the entire city.

You could argue no player has ever meant as much to his franchise as Ray Lewis has meant to the Baltimore Ravens. For over the past decade, he's been more than the cornerstone of their great defensive tradition. M&T Bank Stadium is the House That Ray Built.

On September 1, 1996, the Ravens played their inaugural game at Municipal Stadium before a crowd of 64,124, the largest crowd to ever witness a sporting event in Baltimore. That afternoon's opponents, the Oakland Raiders, scored 14 unanswered points to take a lead going into halftime. In a sign of things to come, Ray Lewis, playing in his first

Ray Lewis has been terrorizing NFL offenses since being drafted out of the University of Miami in 1996.

professional football game, led a second-half charge that resulted in a thrilling 19–14 victory. After giving up 189 yards of total offense in the first half, the Ravens defense held them to 49 in the second half. In fact, Baltimore didn't even let the Raiders cross midfield, holding them to just three first downs. The rookie's tenacity—nine tackles plus a crucial end-zone interception—earned him AFC Defensive Player of the Week honors. "There's no second speed for Ray," said former Ravens owner Art Modell. "It's all out. He's as good a middle linebacker as I've ever seen. The only one who can give him a run for his money would be his coach [at the time], Mike Singletary."

After two straight Pro Bowl appearances, Ray Lewis appeared to be on the expressway to stardom. But his fortunes reversed dramatically at a Super Bowl after-party in Atlanta on January 31, 2000. A street fight broke out that ended with two dead—Lewis and two of his friends were charged with six counts of murder. Midtrial, the murder charges against Lewis were dropped and, in the end, he pleaded guilty to just one misdemeanor count of obstruction of justice, based on the false statement he gave cops right after the incident. (No one was ever convicted of committing the murders.) "Was he in the wrong place at the wrong time?" asked former Ravens coach Brian Billick. "Absolutely. Did he handle the situation badly with the police the first night? You bet. But that's a long way from being a murderer or any of the other things he's been accused of." Lewis' reverend Richard Harris put it this way to ESPN's *Outside the Lines*, "What he's learned from all of this is that he has to be very, very careful about who he allows in his inner circle or inner sanctum. There's nothing wrong with having a posse. Jesus narrowed his down to 12, and maybe Ray has to narrow his down to even fewer than that." But the support of his reverend and coach wasn't enough to sway public opinion in his favor. Months of national media coverage of the case had left Lewis' image in tatters.

In 2000 Ray Lewis came back more determined than ever and, as the heart and soul of a tough, swarming defense, carried the Ravens to a convincing Super Bowl victory over the New York Giants, the first title in Baltimore since the 1983 Orioles. Along the way, the Ravens defense set a 16-game-season record for the fewest points allowed (165, 10.3 per game), surrendered just 970 yards on the ground (60.6 per game), and managed four shutouts. The 2000 Ravens defense never got a catchy nickname like the Steel Curtain or Doomsday Defense, but they belong among the all-time units. Consider that they won two games in which the offense didn't score a single touchdown, and, in four postseason games, allowed just one touchdown and a total of 16 points.

Over his first five years, Ray Lewis had yet to score a touchdown. He had to make his first one count. With less than six minutes remaining in a 2000 playoff battle against the Titans, and an early installment of their bitter rivalry, Lewis picked off Steve McNair and raced the ball back for a 50-yard touchdown return. But Lewis saved his best effort for the biggest game. In a 34–7 Super Bowl victory, Lewis was a one-man army, as he collected five tackles and got his big mitts on four passes in an MVP performance.

The following season, in a preseason game with the Giants, Lewis showed why he's considered one of the most intense guys to ever put on an NFL uniform. "Lewis began taunting the Giants at the coin toss," Mike Freeman writes in *Bloody Sunday*. "The Giants won and chose to receive the ball. 'I don't know why you're taking the ball,' Giants players claimed Lewis said, 'because that just means I'm going to knock out Dayne faster.' Ron Dayne was never knocked out, but Lewis made his usual assortment of eye-popping plays: hitting hard up the middle, making heart-stopping blitzes, covering fast running backs out of the backfield without help, and displaying his uncanny ability to squeeze his muscular 243-pound frame into running lanes to stop a play cold."

Asked about Ray Lewis' gift for gab, former linebacker coach Mike Singletary said, "Ray Lewis talks nonstop for the whole game. I don't know where he gets the energy, but he backs up every word." In some games, Lewis' big mouth proved to be an effective weapon. Sports columnist Ralph Wiley recalled how his "incessant and profane chatter finally got into running back Eddie George's shaven head, and George all but handed the football to Lewis for an interception return for a touchdown in the AFC divisional playoffs. We had no idea why he did that. Because he was distracted. Because Lewis had gotten underneath his helmet, in his dome. He started talking back to Lewis. Trying to match him. He lost."

Over his career, Lewis was also notorious for his spastic pregame dance, which energized his teammates as much as it infuriated opposing fans. Once while playing against the Ravens, agitator extraordinaire Terrell Owens mimicked Lewis' trademark moves after scoring a touchdown. In February T.O. changed his tune as he reached out to Lewis and tried to convince the free agent to join him with the Cowboys. Lewis might be the king of loud, booty-shaking swagger, but Peyton Manning says it's a mistake to overlook the linebacker's intelligence. "You can tell he studies a lot," Manning said. "There have been plenty of times where

Ray has called out the play we're running, and he's fairly accurate. If he's right, I'm not saying you can't execute the play, but it is extremely impressive the way he prepares for the mental aspect of it."

Rich Eisen, who worked with Lewis on *NFL Total Access*, described him as "soulful," "professional," and "charismatic." He tells a story in his book *Total Access* about how Lewis once insisted on teaching him how to tackle at the end of a segment at the Pro Bowl in Hawaii. "Ray Lewis, the most ferocious hitter of his day, suggested we grab a sand-filled tackling bag from the practice field and he'd teach me how to hit and wrap. Rod Woodson said he'd hold the bag while I hit it," recalled Eisen. "I leapt toward the Weebles-like bag and smoked it—and then went *through* it, flying toward the ground on the other side. I hit the grass and rolled over my right shoulder as my watchband unsnapped on my wrist." As Lewis doubled over in laughter, Eisen quickly leaped up. "'What time is it?' I yelled, mimicking the chant Lewis bellows out to his fellow Ravens before every game. Then I did the Terrell Owens eagle-flap dance as the show faded to black." When it turned out that Eisen had sprained his AC joint, he bragged to Lewis that he had "got injured" at the Pro Bowl. Lewis marveled, "All right, Rich!"

While Lewis has moved on from his troubling associations, thankfully he has not abandoned his gift for brash, honest opinions. In 2001 he told Mike Freeman of the *New York Times* that in terms of past middle linebackers "only a couple could play today. Nowadays the speed factor is almost out of control. You have running backs literally running 4.2 and 4.3 in the 40. And coaches tell you, 'Cover him.' I mean, do you really think Dick Butkus could cover Marshall Faulk one-on-one?"

In a tremendous image makeover, Ray Lewis has gone from accused murderer to popular spokesperson for companies such as EA Sports and Reebok. "He had made quite a comeback," said Bob Williams, CEO of Burns Sports & Celebrities. "A guy who was really persona non grata in terms of endorsements has turned it around in a big way."

As well, he has become a popular mentor to younger NFL players. "He's my spiritual father when I'm having problems," said Chad "Ocho Cinco" Johnson. "Ray has been there for me through everything." He has also made a strong effort to be actively involved in humanitarian projects. According to the Ravens' website, "Ray donates a tractor-trailer load of food and personal care boxes annually to 440 of Baltimore's neediest families to enjoy a Thanksgiving meal in the privacy of their homes." And while there are many who question his spiritual and moral conversion, he remains one of the most beloved figures in Baltimore. "It's hard to compare the Ravens' popularity with Baltimore's love affair with the Colts just yet because of the longevity factor," said Scott Garceau, Ravens radio announcer. "But I don't think the passion for the Ravens is any less. Ray Lewis and Todd Heap are just as popular today as Johnny Unitas and Raymond Berry 45 years ago."

Then Mike Haynes Said...

Intimidation comes in all forms. Mike Haynes is the proof. Since the 1960s, the Raiders' team has been about scaring opponents with the threat and use of force. It's been about delivering nasty, unforgiving licks that make you forget what year you're from. In other words, the Black and Silver had always been about the black and blue. But in the 1980s cornerback Mike Haynes showed you could put terror in the heart of wide receivers without ever laying a hand on them. Taking advantage of his lethal mix of size and quickness, he would blanket the wide receivers up and down the field. No amount of zig-zagging, shoulder fakes or sudden cuts could shake him loose. Going man-to-man against Haynes was like a slow suffocation where at the end you're as mentally beaten as you are physically. To Haynes, victory didn't come with a quick knockout, but through 60 minutes of relentless, tight coverage. As a Pro Bowl corner in New England and, later, a key member of the Raiders team that beat the Redskins in Super Bowl XVIII in Tampa in 1984, Haynes proved that a superior mind—not to mention strength and tireless stamina—often results in the worst abuse of all. We talked to the Hall of Fame player, who is now the NFL's VP of player and employee development, about the dangerous Hayes-Haynes tandem, the hit that paralyzed his good friend Darryl Stingley, and the vital need to invest in the growth of players away from the game.

In *Tales from the Patriots Sidelines*, former New England GM Patrick Sullivan told Michael Felger that he believed, in terms of pure talent, the 1976 team was the best in franchise history, even better than the Belichick-era teams. As somebody who played on the '76 Pats, do you agree?

That's a hard comparison to make because the game has changed in terms of the way that offenses play. But to say that, I think Patrick is saying that Bill Belichick is an even greater coach. Because that would mean we had the better athletes, but didn't have the same kind of success. For me, though, you have to look at the records. You compare the record during our time and the record during this time.

Did fans around the league treat you differently when in 1983 you went from the Patriots to the Raiders?

Well, I'll say this. When I played for the Raiders, people genuinely hated us. They *hated* us. I once played in a charity softball game in Kansas City. They had hats there for sale that said "Raider Hater," and they were selling out like crazy. And a woman came up to me and asked me to sign the brand new hat she had just purchased that said "Raider Hater" on it. I signed the hat for her, but I scratched the "Hater" part off. She was livid.

In New England, you were teammates with Darryl Stingley, who was paralyzed after taking a vicious hit from Jack Tatum. How did you and your teammates respond in the days and weeks following Darryl's accident?

Well, a lot of us would get together and pray for him. We all felt that Darryl would be healed and that he'd be able to walk again. We couldn't wait to see him, and we couldn't wait to get good news. It never came. We never got any good news.

When he finally did come back to the stadium in a wheelchair, it must have been emotional.

Oh, yeah. But he was high-spirited. I guess he had accepted what had happened in his life. He was not down. He was upbeat. In a lot of ways, his spirit and his emotion were what they had always been.

How hard was it to then go to the Raiders in '83 and be part of the same locker room as Jack Tatum?

Cornerback Mike Haynes blanketed receivers for seven years as a Raider and was inducted into the Pro Football Hall of Fame in 1997. Photo courtesy of Getty Images.

Darryl was a really good friend. We lived in the same little town in Massachusetts. We spent a lot of time together. We'd go to practice together. So it was tough to go to the Raiders. Had they still been in Oakland, I'm not sure I could have done it. I justified it by saying that, because they moved to Los Angeles, they were a new team. It wasn't the Oakland Raiders. It was the Los Angeles Raiders. That allowed me to at least go. But it also allowed me to start dealing with some of these issues.

What were those issues?

That one incident had a huge impact on me and the other players around the league. Then Tatum came out with a book, and the things he talked about trying to do on the field were things that a lot of defensive backs were trying to do; that defensive coordinators might have been encouraging players to do. They were things I was trying to do. I would say, "I'm going to try to knock this guy's lights out." Not that I did. But for me, that hit was the beginning of a change—how I approached the game, even how I approached life. Because it could have been me that made that hit. It could have been one of my teammates.

Did you ever speak with Tatum about the incident?

When I came to the Raiders, it was really important that I got a chance to talk to Jack.

A lot of people had the feeling after the incident that he would be proud of what he did. Meeting with him, I can tell you he *wasn't* proud of it. He was sick by it.

Did he explain to you why he didn't apologize in his book or visit Stingley in the hospital?

Basically, he was being counseled to stay away. I don't know if it was by legal people or not. He wanted to make contact, he expected to make contact. It might not have been such a great idea to come out with the book. It made people think he was doing things consistent with his bad-guy image. But after I had a chance to talk with him, I had a better understanding of who he was, and what he was thinking about when he wrote the book. Over time, Jack and I actually got to be very good friends. I would go golfing with him, and I did a lot of charitable functions with him. I know it's not water under the dam for a lot of Patriot fans, but for people who've talked to him, I think they have a better understanding.

What impact did that play have on the game itself?

I do think there was a time when guys would use their helmets as weapons. Back then, the attitude on defense was: we need to get a guy out of the game. Our best chance of winning is if he's not playing. So that meant hitting a guy in the head with your helmet. Or with your forearm. Using the momentum of your body. Now the league tries to educate players on those kinds of hits. Head-to-head contact is a very dangerous thing. You can hit somebody hard without putting their lights out.

Did all that booing bother you and rest of the Raiders?

I remember after we won the Super Bowl in 1983, the team had a banquet to celebrate. Al Davis was addressing us and he said, "All those boos are like cheers for the Raiders. Those boos are what keep you going. Those are what wind you up." After that, I kind of looked forward to the boos. I started seeing it as a sign of how much they respected the Raiders.

How did you get along with Al Davis?

I came to have a tremendous respect of Al Davis. The way he supported players, took on the league on a lot different issues, even the way I became a Raider. He wanted to win at all costs. He would bring in the right players and the right coaches so that the team could be successful. I wasn't used to that. During that time period, there were a lot of guys who were looking forward to one day playing for him. So I felt very privileged to be there. I don't always understand him. I don't always understand some of his moves. But I respect him.

I'm curious about your former Raiders teammate Lyle Alzado. He was a wild child. Super Bowl hero. Defensive Player of the Year. Movie star. But, ultimately, a poster child for excessive steroid use, which hastened his death at the age of 43.

I think it's terrible that when people talk about Lyle Alzado the only thing they talk about is his steroid use. He was a guy with a lot of different personalities. Believe it or not, we would have Bible study over at Lyle's house. He was a great father, a great husband, a great leader, and a great speaker. He was a role model for guys like Howie Long, Bill Pickel, and Greg Townsend. All these young Raiders looked to him for guidance. I'd even be willing to bet Howie would give Lyle a lot of credit for helping him to have a plan in life, knowing that you're not going to play forever. He had that kind of influence on people.

How did his steroid use affect his personality?

I saw how certain things would upset him, how he would go in a rage. Later, I learned that was all related to steroid usage. There was this woman, an artist, who had been following our team around all through training camp. She had been doing these little sketches of us. One day, during a preseason game, she was doing a sketch of Lyle sitting on his helmet with his knees up in his chest, watching the game. I walked over and saw what she was doing, and I said to her, "What is that?" She had drawn this thing on Lyle's hip. She said, "I don't know what that is." My guess is that's probably where he used to shoot himself up with steroids.

You and Lester "the Molester" Hayes are considered one of the all-time best cornerback combos in NFL history. Had you guys met before you came to the Raiders in '83? And how did you react to his severe stuttering problem?

I actually met him at the Pro Bowl in 1980, right after he and the Raiders had won the Super Bowl. All the defensive backs had their lockers near each other. I said to him, "Congratulations on such a great season." He took so long to answer that I thought he was blowing me off. But then he finally got out, "Thank you, big fella." It was apparent that, at least initially, I would need to have patience when talking to him.

But he was unabashed by his stutter. In fact, he was an incredibly funny, talkative guy. I heard his favorite subject was *Star Wars*, and that he had watched *The Empire Strikes Back* more than 300 times. Did you ever watch it with him?

(Laughs) No, I never did. But he talked about it constantly. As a matter of fact, when reporters interviewed him, he would say things like, "I talked to Luke, and he said we were going to win by three touchdowns."

I heard he also once declared, "I'm the only true Jedi in the National Football League." Any there any other players you would define as a true Jedi?

(Laughs) You would really have to ask him. But he would probably say there were Raiders like Ted Hendricks, Rod Martin, Mike Davis who knew about battling. Guys who were experts on warfare.

Those Raiders teams of the '70s and '80s have been called a "freewheeling cast of menacing oddballs and goofy misfits" that "unnerved the NFL with boozy escapades, dirty tricks, and bizarre bacchanals." Tell me about Camaraderie Night.

Every Thursday after practice we all went to a place on El Segundo called the Stick & Stein. It was a little local bar where you could get hamburgers and fries and beers. Players could unwind and have some fun together. Then the married guys would go home and a lot of the single guys would break off into different units—the offensive linemen, the defensive linemen, the defensive backs—and go to dinner together. Then, often times, we would meet up at a club or something like that, for those who wanted to continue the night.

As the NFL's VP of player development, you're on the other side now, trying to make sure players in the league stay out of trouble. That's obviously not the easiest task.

These guys are football players. That's the profession that they've chosen. But we ask them to be more than just great football players. We ask that when they step off the football field, they be great people. We ask them to be great role models, to be an example to others, and to promote our great game. Some guys do it willingly, successfully, and with pride. Other guys really struggle.

Why is it do you think certain players struggle?

I can talk to guys in their twenties who play in the NFL and already know that they're going to do the wrong thing. They know how they handle this one situation that could get them in trouble. They already know it. They say, if this person does this to me, then this is how I'm going to react. And there's nothing we can do but tell them, if you do it, you're going to jail. Then you talk to them when they're 35, and they've matured and they tell you how they would handle the problem differently. I'm just thankful that the NFL has an organization now, player development, that was created to help those kind of guys before those poor decisions are made. These same men that struggle when they're younger can become tremendous role models. They become great leaders.

Does O.J. Simpson, somebody who has tarnished his legacy with his actions off the field, deserve to be in the Hall of Fame?

Absolutely. Pick a famous artist. Leonardo da Vinci. We know him for his art. We recognize him for his talent. What he did away from his

Who's the Boz?

Mouthy mullet-sportin' draft bust **Brian Bosworth**, or "the Boz" as he anointed himself, was "one part Mr. T, one part Flock of Seagulls, and one part Hulk Hogan," at least according to Sportshair.com. The only two-time Butkus Award winner, given to the nation's top college linebacker, failed to live up to the initial hype he received when he burst onto the NFL scene in 1987.

His career lowlight as a Seattle Seahawk came that year in a *Monday Night Football* game against the Raiders. Seattle's defense was trying to stop the Raiders from scoring from the 2-yard line when rookie phenom Bo Jackson barreled over Bosworth like he was a stick figure on his way into the end zone and Raiders record book; he finished with 221 yards rushing in a 37–14 victory. "He knocked me on my butt," said Bosworth. "I'm sure they ran that one back a few times in the ABC booth." The Boz went on to play three injury-plagued seasons for the Seattle Seahawks—a total of 24 games—before hanging up his cleats, briefly reinventing himself as a Steven Seagal–wannabe in action flicks like *Stone Cold*, *One Tough Bastard*, and *Midnight Heat*.

art is not going to affect our opinion on that art. And so I think we have to separate what O.J. did on and off the field.

He was an outstanding football player, who in his time set records. He's in the Hall of Fame because of his ability to play football. Nobody likes the fact he's in prison now. Nobody likes all the incidents that have occurred during his lifetime. But there was a period of time that he played in the NFL and was one of the best ever. Off the field, there were a lot of challenges he wasn't able to overcome.

Do you understand why it's hard for people to give Michael Vick a second chance?

I'm not speaking for anyone else here. I'm not the commissioner of the NFL. I'm not an NFL owner. But if, for one moment, I can just be a guy who loves football and who also played the game, I think as long as he has the talent he should be able to use that talent. Michael Vick is an outstanding football player. There was a penalty for his off-field issues. He is paying that penalty. I don't know that people will ever be able to look at him the same way. But, hopefully, he'll get back to doing what he loves doing.

Steve Largent, Jerry Rice, Art Monk—how was each different to cover?

All three of those guys loved to compete. That's what I remember most about them. Art Monk: talented receiver. Strong. Fast. A great ability to get open. Steve Largent: not great size but unbelievable balance and shiftiness. Strong ankles. Great hands. Great concentration. A guy who loved to compete. Jerry Rice: a tall, strong wide receiver. Great hands, great concentration, and a real nice guy. He felt the ball should be thrown to him even if the defender was right on him. He made so many catches, I'd have to agree. He wasn't the fastest guy, but when the ball was in the air, he had world-class acceleration, like a sprinter. Larry Fitzgerald is the same kind of guy.

If you had to cover Fitzgerald, who's coming off a breakout season and terrific Super Bowl game, what would be your secret to shutting him down?

I wouldn't have any secrets. I don't know what I would do. A lot of times, if a defensive back has great coverage, he knows the quarterback is not going to throw it. The most important thing is to know that even if I had great coverage, Kurt Warner is still going to throw the ball to Fitzgerald. I think we saw that in the Super Bowl, that the Cardinals felt that if they just got the ball in his general area that somehow he was going to come up with it. I think he and Anquan Boldin are going to have big careers if they continue on the track they are on.

chapter 6

The Punishers: Offense

Great defensive players live to crush quarterbacks. They also delight in smashing ballcarriers, pulverizing receivers, and hammering tackles into the ground. From the early days of the NFL until the present, there's been a special breed of offensive player who hits every bit as hard and violently as the defense does—hey, they ask you, why should those guys have all the fun? These human sledgehammers deliver a wallop of jaw-breaking impact with every run, catch, and block. Rather than shy away from collisions, they actively seek them out. They meet each menacing glare with unflinching resolve, every snarling taunt with raw defiance. They don't just match their aggressors' toughness, they exceed it—pounding the rock, over and over again, until the defense is not just beaten but deflated. They achieve victory in merciless fashion, hammering away at the powerful enemy until they have broken their will. Few possess the strength, tenacity, and heart to turn the odds in their favor. Those who do belong to an elite club: offensive punishers.

Bronko Nagurski

There's no better example of the hunted becoming the hunter than Bronko Nagurski. The Chicago Bears' fullback, the heart and soul of the original Monsters of the Midway, who dominated the league in the 1930s, reduced the most intimidating tacklers of his era into trifling gnats. As the Bears' frequent opponents, the New York Giants were often on the receiving end of Bronko's bone-rattling punishment. "If you went at him low, he would stomp you to death," recalled Hall of Fame Giants linebacker Mel Hein. "If you went at him high, he just knocked you

Ghost Rider

In the 1920s Red "the Galloping Ghost" Grange, the son of a lumberjack, catapulted the NFL to national acclaim. Up to that point, the pro game was considered a joke compared to the wildly popular college game. As the league's first big attraction, the Chicago Bears' running back would travel around the country, drumming up interest with his daring feats of gridiron agility. As word of his legend spread, everyone wanted to see him up close. Even Babe Ruth once showed up to witness Grange's pro exploits, making an impromptu visit to his hotel room to meet the young star. "Kid," the slugger reportedly told him, "don't believe anything they write about you, and don't pick up too many dinner checks."

down and ran over you." Big Blue defender Benny Friedman described the joy of facing Nagurski in a game played at Wrigley Field in 1933, "Bronko split the middle of the line on the 22 [yard line] and broke into the open with only me between him and the goal. There were 50,000 people in the stands, but Bronko was such a frightening sight that my first impulse was to run away. I think I would've done it, too, if it hadn't been for a four-foot fence around the field that hemmed me in. I had no place to go but toward Bronko. It was like ordering a switchman to stop a locomotive with his bare hands."

So determined was New York Giants coach Steve Owen to stop this runaway train that one game he loaded the defensive line with as many players as he could—bringing up an extra linebacker to stuff the run. On the first play of the game, Nagurski took the hand-off. Owen recalled how his strategy didn't work quite as expected, "Two things happened that we hadn't counted on. One, Nagurski gained eight yards. Two, the linebacker had to be carted off the field." After that failed experiment, the opposing coach proclaimed there was only one way to stop Nagurski: "Shoot him before he leaves the clubhouse."

The late football legend was born in Ontario, Canada, in 1908 and raised in the small Minnesota town of International Falls, where he ran four miles each day, back and forth in the biting cold from his family farm to school. If that sounds like one of those tall tales, wait until you hear how University of Minnesota coach Clarence "Doc" Spears supposedly discovered Bronko. The story goes that the coach was traveling the state looking for recruits when he got lost down a dirt road in the north woods. He slowed his car when he spotted an unusual sight up ahead: a young man pushing a plow *without a horse*. "Which way to the nearest town?" inquired Spears. "Thataway," said Bronko, pointing one hand down the road while the other was holding up the plow. "Right then and there I signed him up at Minnesota," Spears recalled. "Anybody who could point with a plow would have to be a prospect."

Interestingly, Timothy Spears, the grandson of Doc Spears, claims that his grandfather denied ever telling the plow story and believes it's an urban myth invented to explain how "a Ukrainian football player as uniquely influential as Nagurski found his way from the coldest place in the nation to the University of Minnesota and then Chicago." Spears thinks the actual roots of the story can be traced to the legend of Paul Bunyan lifting his plow and ox around when he started a new row. "In 1937 the town of Bemidji [Minnesota] built two large statues of Bunyan and his ox to honor the local folklore and boost the region's sagging timber economy.... Not incidentally, Nagurski attended high school in Bemidji his senior year before going to the University of Minnesota...these gargantuan figures represent the populist spirit of the Midwest."

Nagurski was indeed a Midwestern hero by the time he left the University of Minnesota, where he became the only player in college history to make All-America the same year in two positions—fullback and tackle. Even his college coach, Bernie Bierman, perpetuated his superhuman reputation. One time, the Golden Gophers team was traveling to a game on a railroad when the train came to a jolting stop. Bierman exclaimed, "My God, Nagurski has tackled the train!"

Twenty pounds heavier than the average *lineman* of the era, the 6'2" fullback joined the Bears in 1930, where the legendary stories continued to pile up. One of the most famous is how during one play, Bronko broke a defender's shoulder and knocked another one unconscious while barreling into the end zone of a game in Wrigley Field. He was running with such straight-ahead ferocity that he collided into the goal post, spun around, and ran a few more feet into a concrete wall. That stopped him. Nagurski lay on his back, staring up at the sky. A teammate came over, looked at the wall, which now had a crack running down it. He heard Nagurski saying to him, as he slowly rose to his feet, "That last guy hit pretty hard."

It took no less than the Great Depression to slow his forward progress; despite quickly emerging as one of the league's top players, and leading the Bears to championships in 1932 and 1933, his salary was cut over a three-year period from $5,000 to $3,700. At the time, the services of agent Drew Rosenhaus were not available. His only choice was to take a second job. Which is why, in February of 1933, he stepped into the dangerous, seedy world of pro wrestling, where matches were often rigged, but the broken bones were real. With a towering size predating Ivan Drago, the Russian fighter in *Rocky IV* played by Dolph Lundgren, who, coincidentally, shares the same November birthday as Nagurski, he won his first match, against Tag Tagerson, in just four minutes. "His favorite move was the 'flying block,'" said Jim Dent, author of *Monster of the Midway*. "He would grab the upper rope in one hand and then slingshot himself across the ring like an arrow. He would slam into his opponent with an arm, a hip, a shoulder, or a leg, often plowing him under. He used the flying block on [Dean] Detton, who went down like a sack of dirt and was out cold for three minutes. When Detton woke up, he asked the referee, 'Who the hell hit me? No, what the hell hit me?'"

Nagurski continued to wrestle to make ends meet during the 1930s. Sometimes matches would cut into football season; nothing like throwing your body around the mat against some turn-buckle lunatic, and then rushing, blocking, *and* tackling for 60 minutes in the brutal cold of Green Bay, Wisconsin, on a football field as soft as concrete. Grumpy George Halas brooded that his star player was turning into one of the wrestling world's biggest draws; mostly because it meant he'd have to offer him more money. It didn't matter that Nagurski had silently accepted pay cuts since 1930; a $1,000 salary bump on his $5,000 rookie contract was not asking much. But Halas, stubborn as a mule, refused to budge on his offer, resulting in the *Chicago Tribune*'s shocking headline: "Nagurski Retires at Peak of Career." The city of Chicago went into mourning. Meanwhile, Nagurski left town to compete on the wrestling circuit, where he won three world titles. Back in Chicago, Halas waited to hear from his favorite player, but year after year went by without so much as a postcard or telegram.

Jim Dandy

Who was Wa-Tho-Huk? Well, many consider him the greatest football player, nay, athlete in history. To the millions of Americans in the first few decades of the 20th century who knew him as **Jim Thorpe**, he was an almost mythical figure.

His legendary exploits are many. Consider that he won both the pentathlon and decathlon at the Olympic Games in Sweden, and led the Carlisle Indian Industrial School football team to a national college championship—in the same year, 1912! Already a pro baseball outfielder, he turned to professional football in 1920, signing with the Canton Bulldogs for $250, a princely sum in those days.

Although "Wa-Tho-Huk" translated to "Bright Path," he fell from the heights of a ticker tape parade in New York City to being scandalized when his two gold medals were stripped from him. (He made a couple of lousy bucks as a poor Indian schoolboy.) After taking a beating on the football field until he was 40 years old, he became his own worst punisher, assuming the life of a brawlin', hard-drinkin' drifter living in a trailer. Also, the NFL was literally built on his iconic shoulders, yet sadly he would never win an NFL championship.

In 1954 the residents of Mauch Chunk, Pennsylvania, honored him by renaming the town after him, and finally in 1982 the Olympic governing committee restored his rightful gold medals—a bright ending for one of the men most essential to the astounding rise of the NFL over nearly 100 years.

Pro football was hit hard in the early '40s by the raging war against the Nazis. Many players were forced to report for combat, including more than half the Bears team. NFL bigwigs even talked of canceling the 1943 season, but after a few economic sacrifices, like Philadelphia and Pittsburgh merging to become the Steagles, the show went on. Even George Halas, who never got over the loss of Nagurski, often pointing out to his players how inferior they were compared to his former workhorse, reenlisted in the Navy. While serving as a commander in the South Pacific, he sent a cable back home, three months before the start of the season: SIGN NAGURSKI AND PAY FIVE THOUSAND. STOP. As Dent told it, "Naval decoders analyzed the message for days, wondering if Nagurski was a Japanese spy."

Battered by years of wrestling, and having missed most of the football season back in 1935 due to a broken back, Nagurski was rejected for military service. Thirteen years earlier, he had taken the league by storm;

now his knees and ankles were as brittle as dry twigs. But when the Bears called for him, Nagurski agreed to leave his family and his farm in International Falls and go forth to the field of battle for one more season. While the *Chicago Tribune* trumpeted the news—"The Old Hero Returns"—old foes met the news of a Nagurski comeback with a mix of despair and prayer. "God help us all," said Mel Hein.

As it turned out, their fears were unfounded: the old bull was relegated to defensive tackle, essentially acting as a symbolic figure for his younger teammates. "Of course, Nagurski wasn't really old at 35," said Jim Dent. "But the crooked nose, the bent fingers, the arthritic joints, and a degenerating hip belonged to a man perhaps twice his age."

In the 1943 season finale, a do-or-die game for the Bears (a playoff spot hung in the balance), they faced off against the crosstown rival Cardinals. Entering the final quarter, the Bears trailed by 10. With the team's fullback Bill Osmanksi having shipped off to the Navy, there was only one last hand to play. "As he removed the black cape and reached for his helmet," said Dent, "the fans at Comiskey Park saw the round stomach and bowed legs. A man in the fifth row behind the Bears bench dropped his flask and shouted, 'Omijesus, he's coming in!' A woman screamed. Then the rolling thunder returned, 'Bronko! Bronko! Bronko!'"

Once Nagurski entered the game, the Bears started feeding him the ball. Putting his shoulder down, he battered his way forward for the tough yards. Academy Award–winning screenwriter William Goldman of *Butch*

Sweet Rose

Though he's known as the ultimate power back of his era, when **Earl Campbell** kicked in the afterburners, he could blow past any defense. The Dolphins learned this when they faced the rookie on the evening of November 20, 1978, in what would become one of the most famous *Monday Night Football* games in history. The Houston Oilers had ridden their rookie workhouse all game long and clung to a 28–23 lead late in the fourth quarter. Everyone watched as the Texas Longhorns' legend known as "Tyler Rose" took the ball for the 28th and last time. As he raced up the sideline, past one diving Miami defender after another, the Astrodome crowd broke into deafening pandemonium. Eighty-one yards later he had a touchdown, and Houston had secured a thrilling victory. Tyler Rose was no longer just a college legend in Texas. He was now an NFL legend, as well.

Cassidy and the Sundance Kid, The Princess Bride, and *Misery* fame, who grew up in a Chicago suburb, recalled watching the scene unfold from the stands: "Again and again the old man gained. Nothing subtle about him, nothing cute—no cuts, no hip fakes—just power. Just legend trying to get along. The Cardinals dropped him on their 11 and waited, kneeling at the scrimmage line. This time as he charged them, they dropped him at the 8, and the play should have been over then. But it wasn't. The old man started to crawl. Clutching the ball, he crawled forward—from the 8 to the 7 to the 6 to the 5 to the 3. At the 1-yard line they all jumped on top and they stopped him. They piled off wearily now as the old man stood, shook himself, and went back to the huddle. The Cardinals dug in, slapping each other, shouting, building up confidence as they bunched at the center of the scrimmage line, waiting for him, for Nagurski. And he came, and they tried, holding him for that moment before they parted, and he was through, free and clear in the end zone."

Grinding ahead for the tying touchdown, and later setting up another, he carried the Bears to a dramatic 35–24 victory, sending fans racing onto the field to hoist the reluctant hero onto their shoulders. "The old man had gained 84 yards on 16 carries in the fourth quarter alone," Dent said. "They would never forget the day Bronko Nagurski came back."

Nagurski's amazing resurrection would culminate a few weeks later as he delivered a stellar performance against the Redskins in the NFL Championship Game. Bears quarterback Sid Luckman, the other hero of the game, told writer Paul Zimmerman, "They measured [Bronko] for a championship ring in 1943, when he made his comeback, and his ring size was 19½." It's reportedly the largest NFL championship ring ever measured. After the game, a proud Papa Bear declared Chicago's fourth title the return of the "terrible Bears." As for Nagurski, he quickly doused hopes for a full-scale comeback, telling the *Chicago Tribune,* "It's not a game for a 35-year-old, and I can't listen to George Halas songs all my life." Without much fanfare, he returned to his farm in the north woods. To his family. To his cattle. To his plow.

Jim Brown

Jim Brown dominated on the football field the way Muhammad Ali did in the boxing ring. The only difference was that every time Ali fought, he faced a guy who intended to beat him to a pulp; every time Brown suited up, he faced 12 of those guys. "I have never seen an athlete be as physically abused and still play at such a high level," recalled former owner Art Modell. "Things were done to Jim that today would lead to players getting arrested." Following a game in 1963, reporters gathered in the locker room around the game's hero, Jim Brown, when they noticed his eyes were all red and puffy. Brown told them it was nothing. The next week, on the set of his TV show, he confided to sportscaster Ken Coleman the reason for his battered eyes: "Whenever we got down into the infield part of the stadium, the Giants were throwing dirt in my eyes. Everything was blurry. They were trying to get me mad enough to get me into a fight and out of the game. I wouldn't fall for it." And so it went, the defenders would attack him like a gang of angry Mongols, Brown would come back at them like a tank. "Grab hold, hang on, and wait for help," was the advice on how to tackle Brown from Giants line-backer Sam Huff, whose legendary tussles with Brown became football's main event in the late '50s and early '60s.

It's not for no reason that the target of so many vicious gang tackles, cheap shots, and dirty tactics had a habit of getting up slowly. "He walked [back to the huddle] as if he were Walter Brennan carrying a safe on his back," recalled Coleman. "Jim would creak his way back to the huddle, and the opposing defense would think they had him. The fans wondered about his health. Was he out of breath? Was he hurt? You couldn't imagine he'd be back for one more play. But the Browns would huddle up, and Jim would take his place behind Milt Plum, Jim Ninowski, or Frank Ryan. On the next play, Jim would explode into the line with an energy that no one else on the field seemed to have late in the game. People remember the long, spectacular runs. I remember those tough, hard yards, and the fact that he got them when the team needed them most." The bruised and bloodied Brown didn't miss one game *or practice* over his entire nine-year career.

The story goes that Sam Huff, the meanest, toughest linebacker in the league, was ordered to hit Brown on every play, no matter if he touched the ball or not. Brown answered Huff like he did every other aggressor—with stoic revenge; the kind Clint Eastwood might inflict on a gang of dirty convicts. Recalling one of their early collisions, when he

Lowdown Game

Conrad Dobler believed in protecting his quarterback by any means necessary. Well, he never shot anybody, but he did once bite a man. It was during a 1974 game against the Vikings. The Cardinals' guard was trying to block Doug Sutherland, a member of Minnesota's legendary defensive line, the Purple People Eaters. "He put his fingers through my face mask, and I don't think they were there to stroke my mustache," Dobler told *Esquire* in 2000. "So I bite one finger in my life, and I don't even chew on it. The legend grew from there. It's almost like I'm worse than Jeffrey Dahmer."

Another time, at the conclusion of the regular season, Giants rookie Jim Pietrzak approached Dobler on the field to give him a handshake. "Good luck in the playoffs," he said. Dobler punched him in the throat. "Thanks," he replied.

was at West Virginia and Brown was at Syracuse (where he was also the nation's top lacrosse player), Huff said, "It was early in the third quarter, and here came Jim Brown through a hole, and there I was to meet him. I hit that big sucker head on, and my headgear snapped down and cut my nose, and my teeth hit together so hard the enamel popped off. He broke my nose, broke my teeth, and knocked me cold. I woke up in the training room with an ice pack on my head and my nose bleeding." Another time, in 1965, Dallas Cowboys corner Obert Logan tried to corral the much larger fullback. After Brown carried the poor defender for several yards, he grinned calmly at him, "Man, you just like chewing gum on my shoe."

After leading the league in rushing eight times in nine years, including a record five straight years, Brown set his sight on becoming the first black athlete to make it in Hollywood. Having already made a splash playing an ass-kicking sergeant in the western *Rio Conchos*, Brown flew to London in 1966 to star in the World War II action thriller *The Dirty Dozen*. "Jim Brown in *The Dirty Dozen*…that was the best when I was a kid," Spike Lee told the *New York Times*. "It was: 'Don't kill Jim Brown! Run, Jim! Run!' But, alas, he got it."

Brown's shooting schedule caused him to miss training camp that summer. An angry Art Modell responded by threatening to fine his star player $100 for each day he missed camp. Of course, Modell should have known better than throw dirt in the proud warrior's eyes—Brown

Despite retiring in 1965 at the age of 29, Jim Brown amassed 12,312 rushing yards for the Cleveland Browns.

told the owner to shove it. "Once Modell realized his mistake, he secretly attempted to woo Brown back," said writer Mike Freeman "[He] dispatched a friend and fellow owner to hunt down Brown on *The Dirty Dozen* set, talk with Brown, and discuss his return to football." But the damage was done, as Freeman explained, "Brown responded belligerently to any perceived challenge. To him, there was no difference between a linebacker attempting to tackle him and an owner trying to coerce him back into football." When in 1972 a reporter asked New York Giants defensive back Spider Lockhart how to stop Redskins star

Larry Brown, he answered, "Same way we stopped Jim Brown. Get him a movie contract."

Since, Modell has expressed regret for hastening Brown's retirement from football, but the truth is that Brown exited the stadium because his 30-year-old body had taken a beating. Even more so, it was Brown's unwavering belief that nobody should ever be satisfied, whether it was with their position in society or their performance on the football field. A man should always thirst for more. In fact, Brown would literally deprive himself of water during long, arduous practices just to put himself in an angry and restless mood before games. As time went on, Brown channeled his anger from linebackers toward racial injustice, even starting the Negro Industrial Economic Union to provide money and support to black-owned businesses.

One of the perks of being an outspoken activist of the early '60s was having J. Edgar Hoover open an FBI file on you. *Congratulations, Jim Brown.* One time, the FBI even sent two agents to sneak into the Hollywood premiere of *Rio Conchos* to keep tabs on the film's leading man. Tragically, Brown would squander his promising start in movies, alienating those in the industry with the same abrasive, anti-authority attitude that made him such a magnetic presence in films like *The Dirty Dozen* and the underrated *...tick...tick...tick....* Brown was quickly pigeonholed as a blacksploitation action hero. But when all is said and done, he broke color barriers in Hollywood in the same fearless, defiant way he broke through defensive lines—perhaps most daring in 1969 when he appeared in the first interracial love scene with Raquel Welch in *100 Rifles*.

By the late '60s, Brown had emerged as a powerful voice in the increasingly radical civil rights movement. One of his most courageous moments came in 1966, when he came to the aid of beleaguered boxer Muhammad Ali, who had touched off a national firestorm by refusing to go to Vietnam on moral grounds. That November Brown organized a press conference at the NIEU offices and gathered eight other high-profile black athletes, including Bill Russell and John Wooten. "I can't stress enough how controversial what Jim did was at the time," Wooten said, speaking of the now-infamous Ali Draft Summit. "There were a lot of people who hated Ali, and because Jim supported Ali, they now hated Jim. Jim really stuck his neck out."

Through their shared conviction, Brown and Ali forged a lifelong friendship. One time the two pals almost met in the ring. Originally, the idea was to have Ali fight basketball great Wilt Chamberlain, and Brown was to serve as manager. But once Ali's manager, Herbert Muhammad, got a good look at Chamberlain's towering frame as he stood next to the champ at a publicity shoot, he asked Brown if he wanted to fight Ali instead. "Nah, nah, nah," Brown told NBC's Graham Bensinger in 2008. "But Ali would want to wrestle with me to see his strength. Because I was stronger than he was. But it was always with a sense of laughter—most of the time. But, no, I never thought about fighting Ali. I couldn't box."

Sixteen years after retiring, Brown once again perceived a direct challenge to his manhood: this time from Steelers running back Franco Harris, who was talking about returning to the NFL to make an assault on Brown's then-record 12,312 yards rushing. Accusing Franco of prolonging his career just to break his record, Brown threatened to make a Nagurski-esque comeback to block the challenge. At age 48, he even challenged Harris, 34, to race him "any time and any place" in a 40-yard dash. "I will represent all the old and fat guys who still enjoy athletics," declared Brown. At the nationally televised event in Atlantic City in 1984, Franco whipped Brown, who pulled up lame halfway through the race. While Brown lost the contest, Franco's mediocre time of 5.16 did support Brown's argument about Franco sticking around past his expiration date.

> "I was captivated by him [Jim Brown]. More because of the things he did off the field. He would stand up for what he thought was right. A lot of times you wouldn't see that. Guys would take the punishment and suffer the indignities. He was a guy who stood up."
> —Mike Haynes

The other good news about Brown's aborted comeback: he wouldn't damage his 5.2 yards a carry average. And while he only played 118 games, he ran for at least 100 yards in 58 of them, including twice for a then-record 237 yards. Over his amazing nine-year career, the NFL's mightiest and most complex warrior rushed for more than 1,000 yards seven times, including a career high of 1,863 in 1963. He won the MVP award in 1957, 1958, and 1965, and many media outlets, including the AP and *Sporting News*, have rated him as the No. 1 greatest football player of all-time. "I absolutely unloaded on him," said oak-tree sized Hall of Famer Merlin Olsen of a hit he once put on Brown in L.A. Coliseum. "I mean *unloaded*. When I picked myself up after that hit, I assumed I would find Brown lying on the ground, with his eyes rolling around the back of his head. Far from it. I looked up and saw Jim still running down the sideline, going all the way for the touchdown!"

Mike Ditka

Fact: Chuck Norris once watched a video clip of Mike Ditka playing tight end for the Bears. He cried himself to sleep.

Okay, that's not technically true. It is true, however, that Ditka stormed the NFL like a one-man Delta Force, bulldozing his way over would-be tacklers with devastating stiff-arms and adrenaline-pumping fury. "He'd still be dragging people 10 to 12 yards downfield," recalled Tom Landry. Those opponents who looked into Mike Ditka's glaring eyes felt their blood run cold, but Ditka claimed his reputation as a gridiron bully is exaggerated: "I'm not mean at all. I just try to protect myself, and you'll notice I don't ever pick on anybody who has a number above 30."

What's amazing about Mike Ditka's becoming the first tight end to be inducted into the Hall of Fame is that he had never played the position until his rookie year in the pros. "I was lucky I was even selected by the Bears in the draft," recalled Ditka. "I didn't have an inkling at that time that Halas was going to make me a tight end—there were three other teams at the time who were very interested in me: the Pittsburgh Steelers, the Washington Redskins, and the San Francisco 49ers. If I was taken by any of them, I would have been a linebacker." Some might say that it didn't matter that he was switched to tight end—he still played like a hard-nosed, maniacal linebacker.

In fact, it was Ditka's reputation for playing every sport like a hard-nosed, maniacal linebacker that earned him the nicknames "the Hammer" and "Iron Mike" at the University of Pittsburgh. This even includes basketball, as Ditka explained: "When I see Jerry West [the Hall

Before coaching the Bears to victory in Super Bowl XX, Mike Ditka was a five-time Pro Bowl tight end during the 1960s. Photo courtesy of Getty Images.

of Fame guard from the Lakers who played college ball at West Virginia], I always remind him I was the guy who guarded him for six points and three fouls in a period of 51 seconds—his six points, my three fouls. He says, 'I thought you were going to kill me.' I say, 'I was trying but I couldn't get close enough.' There's another story of Ditka, then an assistant coach in Dallas, playing tennis against Tom Landry. According to Landry, he would slam his racket so frequently on the ground that it began to resemble an "aluminum pretzel."

The tight end's primary assignment was that of blocker in those days, so to use him as an offensive weapon was nothing short of revolutionary. In Ditka, Coach Halas had found perhaps the one player with the full package—speed, size, and hands—to carry out his vision. But even Halas had to be shocked at how quickly Ditka reinvented the position. By the end of his rookie year, Ditka had put up numbers that were unthinkable for a tight end: he caught 56 passes for 1,076 yards and 12 touchdowns. His 19.2 yards per catch would be impressive even for today's deep-threat receiver.

Believe it or not, before he was Iron Mike, the fire-breathing midway monster, he was a scrawny kid barely clinging onto a roster spot on his high school team. Son of an ex-Marine, Ditka grew up in a tough, blue-collar mining town in western Pennsylvania.

Ditka's signature play came in a game on November 24, 1963, two days after John Kennedy had been shot and killed in Dallas. With the entire country still deep in shock, commissioner Pete Rozelle made the controversial decision to go ahead with a full schedule of games. The Bears, fighting for a division crown in Pittsburgh, had the ball on their own 22-yard line, down 17–14 late in the fourth quarter. "I was dead tired," recalled Ditka, a home-state hero. "I came into the huddle, and [quarterback Bill] Wade asked me if I could run a deep pattern, and I said, 'No. Maybe I can hook up 10 yards, see what we can get out of it. But that's it." Wade connected with Ditka on a five-yard pass—Iron Mike took it from there. "With up to a half a dozen Steelers hanging onto him, he carried them a good 20 yards, maybe even farther, before they could drag him off his feet," marveled Steelers owner Art Rooney. "Incredible," remembered Bears flanker Johnny Morris. "He knocked down everybody who touched him. I remember feeling terribly disappointed when the last guy tackled him. If anybody deserved to go all the way, Mike did." While Ditka failed to score, his superhuman effort did not go unrewarded. His run set up a game-tying 18-yard field goal, giving them a half-point edge over the Packers in the final standings and a ticket to the NFL Championship Game, where the Bears defeated the Giants 14–10.

After a few down years with the Philadephia Eagles, Ditka looked to be washed up. Believing he still had some fire left in his belly, Tom Landry brought Ditka to Dallas. He rewarded Landry's faith by helping the Cowboys to their first ever Super Bowl, even catching the final touchdown in a 24–3 victory over the Dolphins. Teammate Walt Garrison recalled the time he got into a car-accident with Ditka after a typical night of raucous partying. "He got his teeth knocked out in the accident," said Garrison. "He went through the windshield and broke his jaw. The dentist told Ditka, 'We can wire your teeth shut, but you can't play tomorrow. Or we can pull them.' Ditka says, 'Pull the sonofabitches.' As it turned out they had to wire his jaw shut anyhow because it was broke. But he played all the same. You could hear him out on the field breathing through his teeth. 'Hiss-haw, hiss-haw, hiss-haw.' Sounded like a rabid hound. And you could hear that mad dog Ditka cussin' even with his mouth wired shut."

When Ditka took over as head coach of the Bears, he coached liked he was still wearing his helmet and pads. "In 1983, his second year leading the Bears, he had been so infuriated after a loss, he punched a filing cabinet with his right hand, breaking a bone in the process," said Rick Telander, cowriter on Ditka's autobiography *In Life, First You Kick Ass.* "At the next game he inspired his team by saying, 'Win one for Lefty.'" Another time Ditka told his team in the locker room before a game, "You worry about the playing, and I'll take care of the coach. I know I can kick his ass." The players cracked up, but the important thing was that the team reflected his tough swagger on the field that day, knocking their opponent all over the place.

In 1985 the Bears embarked on one of the wildest—and most dominant—seasons of any team in history. The eventual Super Bowl champs were littered with outrageous personalities like Jim "Punky QB" McMahon, Steve "Mongo" McMichael, and William "the

Justice Whizzer

Some players find themselves on the wrong side of the law. Former NFL star **Byron "Whizzer" White** was the law. When White joined the Pittsburgh Steelers in 1938, he got paid a $15,800 salary, making him the highest-paid player in NFL history. Although he won the rushing title his rookie year, he went off to Oxford on a Rhodes Scholarship. While studying at the prestigious institution, he would meet a young classmate, whose father was the U.S. ambassador to the United Kingdom.

Later, as a World War II navy officer, White cowrote the official report of the famous PT-109 incident, where John F. Kennedy reportedly saved the other members of his sinking ship, earning him national war hero status. Nineteen years later, in 1962, President Kennedy appointed his friend to the Supreme Court, where he spent 31 years ruling on America's biggest cases. For all his lofty accomplishments, White could never shake the nickname, disliked ever since a newspaper scribe gave it to him back when he was a Heisman candidate at the University of Colorado. Once, in 1961, White, then a deputy attorney general, was eating lunch in a D.C. restaurant when a waitress approached. "Say, aren't you Whizzer White?" she asked him. "I was," he retorted.

Refrigerator" Perry, but nobody captured the public's imagination more than Da Coach. Ditka's tough-guy persona and sideline explosions made him a beloved figure in the Windy City, even inspiring a hilarious *Saturday Night Live* skit starring Chris Farley and George Wendt as thick-mustachioed, kielbasa-eating Ditka disciples. "We call him 'Sybil' after the girl in that movie," recalled the rebellious McMahon. "You know, the one who had all those different personalities. Mike will be calm one minute, then throw a clipboard the next. People don't understand that, but we do. The players figure he's just going from one stage to another. He's merely 'Sybilizing.'"

Ditka mellowed over the years, using his trademark wit to reinvent himself as an entertaining TV analyst and popular pitchman for everything from Coors beer to erectile dysfunction pill Levitra. He has also been a committed leader to get much-needed medical benefits to retired NFL players. His straight-up, no-nonsense perspective on life has made Da' Coach an unexpected source of wisdom, with favorite sayings such as, "Before you can win, you have to believe you are worthy," and, "If you're not in the parade, you watch the parade. That's life." But his charming ability to peacefully accept life without accepting a too peaceful life is best reflected in this quote: "I always tell people I want to live to be 150, and they say, 'Why would you want to do that?' I say, 'Well there's a few people I haven't made mad yet. I want to get them.'" He will, after all, always be Iron Mike. The same man who once chased Chuck Norris' beard off his face with a hard stare.

Walter Payton

Walter Payton should have come with a disclaimer. Marvel at the grace with which he cuts on a dime, and then bursts through an open seem. However, those attempting to tackle him may suffer such side effects as bruising of the face, battered limbs, trouble remaining upright, and shock-induced diarrhea. "For Walter, it very seldom looked easy for him," said his former coach Ditka. "He was always knocking people down, running through people, breaking tackles. He was always busting, kicking, scratching, banging."

While Payton was not the biggest or fastest running back, he made up for these deficiencies with furious striking power. "He took a lot of pounding," said McMahon "But he dished out a lot of pounding, just like Jim Brown used to do. He's a solid rock coming at you." While the threat of Franco Harris breaking his record angered him, the Cleveland Browns legend had nothing but glowing reviews for Sweetness, who passed his record mark in 1984. "He would fight you for every inch, all day long," said Brown. Years later, when former teammate Jeff Fisher became coach of the Tennessee Titans, he'd tell each of his defensive backs the same thing: "You better be careful when going for Walter near the sideline because I've seen him knock out defensive backs with a forearm, and he's not going to go out of bounds. Better take him low, and good luck."

Getting Payton down was no easy task—unless, of course, you were carrying a shotgun. The story goes that Payton, an avid hunter, would bring players up to his camp in the Wisconsin woods to shoot birds. "One time we took one player, and he couldn't hit nothing," recalled fellow Bears running back Roland Harper. "Finally we came on a bird that wouldn't take off. It was just running around on the ground. He was chasing it with the barrel of the gun up, just waiting for it to take off so he could shoot. The pheasant started running right towards me and Walter, and we looked up just in time to see this guy coming at us pointing his gun. We hit the floor so fast it hurt. Sometimes it's a miracle we made it back."

Astonishingly, despite his aggressive style of running, the nine-time Pro Bowl selection missed only one game in his 13-year career. "Shit, I've missed eight games a year," said McMahon. Years later, Jeff Fisher recounted Payton's work ethic to his Tennessee team: "I refer to him probably three or four times a year to my players, usually when it's right before a game and a player is knocked down with something like the flu or food poisoning. That's when I tell them about the time Walter set the NFL single-game rushing mark (275 yards against the Vikings) with a temperature of more than 102 and being sick to his stomach. When I bring that up, I always get a smile from the player I'm telling this to, letting him know that it's possible to play when you're sick."

Payton's durability is more amazing because he didn't take any downs off, rather he threw himself into every play, even if he wasn't running the ball. "If you ask other coaches around the league who watched Walter Payton block, they'd say he was the best blocker by far that they've ever seen at running back. He got the job done. As a receiver coming out of the backfield, or throwing the ball, or carrying out a fake, or chasing down the opponent on an interception or fumble. He did everything." That even included taking over signal-calling duties. In 1984 the Bears were hit with a rash of injuries at quarterback. It got so bad that, in the first half of a game against the Packers, Ditka inserted Payton into the shotgun. He took six snaps: one incomplete pass, one interception, and four rushes for 25 yards. "I wouldn't want to do it for a living," Payton declared after the game. His teammates were a little more impressed with his spell at QB. "He took charge," said center Jay Hilgenberg. "One time he said, 'Screen left to Cal over there.' The rest of the time he had it all right." Defensive tackle Jim Osborne added, "The man can do everything. His first year, I saw him catch a punt in practice—behind his back. He was doing it as though he does it all the time."

Emmitt Smith might have won the disco-ball trophy for winning *Dancing with the Stars*, but when it comes to pulling off the slickest and most stylish moves, you gotta add some Sweetness. Long before Walter Payton was pirouetting out of tackles, he was showing off his fancy footwork on the dance floor. He's even credited with creating one of the first ever hip-hop moves, which he called—wait for it—the Cock Walk. "As a [high school] sophomore," explained Don Yaeger, coauthor of Payton's autobiography *Never Die Easy*, "he even entered a local dance contest, which was broadcast on a Jackson TV show called *24 Karat Black Gold*. Walter and his partner performed the 'Cock Walk,' a forefather to today's hip-hop moves, and won the contest. That earned the two of them a free trip to Los Angeles, where they appeared on the legendary show *Soul Train*. Walter and his dance moves were broadcast nationally in the *Soul Train* line long before he became a household name as a running back."

As a kid, Payton called himself Spider Man. It makes sense therefore that as a player Payton wouldn't want to draw attention to his superhuman exploits, none more heroic than the time he captured the all-time rushing record. ESPN'S Rick Weinberg recalls witnessing the glorious six-yard carry against the New Orleans Saints at Soldier Field on October 7, 1984, "Payton bounces right up from the grass, as he always does, shakes the hands of Suhey and Bortz and the rest of teammates, and then waves to the 53,752 fans surrounding him. The game stops. An official quickly races over to pick up the ball and hands it to Payton, who is then engulfed by his teammates and even several Saints. Payton walks over to the Saints' sideline and shakes the hand of Bum Phillips, the Saints coach. Then he walks the ball off to the sideline, hands the ball to Pete Elliott of the Pro Football Hall of Fame, then asks everyone to get off the field. 'I didn't want to stop the game and stop our momentum,' Payton would say later. 'The thing I was thinking about most was getting the photographers off the field and to start playing again so maybe we could get a quick score. We didn't have enough points. I wanted to get everybody off the field so we could score some more.' As the Bears return to the huddle, Payton tells his teammates, 'Forget the record. Just go for the win.'"

Later in the game, Payton would shatter Brown's record of 58 games rushing for at least 100 yards. But perhaps his finest moment was the heartfelt locker room speech he gave after the game to the surrounding media: "The motivating factor for me has been the athletes who have tried for the record and failed and those who didn't have an opportunity, such as David Overstreet and Joe Delaney and Brian Piccolo [players who suffered tragedy and death].... It's a tribute to them and an honor for me to bestow this honor on them." But he wasn't quite done yet, as Bears historian Roy Taylor explained, "Injecting his typical playful antics into the day, Payton finished his postgame press conference by speaking to President Reagan and asking him to give his best regards to Nancy."

Payton's shy nature—he was a serious loner as a kid—made him uneasy around those he didn't know, especially those in the media, but with his teammates, it was quite a different story. With his football mates, he was known as a high-energy prankster, quick with a funny quip or a wild scheme. Many of his local friends and teammates recalled getting stung by Payton's infamous phone pranks. One such victim was hunting buddy Ralph Cianciarulo. "I had gotten married in 1993," Cianciarulo recalled, "and he would call up Vickie because Vickie didn't really know him at the time, and in his high-pitched voice he goes, 'Is Ralph there?' And Vicky is like, 'Who's this?' And he would go, 'Is Ralph there?' And again, she would go, 'Who is this?' Then he would say, 'If he

A Noble Sacrifice

In 2004 **Pat Tillman** became the first NFL player killed in combat since 1970. While his name is less known, **Bob Kalsu**'s sacrifice is equally noble. The Bills didn't take him until the eighth round of the 1968 AFL-NFL Draft but, against all odds, he became the team's top rookie. After the season was over, Kalsu entered the army to satisfy his ROTC obligation. In November of 1969 he found himself on the frontlines of the bloody battle in Southeast Asia.

"I am proud to say that I served under Lt. James [Robert] Kalsu at Firebase Arsenal in 1970," said Dr. Larry Taylor, a former gunny. "We had a ground attack by enemy sappers one night, and the whole hill was lit up with everyone running pell-mell to their posts. Lt. Kalsu made his rounds during the night, seeing to everyone's security and was very much in control of the situation. He never barked out orders that I can remember, but carried a voice of authority that was matched by his character and genuineness as 'one of the men.' I was stunned by hearing he was killed."

The day his wife received word of his death, she was lying in her hospital bed, having just given birth to their second child. While 19 NFL players were killed in World War II, the Vietnam conflict took but a single life: first lieutenant Bob Kalsu.

ain't there, would you please tell him for me that he left his underwear here?' That was Walter, always kidding around." His teammates were not immune either, as Matt Suhey explained, "Once the guys were able to convince their wives it was Walter playing a prank, the wives would say, 'Jeez, who is this guy?' He did it to Calvin Thomas and almost got Calvin Thomas divorced or killed."

From the time he played for the first integrated football team in his hometown to his time as leader of the Bears' clubhouse, Payton had shown a special ability to forge bonds between people who might not normally be friends, let alone be on speaking terms. Perhaps nobody had traveled more different paths than Payton and his new running partner in 1980, fullback Matt Suhey, a product of hallowed Penn State. "We were Ebony and Ivory before Stevie Wonder and Paul McCartney," recalled Payton. "I think our relationship really broke down a lot of lines, a lot of racial lines, on the team and, some said, in the city. Here were two guys who had to have each other, and everything just clicked. Remember, I came from an all-black college in the Deep South. Matt was one of the first white guys I really got to know.... Without sports, how would I have ever met a guy like Matt? I probably wouldn't have. And he turns out to be one of the best friends I've ever had."

On the field Payton was as tough and hard-nosed as anyone who played the game, but off the field he displayed uncommon humility, opening his big heart to people of all stripes of life—it could be showing up early in the locker room to comfort a kicker who had just been cut after 10 years on the job or palling around with a young cancer-stricken fan before practice. "Walter sat down on the [blocking] dummy, and the kid sat down facing him," recalled Bears administrator Bill McGrane, who watched from the fence. "And Walter real, real quickly snatched this kid up and snapped a baseball cap off this kid's head and put his helmet on him. And then he put the cap on. And they talked for 15 minutes or so, and that was that. And the kid died in the fall, his parents called and told us. And I told Walter, he said, 'It's okay, it's okay. We talked, and he was okay with this.'"

Cruel irony would strike when in 1999 Payton announced that he had a rare form of liver disease. Despite his illness, he did everything in his power to protect his beloved wife, Connie, and two children, Brittney and Jarrett, from the media's morbid curiosity. He even managed to hold onto his wonderful sense of humor with friends and family. "I started joking with Matt [Suhey] about how in *Brian's Song*, the movie about Brian Piccolo and Gale Sayers, they had a relationship like ours," wrote Payton in his autobiography. "But in that one, the white guy gets sick and dies. I said I wondered how come I couldn't have been in that movie." Suhey frequently visited him and his family in the hospital until the very end. On November 1, 1999, nearly 12 years after retiring from the game, No. 34 lost his battle to bile duct cancer. While his sudden and unexpected passing saddened millions, his family set up a fund in his name, which has since raised huge amounts of money for cancer research. Additionally, the courageous way he conducted himself as a player, a father, and a friend has served as a powerful inspiration to millions. "Never die easy," Payton said, recalling the words of his college coach. "Why run out of bounds and die easy? Make the linebacker pay. It carries into all facets of your life. It's okay to lose, to die, but don't die without trying, without giving it your best." Sweetness had done just that.

In other words, he was okay.

Anthony Munoz

Of the young men who've dreamed of NFL stardom, there are thousands for whom that dream was robbed, in a cruel twist of fate, by injury. Anthony Munoz should have been one of them. Instead, he went on to become the greatest lineman in NFL history.

The hope of every kid from L.A. who plays football is to become a USC Trojan and win the big game, the Rose Bowl. But for a kid like Anthony Munoz, growing up in a drug- and gang-infested part of Los Angeles, devoid of a father to teach him how to throw a block, the only thing greater than the obstacles in his path were the stakes should he fail. Refusing to be denied, Munoz dedicated himself to excellence in the classroom and on the football field. His drive and discipline were rewarded with a scholarship to the University of Southern California.

Nine games into his freshman season at USC, Munoz sustained a serious injury to his right knee, requiring surgery. During his rehab, he made two discoveries that would sustain his faith in the dark times ahead: first, he found a spiritual purpose in life beyond football and, second, he

Protect and Serve

If you've ever wondered if any American has enjoyed the kind of protection that the secret service provides the president, the answer might be **Dan Marino**. Over the course of the 1988 season, his offensive line allowed the Dolphins' quarterback to be sacked a total of six times, the fewest number in NFL history. Even more amazing, the unit didn't include one Pro Bowler, and starting center Dwight Stephenson was MIA that season with a knee injury that ended his career. While one could argue that Dan Marino's lightning-quick release kept him upright, Paul Zimmerman, writing in *Sports Illustrated* back in '88, made this case for the big guys up front: "Well, he also throws off a deep drop on occasion, which means the offensive line has to hold its blocks an extra couple of seconds, and opponents use all sorts of intricate schemes to put pressure on him." And why not give the least recognized group in the NFL their moment to shine?

fell in love with a girl named Dee-Dee, whom he met during a pick-up softball game in which he robbed her of several base hits.

His junior year, Munoz started out like a house on fire, quickly emerging as a candidate for the Outland Trophy, awarded to the nation's top lineman. Then, in the seventh game, he suffered a second injury to his right knee. More torn ligaments. Another surgery. A second Rose Bowl missed. Munoz came back his senior year ready to dominate, only to suffer a nightmare in the season opener: he ripped up the ligaments in his left knee. Doctors would have to perform a third knee operation.

After waking up in the hospital with a cast on his leg, he was greeted by a local TV sports anchor by the name of Bryant Gumbel. As Gumbel brought the microphone forward, he asked, "Anthony, when are you going to quit? When are you going to give up? This is ridiculous. This is your third knee surgery. Why are you going through all of this?"

Munoz had a look in his eyes. Punishers don't quit. They fight.

Still, Dee-Dee was worried that Munoz was getting his hopes up only to have them crushed. After all, the Rose Bowl was only a few months away, and that's if USC even made it to the big game. "Anthony came home from the hospital and started jumping rope on one leg with the cast still on the other leg," recalled Dee-Dee. "He started lifting weights before the cast came off, and was running as soon as it came off."

With Dee-Dee by his side, and a fierce desire to make it to the Rose Bowl, he battled through weeks of excruciating physical therapy. But when Munoz went to tell his coach, John Robinson, he was ready to suit up, Robinson responded with laughter, "Yeah, we'll put you in at wide receiver." Munoz went home and cried.

On New Year's Day in 1980, USC faced an undefeated Ohio State team in the Rose Bowl. Robinson, running low on available tackles, decided to send Munoz into the game. Once Munoz got his shot, he started busting open lanes for tailback Charles White like a man possessed. Down 16–10, the Trojans tried to stage a comeback in the fourth quarter. The hand-off went to Charles White. As he rushed with the ball, Munoz delivered a punishing block on an Ohio State defender, allowing White to break free for the game-winning touchdown.

Not until late in his career at USC did Munoz even consider playing in the pros, but now it was all he could think about. Then came yet another setback: he failed physical exams for 14 different NFL teams. One of the doctors who gave Munoz a failing grade was Dr. Pierce Scranton, the team physician for the Seattle Seahawks for more than 18 years. "Five knee operations!" Scranton marveled. "There was a good chance his injuries had diminished his potential playing time and shortened his career. Worst-case scenario: maybe he would hurt his gimp knee in his first training camp. Maybe he would never play a down in the NFL. There were plenty of snickers among the combine doctors when the Cincinnati Bengals took Munoz in the first round of the 1980 draft."

Luckily for Munoz, Cincinnati Bengals founder and GM Paul Brown happened to be in Pasadena on New Year's Day in 1980 to witness Munoz's heroic performance. To follow up on his hunch, Brown sent his new head coach out to USC to check out Munoz for himself. In a twist of fate, the head coach was none other than Forest Gregg, the legendary Green Bay Packers lineman from the '50s and '60s, whom Vince Lombardi once called "the greatest athlete I ever coached." After Gregg arrived on campus, he brought Munoz down to the field. He then faced the senior and told him to try to stop him. Sure, Gregg had a few years on him, but still, this was maybe the greatest ever to play the tackle position. After Munoz stopped him a few times in a row, Gregg decided to catch him off guard with a quick, veteran move. "I rushed like I was going inside and then went outside on him. He reacted like a football player would. He jammed me on the chest with both hands and knocked me on my rear. He was very apologetic, and I said, 'No, no, no, you did what you were supposed to do,'" Gregg recalled. "I thought, *We've got to have this guy.*" On draft day in 1980, the Bengals ignored the warnings, selecting Munoz as the third-overall pick.

In Cincinnati, Munoz would quickly become a quarterback's best friend: the year before he arrived in Cincy, Ken Anderson and the other Bengals quarterbacks were sacked 63 times, compared to only 37 when Munoz started blocking for them in 1980. Later, he would be Boomer Esiason's personal bodyguard on the left side. "If I were as good at my position as Anthony is at his," Esiason said, "then I'd be 10 times better than Joe Montana."

Some punishers growl and scowl and spit blood, but Munoz bull-rushed defenders like Jason or Michael Myers, silently, relentlessly, efficiently. Recent Hall of Fame inductee Bruce Smith recalled how Munoz didn't trash-talk in the heat of battle. In fact, Smith said he only remembered Munoz speaking up one time. "I think it was after he stuck his hand in my face mask," recalled Smith. "He said, 'I'm sorry.'" Then Smith went on to pay him the highest compliment: "There are no comparisons between him and other tackles. He's proven it year after year that he's the best."

Munoz's superb play at left tackle was the foundation for Cincinnati's three AFC Central Division titles and two Super Bowl appearances in eight years. Fittingly, in 1981 he helped make Forest Gregg only the second person ever to play in a Super Bowl and then later be a head coach in one. Although the Bengals lost Super Bowl XVI to the Montana-led 49ers, they mounted a valiant comeback, down 20–0 but losing in the end 26–21. "After Munoz spent more than a decade in professional football and made 11 appearances in the Pro Bowl, Cincinnati got the last laugh," recalled Dr. Scranton. "Some of the things we can't measure at combines are heart, confidence, focus, and determination. Every draft day since 1980, Chuck Knox was kind enough to point out that I had flunked Anthony Munoz. Medicine is not an exact science."

Not exact, indeed. Munoz would go onto become the most consistent protector of the 1980s, starting 147 of 148 games in that 10-year span. "When Anthony came here," said his former offensive line coach Jim McNally in 1990, a decade into the tackle's career, "most of the defensive ends were 250 pounds. Anthony would get 15 to 20 of what we call 'pancakes' in a game. That's when you drive the guy off his feet, and he winds up on his butt. Now, most of the ends are going 280. So Anthony might get only five or six pancakes a game. But I don't see where he's lost anything."

In 1998 Munoz became the first Latin player to be inducted into the Pro Football Hall of Fame. "Todavia no lo creo. Es un honor increíble [I still don't believe it. It's an incredible honor]," declared Munoz. In addition to receiving the Hispanic Heritage Award in 1999, Munoz has been recognized several times for his tireless charitable works, during and after his playing days. His Anthony Munoz Foundation has raised more than $5 million for kids in Cincinnati and the Tri-State region, and he has traveled the country speaking to military units as well as going to small towns in Mexico to assist in football camps. Striving to become an active leader, despite his status as a Hispanic minority in a mostly white area, he and his wife, Dee-Dee, helped found the Hope Evangelical Free

Twice the Action Jackson

College athletes who play multiple sports know that once they go pro, they have to pick one. **Bo Jackson** knows better. Which is why, in the middle of the baseball season, the Kansas City Royals outfielder signed a contract to play for the Raiders.

As Jonathan Rand wrote in *300 Pounds of Attitude*, Jackson explained the move to his Royals teammates this way: "Football's my hobby, like hunting and fishing." When a reporter asked his teammate Willie Wilson about the comment, he said, "How can having Howie Long running into you be a hobby?" When the Raiders' defensive great heard what Jackson had said, he shot back, "It's like *One Flew Over the Cuckoo's Nest*. Bo must have had a frontal and rear lobotomy."

But from the fall of 1987 to the winter of 1991, he pulled off the most successful two-sport run since Jim Thorpe. Even working part-time for the Raiders, he managed plenty of pyrotechnics. In 1987, just a month into his pro career, he scintillated *Monday Night Football* viewers, abusing the Seattle defense for 221 yards rushing. During the game, he ripped off a 91-yard run. Two years later he had a 92-yarder against the Bengals, making him the only player in NFL history to register two rushing touchdowns of 90 yards or more.

Church in Mason, Ohio. "If pro sports could point to one guy who would be the ideal to look up to, Anthony would be it," says his former head coach Sam Wyche. "All of us try to set examples until something goes wrong, and then we reveal our true selves. Anthony's real self is the one the rest of us try to be."

Then Sal Paolantonio Said...

Among the greatest Super Bowls of all-time, where would you rank the epic clash between the Pittsburgh Steelers and the Arizona Cardinals in the 2009 Super Bowl?

I think it ranks as the fourth-greatest Super Bowl of all-time. The greatest Super Bowl ever was, without a doubt, Patriots versus Giants in Super Bowl XLII [2008]. The Patriots were undefeated. The Giants were severe underdogs. And they beat what was arguably the best regular season team of all-time. I think the second greatest of all-time was Super Bowl III [1969]. The third would have to be Super Bowl XXXVI [2002], when the Patriots beat the St. Louis Rams. New England was an 18-point underdog in that game. Last year's would be fourth, and the fifth greatest would be the 49ers beating the Bengals in Super Bowl XVI in 1982.

You wrote in your 2007 book *The Sal Paolantonio Report* that you believed the 1985 Chicago Bears were one of the most overrated Super Bowl teams?

They were a great team. They are currently one of the 10 greatest teams of all-time, but a lot of people have them one or two. I don't, for a number of reasons. On their road to the Super Bowl they played some really bad teams. They played the L.A. Rams in the NFC Championship Game. The Rams' quarterback, Dieter Brock, has never been heard from, before or since. The Rams were a horrible team. That year the Bears played arguably one of the worst Super Bowl teams of all-time in the New England Patriots, where their quarterback, Tony Eason, got benched in the middle of the first half. And what's more, that Bears team was supposed to have been built to last, and they only won one Super Bowl. In fact, they only appeared in one Super Bowl. And in the 1980s, at a time before the salary-cap and free agency, when other NFC teams

Sal Paolantonio has been covering the NFL and interviewing the game's biggest stars for ESPN since 1995. Photo courtesy of Getty Images.

like the 49ers, the Cowboys, the Giants, and the Redskins were building dynasties, the Bears were one and done. This is not a knock on the Bears—they had one of the all-time greatest defenses—it's a knock on the media for over-hyping and over-elevating them.

After your book came out, did you call in sick to work for the next several months, knowing you'd probably run into Coach Ditka in the halls of the ESPN offices?

I know he's not happy about it.

Did he tell you that?

I have not spoken to him about it, but I've heard through various people that he was not happy about it.

Mike Ditka feuded famously with his defensive coordinator Buddy Ryan. What do you think is the all-time best NFL feud?

Ditka and Buddy were both taciturn individuals who were both looking for equal parts credit for what was going on in Chicago, and I think Ditka was always jealous that Buddy got a lot more credit than perhaps Ditka thought he deserved to have, and Buddy was always envious of Ditka for getting more credit then perhaps he thought Ditka deserved to have. But the greatest feud of all-time has to be now with Bill Belichick and Eric Mangini. Here was the son growing up to betray the father. That's Shakespearean. That's Richard III stuff. Here Belichick had groomed Mangini from the time he was making copies in the press room with the Cleveland Browns. Brings him under his wing, teaches him everything he knows about evaluating football players, and how to do the job. Brings him to New England. Makes him the defensive backs coach, the most coveted job to Belichick; that's what he did under Bill Parcells in New England. Then makes him defensive coordinator. Tells him, don't go to the Jets. Mangini goes to the Jets, and once he's there he turns Belichick's organization in for spying, something Mangini did when he was with the Patriots. That's a nasty feud.

The son betraying the father. Sounds like Luke Skywalker and Darth Vader.

Oh yeah, it's George Lucas material.

Except that Bill Belichick hasn't cut off Mangini's arm yet.

No. And Mangini hasn't had to save Belichick from the evil lord emperor.

Who I guess would be Robert Kraft?

Yes, it would. *(laughs)*

Who do you think was the most underrated Super Bowl team?

The 1976 Oakland Raiders. Without a doubt. They should be considered in the top five all-time.

What's the case for them?

They had eight players and coaches on that team go to the Hall of Fame. No other Super Bowl team is even close. They had to beat two of the greatest defenses of all-time to get there. The Steel Curtain and the Purple People Eaters. They only lost one game that year, the same number that the Chicago Bears lost in 1985. The '76 Raiders beat a phenomenal football team in the AFC Championship Game, the Steel Curtain–era Steelers; the '85 Bears played the Rams in the NFC Championship Game, a joke. The '76 Raiders should be in the same conversation as the '85 Bears, and they're not. They're a very, very underrated Super Bowl team.

I have a section on the all-time greatest defensive punishers. Huff, Nitschke, Marchetti, Butkus, Jones, Tatum, Greene, Lambert, Taylor, and Lewis. What do you think?
Sam Huff should not be on your list. Was he a great linebacker? Yes. Was he a Hall of Fame linebacker? Yes. Was he one of the 10 best linebackers of all-time, not even close. No way.

Why do you think he's such an overrated linebacker?
He was the beneficiary of some genius marketing by the Giants. And then Paul Brown drafted Jim Brown, who made Sam Huff look like a child.

So who do you think is the greatest defensive punisher of all-time?
I think the top punisher is Dick Butkus, number one. He put real fear in the mind of the offensive player. You did not want to get hit by him. He was menacing. I would say Ray Lewis, number two, and Lawrence Taylor, number three.

How come Ray Lewis deserves to be ranked over Lawrence Taylor?
He's just as fast as Lawrence Taylor but more powerful.

Who was a better running back, Emmitt Smith or Barry Sanders?
Emmitt Smith, in my opinion, is far and away a better back. He did it when it counted. Barry Sanders is the most overrated Hall of Famer of all-time.

Couldn't you argue that Barry Sanders didn't have the supporting cast to get him to the big game?

That's not true. Barry Sanders had one of the greatest offenses ever put together. In 1995 they had three great wide receivers: Herman Moore, Brett Perriman, and Johnnie Morton. Scott Mitchell was the quarterback. And Barry Sanders performed horribly in the playoffs [against the Eagles] with a great offensive team.

Which of these quarterbacks do you think will become a great champion quarterback: Matt Ryan, Jay Cutler, Joe Flacco, or Sam Bradford?

I think only one—Matt Ryan. He has great accuracy, poise, and leadership ability. He's smart. He has great character. Players immediately gravitate toward him. Like Joe Montana. Like Tom Brady.

sources

NFL Films
NFL.com
ProFootballHOF.com
Pro-Football-Reference.com
SI.com
ESPN.com
NBC.com
SportingNews.com
NYTimes.com
ChicagoTribune.com
BleacherReport.com
Sports.Jrank.org

about the author

Matthew Shepatin is a New York City–based author and journalist. His stories on American culture, entertainment, and sports have appeared in *Esquire*, *Slate*, the *Los Angeles Times*, *Playboy*, *Radar*, *Time Out New York*, and the *Village Voice*. A regular columnist for *New Jersey Monthly*, he is also a contributing writer on *The Enlightened Bracketologist: The Final Four of Everything* by Mark Reiter and Richard Sandomir, and *The Mad Dog Hall of Fame: The Ultimate Top-Ten Rankings of the Best in Sports* by Chris Russo and Allen St. John.